Advance Praise for

THE NEXT ONE IS FOR YOU

"In the 1970s, a small circle of Philadelphia residents fueled brutal street warfare 3,000 miles from the Liberty Bell. Unflinching and meticulously reported, *The Next One Is for You* is a gripping tale of the Troubles, told for the first time from this side of the Atlantic."

— Tom O'Neill, author of *Chaos: Charles Manson, the CIA, and the Secret History of the Sixties*

"The remarkable story of the Philly Five will serve for many as a riveting companion piece to Patrick Radden Keefe's *Say Nothing*. But that doesn't do it justice. In Ali Watkins's capable hands, it stands proudly alongside that modern classic as its own gateway into the Troubles. A powerful, gritty, emotional read."

— Julian Sancton, author of *Madhouse at the End of the Earth: The Belgica's Journey into the Dark Antarctic Night*

"*The Next One Is for You* is nonfiction at its best: an intense, clear-eyed, and brilliantly reported story that takes the reader on a very human journey. In revealing how a flood of weapons from Philadelphia suddenly transformed the urban battlefields of Northern Ireland, Ali Watkins also brings to life two parallel subcultures: the Irish nationalists who left for the United States and those who stayed behind. Powerful and compelling, this book is a must."

— James Risen, author of *The Last Honest Man: The CIA, the FBI, the Mafia, and the Kennedys — and One Senator's Fight to Save Democracy*

"Written with the meticulousness of forensic investigation and the narrative intensity of a novel, *The Next One Is for You* is a definitive, sobering exploration of legacy, insurgency, and the Irish question. Ali Watkins masterfully unravels the covert history of how a small band of Irish Americans shaped the course of history."

— Elaine Feeney, author of *How to Build a Boat*

"Ali Watkins is an intrepid guide to the intersection between violence, identity, and power. Now she proves herself to be a riveting storyteller, to boot. *The Next One Is for You* is a masterpiece of investigative and true-crime reporting: a white-knuckle ride through 1970s Philadelphia and Belfast, two cities that will now be forever linked in American memory."

    — Mark Leibovich, author of *This Town* and *Thank You for Your Servitude*

"An important, fascinating exploration of how American guns became central to the course of an Irish war."

    — Toby Harnden, author of *First Casualty: The Untold Story of the CIA Mission to Avenge 9/11* and *Bandit Country: The IRA & South Armagh*

"A harrowing epic of crime and betrayal, a surprising story of the Irish diaspora, a masterful work history: Ali Watkins's *The Next One Is For You* chronicles the overlooked chapter of America's role in the Troubles, and is the next must-read for those interested in one of the world's oldest sectarian struggles."

    — Dan Slater, author of *The Incorruptibles: A True Story of Kingpins, Crime Busters, and the Birth of the American Underworld*

THE
NEXT
ONE
IS
FOR
YOU

THE NEXT ONE IS FOR YOU

A True Story of Guns, Country, and
the IRA's Secret American Army

ALI WATKINS

LITTLE, BROWN AND COMPANY
New York   Boston   London

Little, Brown and Company
Hachette Book Group
1290 Avenue of the Americas, New York, NY 10104
littlebrown.com

First Edition: March 2025

Little, Brown and Company is a division of Hachette Book Group, Inc. The Little, Brown name and logo are trademarks of Hachette Book Group, Inc.

The publisher is not responsible for websites (or their content) that are not owned by the publisher.

The Hachette Speakers Bureau provides a wide range of authors for speaking events. To find out more, go to hachettespeakersbureau.com or email hachettespeakers@hbgusa.com.

Little, Brown and Company books may be purchased in bulk for business, educational, or promotional use. For information, please contact your local bookseller or the Hachette Book Group Special Markets Department at special.markets@hbgusa.com.

Print book interior design by Bart Dawson.

ISBN 9780316538275
LCCN is available at the Library of Congress

Printing 1, 2025

LSC-C

Printed in the United States of America

For Patsy Drumm

CONTENTS

CONTENTS

PROLOGUE

ANDERSONSTOWN, NORTHERN IRELAND, 1973

AT SEVENTEEN AND eighteen, they were hardly old enough to be soldiers. But here they were, two girls moving quietly through the dark, a single rifle between them.

The streets of Andersonstown took on a new, more dangerous texture under the cover of night. These were the blocks on which the girls had come of age, and where they learned the hard reality of their circumstances. Like so many other young residents of Andersonstown, the teenagers and their families had been pushed into this neighborhood — one of West Belfast's fortified, Irish Catholic ghettos — as the sectarian lines bisecting the heart of the city dissolved into violence.

Nothing in Andersonstown was as it seemed, and understanding that was key to survival. The community was its own cipher of hidden loyalties and hiding places, and freedom depended on knowing the code. Which homes were safe and which weren't? Which families were sympathetic and which were indifferent? Which alleyway had a soldier hidden around the corner and which could get you home uninterrupted? Already, the girls had collected these sorts of street smarts, the capacity to read a block not only for what it showed, but for what lay beneath.

Their teenage years should have come with lower stakes, especially on a night like this. It was a September evening, the edge of an Irish autumn, the sort of bittersweet chapter that was meant to mark the last days of adolescence, when the biggest risks should have been fast cars and skipped classes. Perhaps life would have been like that, if this had been a normal place. If adolescence could exist here.

But nothing was normal about growing up in West Belfast — especially not in 1973 Andersonstown. Summer had landed in the city like a bomb, the entire place stumbling through the season in a sort of bewildered, heady daze, hardly able to pull itself from one pile of rubble before the next appeared. The streets were volatile, explosively violent like a shock after built-up static. Released from five decades of restraint, West Belfast bucked and hurled in unrest.

The buildup to this moment was slow but inexorable. For the entirety of time that the girls had been alive, their home of Northern Ireland had never found more than the most fragile of peaces, and even those were regularly shattered. When they were born, in the late 1950s, the Irish Republican Army — the guerrilla force of nationalist Ireland, founded in 1913 to free the island from the British Empire — was in the midst of a doomed, armed campaign, waging attacks along the border that partitioned British-ruled Northern Ireland from the independent Irish Republic. While the girls were growing up, in the 1960s, a new movement of protest and civil unrest — inspired in part by the civil rights protests in America — was sending hordes of young people to march in the streets. Then, in 1969, on the cusp of their adulthood, they watched as the region careened into war.

They were born into a land of tangled identities and loyalties, raised in a place that had never been entirely itself and wasn't quite sure what that looked like anyway. Nowhere was the conflict more distilled than in Belfast and Derry, Northern Ireland's wily border city to the west.

The realities, by 1973, were stark: Northern Ireland's Irish Catholic residents had been marginalized, ostracized, and strategically oppressed by the mostly Protestant, Unionist powers that controlled the region for the British Crown. The struggle had been going on and off for centuries, ever since Great Britain had invaded its neighbor in 1169, culminating in the Irish War of Independence and a 1921 treaty that freed most of the island but left Northern Ireland as a British territory. By 1973, the plight of Northern Ireland's Catholics was laid bare: there were few jobs, poor housing, and threadbare resources. British-backed police and soldiers seemed to relish the imbalance, muscling into Catholic homes, harassing schoolchildren, and shooting their way through West Belfast's Catholic ghettos. It didn't matter whether you were in the IRA or not; being Catholic was enough to get you detained. And so, even those who had shied away from armed resistance in the beginning started to realize what the girls understood: perhaps, in the tortured fight to reunite Ireland, there was no other choice.

Such were the forces that had driven the two girls into the streets of Andersonstown that night. The younger of the two came from a Republican family, and was well familiar with the nighttime mechanics of secret revolutions. But the older girl, with her long dark hair and wide, sad eyes, had only just pledged herself to the IRA. Though she hadn't grown up in a Republican family, her decision to join became inevitable — her adolescence was defined by the brutality of British troops and the Loyalist mobs that prowled Catholic ghettos, attacking and maiming her neighbors. It had pushed her family to move west from their home on the Lower Falls to Lenadoon, a claustrophobic housing estate in Greater Andersonstown. Many of Belfast's Catholics had fled there in the violent haze of the early 1970s, when British troops flooded the streets, raided homes, and generally terrorized Belfast's Catholics, tossing hundreds in jail without charge. Things had only grown more fraught since, as Lenadoon and Andersonstown had become the front line of a boiling sectarian conflict. The working-class Catholic ghettos were surrounded by British military barracks, Loyalist neighborhoods, and the looming shadow of Divis and Black Mountain, the sparse hills to the city's west, from which the British Army looked down upon its targets. Pushed to defend itself from all sides, West Belfast quickly became an incubator for a new generation of fighters like the girls.

Most shocking was that they were holding their own. By 1973, there was a big reason. Not only did the IRA have a flood of new recruits, the group had also received an influx of high-powered guns.

Amid all the other changes that summer, that one was paramount. What had changed on the streets of West Belfast were the guns. For decades, the scrappy, outgunned IRA had fought against looming odds, desperately confronting the might of the British Army with rusty triggers and expired bullets. But what had begun as a trickle in 1971 became, two years later, a miraculous flood: nearly overnight, the Catholic ghettos of West Belfast were full of deadly American ArmaLites and tens of thousands of rounds of ammunition.

The ArmaLite guns were sleek and versatile, light and easy to carry, so distinctive in shape that their ominous profile would one day be inextricably associated with the IRA and the Troubles, as the conflict would become known. Each semiautomatic rifle also carried with it a small nudge of solidarity, a reminder that the island's war had expanded far beyond its shores: the ArmaLites were American guns, secreted into Northern Ireland by a core group of IRA supporters overseas who believed deeply in the guerrilla army's mission — and were determined to help them succeed.

Thanks in large part to these guns, by 1973 Andersonstown's IRA volunteers were well armed, and the cloistered front had played host to the IRA's tit-for-tat shooting war with the British soldiers and the Royal Ulster Constabulary. Though ostensibly in the territory as peacekeepers, the British Army had proven just as ruthless as the police; its soldiers had invaded the labyrinthine streets of Andersonstown like conquerors, transforming residential neighborhoods into Army fortresses and police barracks.

There were seventeen military installations in Andersonstown alone, observation posts and bases like the Woodbourne House, a former homestead of a British lord that had been repurposed as Army barracks. The outposts were stark symbols of the oppression that Belfast's Irish had for centuries associated with the British flag. To volunteers like the two girls, each of these installations was a colonialist, militarized wart — and a target.

Hence the girls' mission: under the cover of that September night, they were dispatched to harass the British soldiers stationed at the Woodbourne House. The girls had started the night as part of a large group of IRA volunteers — mostly men — but by the early evening, they decided that only one among them would be armed. The older girl would carry the gun, an initiation ritual for her first night on duty. The ArmaLite rifle had only recently arrived from America, and it was part of a tightly rationed arsenal maintained by the brigade in Andersonstown.

As they neared the neighborhood's southernmost boundary, at the corner of Suffolk and Stewartstown Roads, the fortress loomed in front of them, its cage-like exterior a shadow against the sky. The night was quiet. The dark road — its streetlights long since shot out by British soldiers — was lit only by buzzing spotlights.

The older girl maneuvered the ArmaLite to her shoulder. This was her moment. She breathed steadily, raised the gun, and aimed.

PART I

A NEW RISING

"ONE WITH US ADDRESS"

THE LETTER ARRIVED in a blue envelope, slipped through the mail slot of a nondescript row house on St. Vincent Street in a quiet residential neighborhood of Northeast Philadelphia. Inside, a man eagerly tore the package open.

He had been in the city for years, but Vince Conlon — nearly forty, slim, and dark-eyed with a long face — still had the clipped brogue of Ireland's border counties. Since first settling in Philly a decade earlier, there had been a steady march of mail from back home, but in recent months the notes were growing more urgent. This particular dispatch, which arrived from Dublin, was typewritten and unsigned, but the writer needed no introduction. As for the message itself — well, Conlon had been waiting to read these words for a very long time.

It was all life seemed to be about those days, and he wasn't good at it: waiting. Impatient even in the best of times, Conlon — a brash, devoted IRA man from Armagh, a deeply divided county along the border in Northern Ireland — had suffered through the last decade, and the last few years especially, as the IRA withered on the vine, its leadership steadily becoming less aggressive and less ambitious than the plucky force he had joined as a young man.

The truth was that for Conlon, there was little about life that *hadn't* been about the Irish Republican Army. This house, this chapter, his family's arrival in Philadelphia: all were tied in some way to the IRA and its cause.

Conlon and his wife, Marina, had landed in the city in 1960 with their newborn son, finding in the leafy, quiet streets a haven from the dismal

Vince and Marina Conlon
on their wedding day,
in Kilburn, London, 1959

economic straits of Ireland and London — and a much-needed break for Vince, who had spent years dodging arrest warrants and breaking out of jail cells along the Northern Irish border. In Philadelphia, he assimilated quickly, settling down in the Five Points neighborhood, a predominantly Irish, working-class area, where he became a well-liked neighbor, an attentive father, and a successful carpenter.

Through it all, though, Vince Conlon harbored a secret.

Far from leaving the IRA behind, Conlon had spent his years in America on a very important mission; and now, in the autumn of 1969, nearly a decade after it started, the operation might finally be bearing fruit. The letter in Conlon's hands almost certainly brought important news from comrades back home — fellow IRA veterans who felt the same way he did, with the same goal: to expel the British from Northern Ireland, whatever the cost.

By the time the letter arrived in Philadelphia, in the late 1960s, the Irish Republican Army was a shell of its former self. He might not have been able to see them at the time, but the signs of its decline had been visible even in the 1950s, when Conlon first joined the organization. By that point many of its veterans, having opposed the 1921 treaty that partitioned the island in two, had long since fled overseas after finding themselves on the losing side of the bloody Irish Civil War.

Those anti-treaty IRA volunteers were carrying on a long tradition of armed resistance against the forces that stood in the way of the full reunification of Ireland's thirty-two counties. Ever since 1169 CE, when Britain had brutally invaded its island neighbor and taken over all of the territory comprising modern-day Ireland and Northern Ireland, Irish nationalists had been mounting periodic attempts to overthrow British occupation. Their attempts culminated in the formation of the IRA, which went on to wage Ireland's War of Independence in 1919. That conflict had ended with a controversial détente, when a large contingent of Irish forces reluctantly agreed to a devil's bargain that partitioned the island into two segments. The southern twenty-six counties would function as an independent state, which in time would become the modern-day Republic of Ireland, while its northern six would remain a territory of Great Britain.

That agreement split the IRA, leading to a brief but bloody internecine conflict in the newly formed free state of Ireland following its 1921 independence from Britain. On one side were militant Irish Republicans who remained known as the IRA, and on the other, pro-government supporters of the Anglo-Irish Treaty, which ended the war and partitioned the island in December 1921. That civil war ended in the decisive defeat of the anti-treaty IRA. It left the army as a stateless rebel group, opposed to the very foundation of the newly created Republic of Ireland and proscribed both there and in the six British-controlled counties in the North.

That region, known as Northern Ireland, would be governed by its own parliament, which was autonomous but beholden to the British Crown. This body in Northern Ireland, known as Stormont for the complex in which it was based, was controlled by Unionist politicians who saw themselves and the region as fundamentally linked to Great Britain, and whose interests aligned as such. Comfortably in control, Unionist officials had created a system that excluded nationalists from Northern Ireland's government, ensuring Irish Catholic residents were powerless, doomed to be an overruled, discriminated-against, and gerrymandered minority.

Northern Ireland, as the region would be known, encompassed the majority of Ireland's Ulster Province, of which six counties made up the entirety of the new territory. (Three Ulster counties — Cavan, Donegal, and

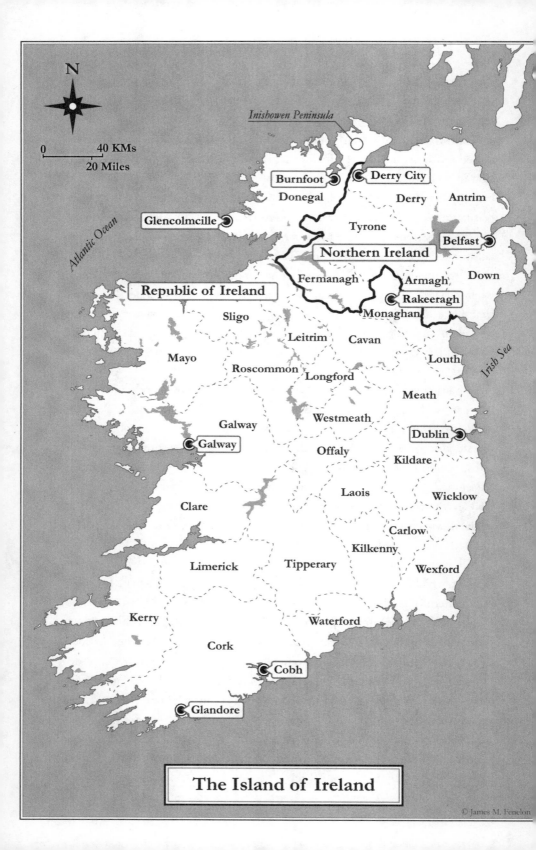

Monaghan — were excluded from Northern Ireland when the borderlines were first drawn in 1921, in an effort in part to ensure Protestant majorities in the Unionist-controlled North.) The island settled into an uneasy peace.

The anti-treaty IRA had been driven from the island in the brief, ugly civil war — but in the shadows and beyond the shores, the IRA never quite went away. The years that followed their defeat were desperate, marked by failures and ignominies large and small; in the late 1930s, the IRA even attempted to forge ties with Nazi Germany, under the pretext that any enemy of the British was a friend of the IRA. It was a doomed escapade that caused the organization untold reputational damage and didn't succeed in advancing the cause of Irish reunification. And yet the struggle for total independence for Ireland — all of Ireland — not only endured in the years after partition, but also became more dynamic, contentious, and fluid.

At its core, the fight was waged by mostly Irish, mostly Catholic nationalists, who believed that Ireland — north and south — should function as an autonomous thirty-two-county state, free from British occupation. Opposing them were the mostly Protestant, mostly British Unionists, who believed Great Britain should maintain control over the island's six northern counties. The nationalist and Unionist designations each had hard-line subsets, mostly among their working class — Republicans and Loyalists, respectively. Diametrically opposed, both these factions were willing to use violence to reach their respective ends, and for as long as they had existed on the same island, such clashes had erupted. But as the 1970s neared, few could have imagined just how much worse things could get.

For many in Ireland's south, the 1920s-era partition of the island was an imperfect compromise. But for hardcore Irish nationalists and most Irish Catholics in the North, it was a deeply flawed agreement that effectively abandoned those residents to the mercy of Unionist, Protestant rulers. By 1969, the arrangement had worked out about as poorly as most Irish nationalists had predicted.

In Northern Ireland, partition resulted in a deeply segregated, unequal society, where gerrymandered districts ensured that Catholic residents would remain in the minority, subject to widespread discrimination in almost every aspect of daily life, from housing to employment to education. Catholic schools were less resourced. Catholic housing was sparse and poorly maintained. A Catholic surname got you passed over for jobs, if you even got the chance to apply. Nowhere, perhaps, were these forces felt as potently as in Belfast and Derry, Northern Ireland's two largest, most deeply divided cities. There, tensions over these skewed realities simmered for years, threatening to boil over at any moment.

In the center of it all should have been the IRA, which remained the outlawed, militant arm of nationalist, Catholic Ireland. Its singular mission was the eradication of British occupation and the reunification of the island's thirty-two counties. As part of that goal, the IRA became widely known as the defender of Northern Ireland's Catholic ghettos, particularly as they faced increasingly dire straits under Unionist rule. But two things had become clear by 1969, when the letter from Dublin reached Vince Conlon's hands in Philadelphia: the situation in Northern Ireland's cities was spiraling, and the IRA wasn't ready.

Attempts to reinvigorate the guerrilla army through the 1940s and 1950s had been tepid, at best; in 1949, the American CIA, long wary of potential communist influences among European radicals, was comfortable enough to note in one internal briefing paper that the IRA's membership rolls were modest, and easily tracked by police and military intelligence in the Irish Republic. Indeed, what little of the IRA existed in the 1950s had stayed together mostly because of men like Vince Conlon, young ideologues from British-dominated Northern Ireland who cared little for their waning odds. Radicalized by the daily discrimination they faced under the British system, most enlisted in the years following World War II — either undeterred by, or ignorant of, the Faustian pact that the IRA leadership had so recently attempted to strike with the fascists who had just lost the war.

Conlon seemed predestined for a life of revolution. Born and raised in the western part of County Armagh, one of the six Ulster counties that were drawn into Northern Ireland, Conlon grew up in one of the IRA's most fervent strongholds. He was surrounded by Republican lore and stories of the 1920s, an era that occupied outsized, romantic real estate in the Irish Republican consciousness. Armagh had a reputation for producing some of the most ruthless militant units of the IRA, eventually earning parts of the region an ominous nickname: "bandit country."

Somehow, Conlon managed to reach adulthood without any particular pull toward joining — in fact, he left the island at eighteen to take a job as a highway construction worker in England. It was a brief, short-lived move that would change his life. Like many young Irishmen who sought work in England, he returned home a different man, battered by anti-Irish discrimination and harassment, with a newfound clarity on the disparities between Northern Ireland and its British overlords. He joined the IRA.

The army's pledge was not meant to be taken lightly, and Conlon carried it with the seriousness of a prayer. He made fast work of establishing himself as a reliable, ambitious soldier, but the island's dire economic straits were hard to surmount. Hoping to find work, Conlon first traveled to Philadelphia in 1954, landing with his older brother, John, who worked as a carpenter in the city's suburbs. But it was a brief inaugural trip — Vince Conlon couldn't stay away from Ireland long. Within a year, he told John his "conscience" required him to return, "to fight and help free Ireland." He set off for Cork Harbor and marched directly back to Armagh, where he quickly rejoined the local IRA brigade.

Vince Conlon arrived back at a busy time: the IRA was gearing up for Operation Harvest, a new campaign that was to take place along the Northern Irish border in the late 1950s. The campaign — planned by Conlon's friend, a man named Sean Cronin — targeted military installations and communication networks in the North. It would be the IRA's first earnest offensive in decades, and as it unfolded, Conlon proved himself as a fighter and leader, organizing trainings and smuggling guns into and out of the North. In the free Irish Republic, deep in the rugged Wicklow Mountains, he helped run a secret training camp for 150 newly minted IRA men, with live ammunition and explosives. In December 1956, the offensive began with an attack in Derry, where IRA volunteers blew up a transmitter for the British Broadcasting Corporation, followed by an attempted attack on a set of barracks in Armagh.

Not long after, Conlon gained renown as an IRA fighter, thanks to his role in one particular mission. On New Year's Day 1957, Conlon drove a stolen delivery truck filled with hidden IRA volunteers to the barracks of the Royal Ulster Constabulary — the British-backed police force in Northern Ireland — in Brookeborough, a small town in County Fermanagh, another Ulster county which was part of Northern Ireland. The group had planned to plant bombs around the barracks and attack the officers there, but things went awry nearly as soon as they arrived. The bombs failed to go off, and Conlon and his unit came under fire. In a chaotic escape, Conlon sped the truck through a hail of bullets and back toward the safety of the Republic, but two of the men — Fergal O'Hanlon and the unit's commander, Seán South — were caught in the crossfire and mortally wounded. The remaining volunteers eventually ditched the truck, fleeing across the border on foot through the tangled forests of the Slieve Beagh Mountains, finally reaching a safe house deep in the thick pine groves of County Monaghan, in the Irish Republic. It was an arduous journey that would bond the Brookeborough survivors for life. There were eleven of them along with Conlon, including a tall, intensely focused Cork man known among IRA colleagues as "the Long Fella" — Dáithí, or Dave, O'Connell.

The raid would fast be catapulted into IRA legend for the daring escape of Conlon and his comrades: "Sean South of Garryowen," named for the dead officer, is still a celebrated Irish rebel song, a mainstay in pubs across Ireland and America. The death of the two young men brought a wave of sympathy for the IRA — their funerals were said to be some of the most widely attended for decades — and the men who were with them became folk heroes. But Conlon didn't waste time basking in such wartime glories. Soon he was back in the field.

Conlon had narrowly avoided capture in Brookeborough, but he wasn't so lucky a few months later, when he was picked up along the Northern Irish border with Thompson machine guns and several other IRA men — "one with US address" the local paper reported ominously, referring to Conlon's ties to Philadelphia. Conlon was dragged into court in Letterkenny, in County Donegal, where he and his fellow volunteers talked over the judge, forewent the polite gestures of taking off their hats, and otherwise completely ignored the proceedings. Unsurprisingly, they were convicted. On the way out of court, one defiantly shouted a traditional cry in support of Irish Republicanism: "Up the IRA!"

Imprisoned for a term in the Curragh, a prison camp operated by Irish authorities outside Dublin, Conlon began trying to escape nearly as soon as he got there. The first attempt was through a small bathroom window: he succeeded and spent two days on the run before being recaptured and sentenced to solitary confinement. The second attempt saw him flee the prison as part of a mass breakout that he helped to organize. This time, Conlon stayed free.

Conlon remained in Ireland for more than a year after his second escape from prison, evading warrants and authorities by bouncing around safe houses. But although technically a free man, he still chafed at the claustrophobia of a life in hiding. One sympathetic homeowner called Conlon "a caged lion" for the way he paced angrily around his room, unable to venture outside lest the authorities get a hint of his whereabouts. He lived in the shadows until the IRA's border campaign petered out and Irish authorities stopped looking for him.

Philadelphia, though, and its Irish network — these were never far from his mind. Conlon was taken with the city, and harbored a deep connection to its Irish diaspora. Even while on trial in Donegal, Conlon gave transatlantic interviews to local Philly radio stations about Irish history and the IRA's cause. His fellow expats may have settled into more robust enclaves along the East Coast, but Conlon was a Philadelphia man, loyal to it over all other cities. His general ignorance of New York — a celebrated city among the Irish diaspora — had earned him the prison nickname "the Bronx," which he was given, in ironic Irish humor, because he knew little about the place. Strangely enough, the nickname fit Conlon well, given the borough's no-nonsense stereotype; Conlon, too, had similarly direct tendencies and little patience for empty talk.

In 1960, three years after the raid that made him a legend, and with the IRA's border campaign on its last, wobbly legs, the hero of Brookeborough slipped away again. This time, he headed back to Philadelphia. Life had taken some turns in the years since his escape from the prison camp in Curragh, not all of them bad; for one, he and Marina, a nurse in Armagh whom Conlon met as a young volunteer, had married, and they had a child on the way. But after years on the run, Conlon was uninterested in hiding away in America. Returning to Philadelphia would, ironically, put him back in the fight — perhaps in his most critical role yet.

CHAPTER 2

THE THIRTY-THIRD COUNTY

AN OCEAN AWAY from Ireland, Vince Conlon was effectively a noncombatant. He was no frontline soldier; not anymore. But although he had left the island behind, there were other ways to serve the IRA besides planting a bomb or firing a gun.

There were many others like him, too. By the time Conlon and Marina relocated to Philadelphia, IRA volunteers had been fleeing to America for decades. They had landed there for plenty of reasons: many had left Ireland after the civil war that followed the island's War for Independence, their staunch, anti-treaty stance leaving them vulnerable to persecution at home. Others had been driven to America earlier, having fled during various points of the centuries-long independence struggle — including Ireland's devastating famine in the 1800s — or later, after the lukewarm efforts of the 1950s and the IRA's failed border campaign. Whatever the reason, by the mid-twentieth century the steady flight of IRA veterans to America had effectively created a shadowy, satellite brigade of Irish Republicans within the country's sprawling Irish diaspora. Like the IRA, it had been loosely organized and mostly dormant for years. But as tension percolated in 1969, something became clear about the IRA's American auxiliary: it was full of people like Vince Conlon, devoted to the cause and tired of sitting on the sidelines.

For over a century, since 1867, America's Irish rebels had been organized under the name Clan-na-Gael, or United Brotherhood. In Irish, the phrase translates literally to Family (or Brotherhood) of Ireland, but American members sometimes called themselves the Children of Ireland, a nod to the group's generational and geographic expansion.

Secretive and hard-line, Clan-na-Gael operated with an omertà that evoked the Italian Mafia, another foreign-born organization that had taken root in the United States simultaneously. But the Clan was no criminal syndicate. It was motivated purely by Irish nationalism: across the nineteenth and early twentieth centuries, Clan-na-Gael, or just the Clan, as it would also be known, was a critical channel for rebellions in Ireland to access a growing network of supporters in the States. The Clan's roster was peppered with well-known Irish revolutionaries like John Devoy and Jeremiah O'Donovan Rossa, and its efforts ranged from chillingly efficient to shockingly ambitious: in the late 1800s, it both ran an effective bombing campaign in London and funded a secret, failed effort to build three submarines in California with the intention of attacking the British navy.

Clan-na-Gael's roots were in New York. But by 1916, as the IRA was forming, the Clan had expanded to establish a firm presence in Philadelphia, too. The bustling mid-Atlantic city, with its easy access to the ocean and its large community of Irish expats, was a harbor of sorts for Irish revolutionaries — radicals who often needed to get off the island of Ireland, and fast. By the late 1960s, New York had become synonymous with the Irish working class, and Boston's Irish had been elevated to the highest echelons of political power, but something about Philadelphia appealed to the militant Irish Republican consciousness long before Conlon even took his oath to the IRA, at twenty years old. By the time he settled there, Philly wasn't just an Irish city; it was a *Northern* Irish city, with a disproportionate number of émigrés from the six partitioned counties from which Conlon hailed. It was an important distinction, and one that set Philadelphia apart from other Irish strongholds along America's East Coast.

As far back as the 1800s, a critical immigration route had sent floods of Irish to Philadelphia from Armagh and other northern counties like Derry and Tyrone; three ships a month left Derry for the city. One agent for the McCorkell steamship company, which ran regular routes between the North of Ireland and Philadelphia, booked more than five thousand tickets between the two regions alone. The émigrés continued to arrive in droves into the 1920s; among them were anti-treaty IRA men. In short, by the mid-1950s, when Conlon first sought refuge in Philadelphia, it had already established itself as a quiet hideaway for rebels who needed to lie low, protected by sympathetic comrades. Smuggled across borders on ships, planes, and caravans, these fugitives could find a bed and a job in Philly, where the Irish managed many of the city's powerful labor unions. Sympathetic leadership helped the men get union cards and fake names. Then they could find work and wait out the heat, quietly. Many of those fugitives would also join the underground brotherhood of Clan-na-Gael, which — in a city full of Irish social clubs — was reserved almost exclusively for veterans of the IRA and expat Republicans. As with the IRA back home, the Clan's mission boiled down to one goal: to reunite Ireland's thirty-two counties.

It was just one part of the wide-reaching community that had flourished in America. The Clan was for Irish-born IRA veterans, but Irish America was full of second- and third-generation descendants who nurtured their own affinities for Ireland's long war. Most never forgot the reason they were in the States in the first place. Theirs was a particular sort of remembering, the kind that sands down nuances to glossy superficialities. But for volunteers like Vince Conlon, that didn't really matter. Irish-American affinity for the cause had the potential to be a vast resource for the IRA, a deep well that they need only tap. Vince Conlon had long believed he knew how.

When Conlon returned to Philadelphia, in 1960, Clan-na-Gael — like the IRA — was a whisper of its former self, rife with discontent and division, and without clear purpose. Conlon, short on patience, immediately set to work fixing it. He had joined the Clan years before as a young IRA fighter, on that first, brief trip to Philadelphia back in 1954. But he returned to it in 1960 as one of the movement's respected veterans, a position that afforded him great credibility to change its course. It was a mission he initially undertook of his own volition, but with the blessing and guidance of IRA leadership in Dublin, which was full of men with whom Conlon had served in the 1950s.

Grabbing hold of the limping Clan, Conlon rallied members along the coast, shaking down for money anyone who would sit still. He quickly rose through the ranks and eventually landed the role of national secretary. He also led the Clan into the open, discarding its code of secrecy: in 1963, in a small motel conference room with a handful of fellow members, Conlon rallied a quorum and passed a new, nationwide mission statement. Clan-na-Gael would no longer operate in the shadows; its fight was a noble one, and to hide it suggested a timidness to which Conlon didn't subscribe. Moving forward, the Clan would be "an organization that gives its support to the IRA and have no other purpose." This was a bold — and dangerous — association, one that perked the ears of federal agents.

Under Conlon, Clan-na-Gael membership in the Philadelphia area exploded, more than doubling in the early 1960s. He was joined at the top of the organization by two other Philadelphia-based Republicans: Brigid Makowski, an organizer from Derry, and Néilidh "Neil" Byrne, a flamboyant, eccentric bachelor from the west coast of Donegal who had served in the US Army during the Korean War. The three were everywhere that the Clan had business. Byrne planned commemorative ceremonies at the graves of local Clan-na-Gael members, and coordinated parades on Saint Patrick's Day. Conlon arranged pickets and demonstrations outside British consulates, and all over the East Coast. In 1963, the same year he announced the Clan's new, public mantra, Conlon was banned permanently from the United Nations, after he stood up in the observer's balcony and loudly heckled the Irish contingent on its policies in the North.

Vincent Conlon carrying an American flag while protesting in downtown Philadelphia, 1969

Clan-na-Gael members at the Saint Patrick's Day parade in Philadelphia, 1970. Neil Byrne is second from left, holding an American flag; Brigid Makowski is fourth from left, holding a Clan-na-Gael banner.

It was in that context that Conlon began restructuring the IRA's American outpost, and he found fertile ground. In the years since the 1920s, a feverish, insular community of Republican sympathizers had spread out across the Philadelphia area, creating a network of bars, social clubs, and union halls; so strong was this contingent that the city's outskirts were sometimes jokingly referred to as the thirty-third county, a nod toward the nationalist battle cry of a thirty-two-county united Ireland. The group was composed mostly of two distinct generations: The younger were Conlon's compatriots, who had grown up under partition. The older were the anti-treaty veterans who had fled the island after their defeat in the civil war. For both groups, nothing short of a thirty-two-county, autonomous Republic of Ireland would do.

Many of those expats had settled in the city's Northeast, the same area where, in 1960, Marina and Vincent landed with their young son, Sean. The various neighborhoods were connected by Roosevelt Boulevard, a wide avenue that took you either west, farther into Pennsylvania, or east, toward New Jersey and the interchange with New York City. Hardscrabble and working class, Northeast Philadelphia was flooded with the Irish immigrants of the

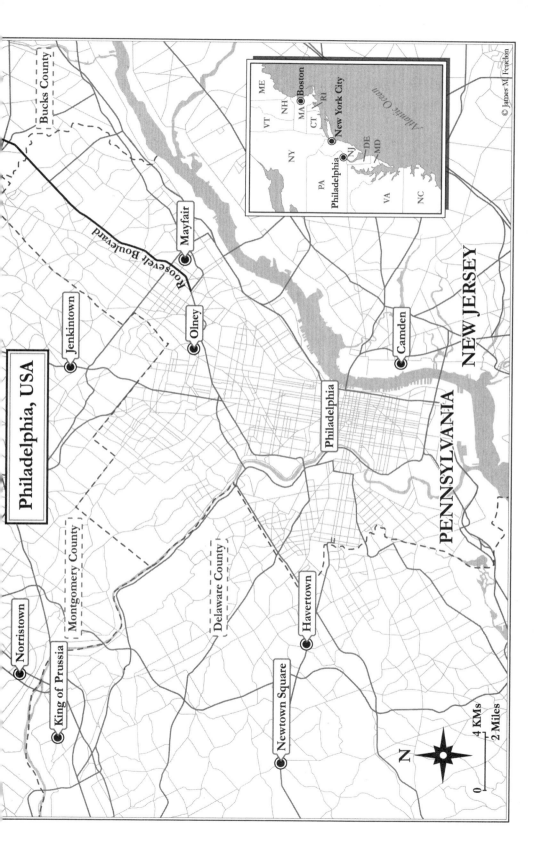

Philadelphia, USA

Bucks County

Roosevelt Boulevard

Mayfair

Jenkintown

Olney

Camden

NEW JERSEY

Philadelphia

PENNSYLVANIA

Norristown

Montgomery County

King of Prussia

Delaware County

Havertown

Newtown Square

N

0   4 KMs
     2 Miles

VT

ME

NH

MA ● Boston

CT   RI

NY

● New York City

DE

NJ

MD

PA

Philadelphia ●

VA

NC

Atlantic Ocean

© James M. Fenelon

1950s who left the inner city for the space and relative comfort of the sub-urbs. Five Points, Mayfair, and neighboring Olney were some of the city's most heavily Irish neighborhoods, and naturally they became strongholds of the Irish-controlled labor unions.

In the decade or so after they arrived, Vince and Marina built a comfort-able life for themselves in Philadelphia. Vince started his own landscaping busi-ness and attended classes at night school, and the couple built a network of close friends. They hosted regular dinners and traditional Irish bands, their living room full of dancing and storytelling, with fellow expatriates from home. But even as their little family grew — in 1969, Marina was pregnant with their fifth child — and even though they occasionally returned to Ireland to visit family, the Clan remained a key priority in their day-to-day. Their children attended protests and group trips, their sons toddling along as Vince led visiting IRA delegations around Pennsylvania's countryside.

For less public endeavors, Conlon gathered the Clan in Jenkintown, a suburban neighborhood on Philadelphia's northeast outskirts. There, a County Mayo descendant and Clan member named Matt Regan owned the MacSwiney Club, a modest pub whose secret attic doubled as Clan-na-Gael's meeting space — a discreet place where Conlon and his fellow members could discuss the organization's affairs.

A Clan safe house of sorts, the MacSwiney Club was part of a larger infra-structure that had grown around Philadelphia's Irish. Not far from Jenkintown and the MacSwiney Club was the nearby Irish Center, where a large auditorium hosted speeches and events on a regular basis. Closer to the city from there was a tavern run by Hughie Breen, a gruff, no-nonsense veteran of the 1920s war. Near to that was the gathering hall for the local roofers' union, whose head, John McCullough, was an ally of Breen's and keen to employ Irish fugitives.

None of this escaped the eyes of American law enforcement, who, alarmed by Conlon's proximity to militant Irish Republicans, began keeping close tabs on him nearly as soon as he had set foot back in the States in 1960. FBI agents quickly amassed a sizable dossier not just on this new, fast-rising leader of Clan-na-Gael, but also on the organization itself, and they kept a watchful eye on demonstrations through a network of informants within the broader Irish-American community.

Conlon had courted much of this attention himself; after all, he made little secret of Clan-na-Gael's loyalties. He might well have agreed with the enterprising FBI officer who observed, in a secret investigative report, that "the IRA, in fact, does not exist in the US, but works through the Clan-na-Gael." The dispatch was written around the same time that Conlon rose to the top of Clan-na-Gael's leadership structure.

Before 1969, Clan-na-Gael had never quite realized its full potential in post-partition Ireland; there simply hadn't been much opportunity for it to show how it could contribute to the cause of Irish independence. But now, after years of fostering this community of supporters, it seemed the moment had finally arrived for the IRA — or at least for some enterprising members — to activate it.

CHAPTER 3

THE SPLIT

BY 1969, AS THE LETTER in the blue envelope arrived in Philadelphia, it had been a decade since Vince Conlon had left Ireland; over a decade since he'd been confined to a prison camp or a safe house.

By all appearances, Conlon had settled into life as an average Irish-American dad: a handsome, successful carpenter raising five children on a leafy street in the city. But this unassuming cover masked one of the IRA's most enterprising, quietly ambitious operatives in America, a battle-hardened veteran who had taken control of a secret society of Irish rebels and reorganized it in service of the IRA's cause. And now, to his immense frustration, the people who were in charge of the army back home were squandering this opportunity — and, it seemed, every other one that fate had handed them.

Although Conlon remained a devoted IRA man, the army's impotence had grown maddening. He had once maintained close friendships with elder IRA leaders, but by 1969 he could no longer ignore the fact that those at the top of the organization seemed content to let the IRA and its American satellite brigade simply limp along, ineffectual and increasingly irrelevant.

One of those old hands, Cathal Goulding, was the official who had first directed Conlon's work with Clan-na-Gael in America, and across the 1960s the two had remained close. Goulding visited Philadelphia regularly; Conlon had even sided with him when the IRA went through a fraught reorganization in the early 1950s. Back then, Goulding was the leader of the movement's more militant faction. But in the run-up to 1969, the friends found themselves on different ends of a stark divide. Under Goulding, the IRA had grown less militant and less ambitious, more interested in Marxist politics than armed resistance. In letters from Philadelphia, Conlon fumed at Goulding for his lackadaisical approach to the IRA. And, separately, he began corresponding with a similarly disillusioned set of army insiders — ones who seemed intent on taking the IRA back to its militant roots.

It was these friends who were sending the steady stream of letters to Conlon in Philadelphia. And what they were describing would be the end of all of them — and perhaps the end of the IRA's mission — if it were discovered.

Only a small, trusted handful of them knew it, but some of Vince's fellow volunteers back in Ireland were staging a coup within the IRA. They felt they had no choice: they needed to shake up the antiquated army and prepare it for a potential war. And they were not alone in their darkening view of the IRA's old guard — including Conlon's increasingly estranged friend, Goulding. For months, this rebellious group kept Conlon apprised as discontent festered and grew within the organization's ranks.

There was much to be frustrated about. By 1969, tensions in Belfast and Derry had escalated significantly. Irish Catholic residents of Northern Ireland had grown sick of living in worse housing than their Protestant neighbors, with worse jobs and worse schools, under constant threat of harassment. But attempts to mobilize against such inequities were met with brutal force by Northern Ireland's Unionist-controlled police force, the Royal Ulster Constabulary. With no civil outlet for Irish Catholics' discontent, a violent confrontation was brewing. Meanwhile, under Goulding, the IRA — which historically had served as the protector of Catholic enclaves in the North — seemed completely unprepared for this new moment.

Among that small group of volunteers, though, momentum was building to break away and form a new, more militant IRA, one that would do what the old guard wouldn't. This was dangerous business, and not just because the end goal would involve a violent campaign to fight British occupation. If the mutiny didn't succeed, its failure could be fatal for all who had chosen the wrong side — after all, the IRA had never taken kindly to such internal dissent, and divisions had generally led to bloody infighting. But as conditions for Irish Catholics worsened, the malcontents were beginning to feel that they had no choice.

Conlon watched from afar, poised like a coiled spring. Whenever a split came — and they came often, in the world of Irish rebellion — he always sided with the more enterprising and ambitious. And so, as the IRA approached this new crossroads, Conlon knew unequivocally which path he would take.

According to the letter in the blue envelope, the time for restraint was nearing an end. As IRA members watched the harsh realities rally more and more Irish Catholics against Northern Ireland's Unionist government, many within the organization were coming to feel that they had to seize the moment. Support for this fledgling contingent was spreading within the IRA, and among Northern Ireland's Catholics more broadly.

Now, according to the letter Conlon had received, the plotters were almost ready to act, and formally break ties with Cathal Goulding. But things were not yet cleanly arranged, the anonymous writer urged, and Conlon needed to proceed with caution. He should lie low until the group of them in Ireland could work out their own structure and divisions of power. What's more, the letter writer explained, there were also competing factions in America, some of whom would likely still support Goulding's more conservative IRA and weren't to be trusted. Conlon would be a valuable asset in the States, but only if he kept his head down for a while longer.

By the time Conlon got to the letter's final page, its tone had pivoted from hopeful to darkly paranoid, and unequivocal in its warning:

"Keep us informed on the basic developments in America. And whatever else you do do not reveal to anyone over there or here however much you trust them that you are in touch with us," the anonymous writer said. "Or we will be sunk."

If such paranoia and peril were felt in Philadelphia, that was doubly so in Belfast, Northern Ireland's largest city and the spiritual home of this mutinous movement within the IRA. Belfast was geographically fated, perhaps, to feel under siege. Wedged between hills to the west and a large, tidal inlet to the northeast, the city — tucked away in County Antrim, in the corner of Ireland's northern Ulster Province — had been contested territory nearly since its founding in 1888, when the British occupied all of Ireland. Its name alone carries that dark history of colonialism: "Belfast" is an anglicized version of the Irish Béal Feirste, or Mouth of the Sandbar. It was a tough city, working class and sharp, with a booming textile and shipbuilding industry that had briefly made it the island's largest metropolis, bigger during the late nineteenth century industrial revolution than even Dublin, in the south. In a trend that defined Belfast, though, such fortunes weren't shared equitably between its Catholic residents and its Protestants. As the 1960s drew to a close, the city housed around 416,000 people in neighborhoods that were stringently divided, mostly according to religion: the majority of Protestant, Unionist neighborhoods sat in Belfast's north and east, while its mostly disenfranchised Catholic, nationalist neighborhoods were in the west.

In a city of fault lines, the neighborhood of Clonard sat at the heart of Belfast's two largest ghettos, both named after their respective main streets: Shankill Road, a Loyalist, largely Protestant working-class stronghold; and the Falls Road, which was nationalist and largely working-class Catholic. The two streets would become household shorthand for their respective ideologies, the arteries around which Belfast unofficially oriented itself. They both extended west from Belfast's city center, with the Falls arching south and Shankill progressing straight before cutting north and ending, serving as the boundary line into Loyalist Belfast. But near Belfast's downtown, the streets converged, nearly intersecting at the small, central ghetto known as Clonard; here, the Shankill and Falls factions were dangerously close.

For as long as anyone could remember, each neighborhood's respective Catholic and Protestant residents had lived in uncomfortable proximity. But as the city's Catholic minority grew more and more desperate under Unionist rule, the day-to-day tensions were manifesting into something more.

It began quietly in 1968, when a group of university students in Derry organized and began protesting British occupation and Unionist rule, inspired partly by the American civil rights movement. The protests and marches led to more violent clashes between protesters and the Royal Ulster Constabulary. Soon, Northern Ireland's Catholic neighborhoods were suffering near-constant incursions by both Loyalist mobs as well as the RUC and its brutalist auxiliary police brigade, known as the B Specials. In nationalist neighborhoods, the successes of the Loyalist mobs bolstered suspicion that these extrajudicial offensives were being planned in conjunction with the RUC — and that the Unionist authorities and Loyalist mobs were effectively one and the same. The regular, violent interventions by the police against nationalist protestors, meanwhile, were also politically loaded, because the RUC — although ostensibly impartial — was in fact overwhelmingly Protestant and inherently Unionist. Nationalists thus saw the RUC as anti-Catholic, while Protestants considered it an important pillar of Unionist politics. In such a charged environment, it didn't take much for these standoffs to spread into a broader conflagration.

The explosion occurred on the morning of August 12, 1969, in a ghetto known as the Bogside, a disenfranchised Catholic area in Derry's west. It was the weekend of the Apprentice Boys' march, an annual Unionist celebration in which Protestant revelers would parade past Catholic ghettos, hurling insults and worse. With little help from the RUC, Derry's Catholics were usually left to face the day's indignities on their own. But in 1969, as the group of Protestant marchers approached the Catholic ghetto that August morning, the residents of the Bogside — hardened by months of unrest — were prepared to defend themselves.

As the marchers closed in, a battle erupted. Petrol bombs were hurled through the sky and tear gas was launched into crowds. Soon, entire pockets of Derry went up in flames. Barricades were erected around the city's Catholic neighborhoods, blocking the areas from their RUC and Loyalist neighbors.

The siege lasted forty-eight hours. No one died in Derry, but it was a dangerous, dark release, both for the city and the North as a whole. The chaos in the Bogside was not an isolated, one-off incident — and the tension in Northern Ireland was not likely to abate; instead, the events in Derry signaled that Irish Republicans and nationalists had reached a tipping point. "There is hope in the future," said one nameless resident of the Bogside. "It lies in the hands of the people of Derry."

The Battle of the Bogside, as it came to be known, forced a decision from British and Northern Irish officials that would have ramifications for decades. Since the partition of Northern Ireland in the 1920s, Northern Ireland's Unionist-majority parliament — known as Stormont — had often been left alone by London politicians, who generally preferred to keep the Irish problem at arm's length. Indeed, while Northern Ireland's Loyalists and Unionists were ardently devoted to the Crown, that same emotional attachment was hardly true of rulers in Westminster, where Northern Ireland was something between a political inconvenience and a liability. This ambivalence on behalf of Great Britain only further radicalized Northern Ireland's Loyalists, who grew to fear not only being overtaken by Irish nationalists, but also being abandoned by an apathetic Westminster.

These simmering political realities were drawn into the open by the Battle of the Bogside. Facing a complete breakdown of order in Derry, Unionist leaders in Stormont reluctantly asked London to send in British troops. With few other choices, a wary Westminster acquiesced, and ordered a deployment of the British Army into Northern Ireland to take over from the bruised RUC police force, which was modestly sized and incapable of reestablishing control. Ironically, it was Catholic residents who welcomed the British soldiers most warmly, seeing them as a definitive mediator between them and Unionism. They hoped the soldiers arrived to do what the RUC and Stormont couldn't: keep the peace. (This perspective was not shared among militant Republicans, who viewed the British and Unionists as the same enemy.)

But the true effects of this military escalation were soon clear. While Stormont still ostensibly maintained direct control over Northern Ireland, the arrival of royal troops signaled a usurpation by the Crown, injecting the politics of the British mainland directly into the territory's day-to-day. Even though the soldiers were being deployed to a semiautonomous region of the British Empire, they were not under the control of Stormont; their orders came from London, and London only. Thus, the deployment marked a fundamental shift in the delicate balance of power between these governments, one a regional power and the other a global one.

Meanwhile, in a desperate attempt to draw the RUC's attention away from Derry that weekend, nationalist civil rights organizers urged followers in places like Belfast to take to their own streets. They did — but so did violent Loyalist mobs who had been triggered by Derry's unrest. They rampaged through the nationalist ghettos of Belfast, prompting a scramble among residents to defend themselves. Both sides converged near the Divis Flats, a housing complex that sat where the Falls Road and Shankill contingencies grew closest, at the city center. It was the natural place toward which a sectarian tide would pull, and on the night of August 14, 1969, as mobs surged through the streets and toward Clonard, it was where the first shots of the Troubles rang out.

The initial volley came from the Catholic side and was answered by a frenzy of machine-gun fire from the RUC. The exchanges escalated from there. By the end of the night, Clonard was smoldering. One Protestant and four Catholic residents of Belfast were dead, including a young Catholic schoolboy who had been killed when an RUC bullet pierced his bedroom wall in Divis Flats. By the following evening, British troops had arrived on the streets of Belfast and Derry.

In times past, this was exactly the sort of attack against which the IRA would have defended the Catholic residents of West Belfast. But on those August nights, no armed IRA men arrived to confront the Loyalist mobs; instead, the rioters burned nationalist streets from end to end, largely unchallenged. In the ruins of Clonard, there was an unavoidable, unsettling verdict: Northern Ireland's Catholics needed defending, and the army tasked with it had failed at the job.

This was why, after August 1969, the IRA found itself at a crossroads. Its older, antiquated leadership — eventually known as the Official IRA — had proven unable or unwilling to defend besieged Catholic ghettos. Faced with that cold reality, a younger, gutsier contingent of nationalist fighters began moving to the fore. This new faction of the IRA came to be known as the Provisionals, or the Provos, and their symbol was a phoenix rising from the ashes of West Belfast.

By the late 1960s, the IRA had been through decades of dizzying rifts and splits. Feuds, grudges, and reinventions had become as closely held a tradition for the IRA as the notion of thirty-two united counties.

But in 1969, the group was on the cusp of the most consequential schism in its modern history. Discontent had festered in the IRA's ranks for years, and the Dublin-based leadership — accused of being antiquated and conflict-avoidant — had long been criticized as out of touch with the struggles of Irish residents in places like West Belfast, many of whom wanted more aggressive challenges to Unionist rule. Never before, though, had there been such a compelling opportunity for mutiny.

Under Cathal Goulding, the IRA had shifted away from armed conflict, orienting themselves toward political solutions and, by some accounts, off-loading their modest armory of weapons to other guerrilla groups. Even in the wrenching aftermath of August 1969, the IRA's core leadership was reluctant to shift to a war footing, cautiously guarding its limited arms and banking on political intervention from both Dublin and London. That hesitancy, though, would incense and motivate younger, more militant volunteers who were growing increasingly desperate as tensions mounted.

The days following August 1969 would make clear the trouble toward which Northern Ireland was headed. Loyalists were organizing their own paramilitary groups in Shankill and other Unionist strongholds: the Ulster Volunteer Force, and later the Ulster Defence Association. The perception within nationalist neighborhoods — one that has since been bolstered by the findings of contemporary reconciliation panels — was that these groups were supported by Unionist politicians, the RUC, and the B Specials, many of whom moonlighted as members of these extrajudicial groups or tacitly encouraged them to attack Catholics. This underscored nationalists' rejection of the RUC's authority. As they barricaded themselves away from Unionist structures, it fell to the IRA not only to defend the neighborhoods, but also to maintain some kind of social and civil order in nationalist areas that had rebuked local authorities.

The Officials approached the moment cautiously, preferring soft power to militancy. But the more militant IRA faction, emboldened by the burning of Clonard Street, began operating autonomously in the weeks following the August riots. This breakaway group rallied their own streams of support and began recruiting younger, more eager volunteers. The rift between the Officials and the Provos thus widened quickly, and support for the mutinous volunteers spread westward and southward, particularly among disenchanted Irish nationalists who had long questioned the capabilities of the conservative Official IRA leadership.

Support for the Provisional IRA faction would pull a group of older IRA men back into the fray. Among them was a group of veterans from the army's failed border campaign in the 1950s — including Vince Conlon — who had never gotten their moment in a full-scale war. It would be the death knell for the IRA in its then-present form. Internal discord within the movement, long whispered but rarely voiced, spilled into public view after August 1969. Rifts and splits tore entire families apart, and the infighting ranged from petty to fatal.

In a last-ditch effort to knit the Irish Republican movement back together, the IRA's Dublin leadership — much of it aligned with the Officials — held a convention in December 1969. Attendees included both the old and new guards of the IRA, in the hopes that they could hash out their differences and reunite the movement.

The convention failed miserably. The Belfast brigade was shouted down by Cathal Goulding's Official IRA. Faced with the unavoidable truth that the institutional IRA cared little for the Provisional's misgivings, the dissidents walked out with their supporters. Among them was a West Belfast native named Gerry Adams — an enigmatic young volunteer who would later emerge as one of the de facto leaders of the rebels. History would label this moment the formal baptism of the Provisional IRA, the group that would soon become the preeminent paramilitary force of nationalist Ireland. Sinn Fein, the main Republican political party, which was closely linked to the IRA, underwent a similar split not long after.

Together, the new Provisional IRA and Provisional Sinn Fein solidified a new Republican front, ensuring a fresh start for the IRA. In the Provisional movement was the new Republican vision. For many young people in Belfast, it was the only one worth supporting, if any were to succeed at all.

The Provisionals may have had the momentum and willpower to start a new armed campaign — but they lacked the means. During the IRA's slow decay, no one had properly kept track of members, money, or guns; indeed, rumors persisted that the organization had discarded most of its weaponry. During the bloody riots of August 1969, desperate cries echoed across Clonard: "Have we any guns?" No one was even sure who among the IRA's volunteers had fired the initial shot that had killed the first Protestant resident to die on the August night that Clonard Street burned. In the weeks surrounding the split, it was difficult to tell who was in charge of the IRA at all.

It remained unclear, moreover, what would happen between the Officials and the new, aggressive Provisionals. Even if the Provisionals could organize themselves into a legitimate fighting force, logistical hurdles stood in their way. For the Provisionals to survive on the streets of Belfast, they would need two things: money and — most desperately — guns.

Surmounting this latter obstacle fell to a well-known veteran of the 1950s, one of the older IRA fighters who had turned against Cathal Goulding. The man's name was Dáithí, or Dave, O'Connell — the storied "Long Fella" from the Brookeborough raid. A quiet schoolteacher who hailed from County Cork, O'Connell moved north to Donegal after the border campaign, where he took over the county's IRA brigade and fell in with the militant faction that would eventually become the Provos. By the time it split off into its own army, O'Connell had become one of the IRA's most reliable, ambitious hands — and was on his way to becoming the Provisional IRA chief of staff.

In the early 1970s, as the Provos were fashioning themselves into an army, O'Connell set off for America, where an old friend was in a unique position to help. This fellow IRA veteran had already proved invaluable to the cause, rallying support from across the ocean, and his efforts in America were not limited to fundraising and social clubs. Luckily for O'Connell and the Provos, what Vince Conlon was particularly good at — and had spent the last decade doing — was finding guns.

CHAPTER 4

THE BROTHERHOOD

BY THE TIME Dave O'Connell left for America in the early months of 1970, Clan-na-Gael was already a high-value asset in the custody dispute between the Officials and the Provos. The organization was the best-established base of IRA veterans in America, and both IRA factions knew it would be hugely valuable to whichever of the two won its loyalty. Recent years might've seen its influence wane, but the Clan had a long history of propping up Irish rebellion, a tradition that had started right in Vince Conlon's adopted home of Philadelphia — and one that Conlon had secretly carried on, even as he brought many of the Clan's activities into the open.

The lifeblood of the Irish cause, nearly since the beginning, had been American weaponry. Back before the IRA even got its name, the first uprisings of Irish nationalists, in the late 1860s, were fought in part with American guns and bullets that were sent across the Atlantic by a network of Irish Americans that would eventually become Clan-na-Gael. Perhaps most recognizably, that group helped arrange gun shipments used by the IRA during its famed 1916 Easter Rising, and kept a steady stream of arms flowing across the ocean to remaining anti-treaty IRA hands.

Central to this effort was Philadelphia, where, around the 1920s, a legendary bootlegger-turned-businessman named Joseph McGarrity had fashioned one of the IRA's first and most successful large-scale gun-smuggling rings. At the time, the IRA was hungry for what was then a new American weapon: the Thompson submachine gun, the infamous tool of choice for many US gangsters. McGarrity, born in Ulster's County Tyrone, would eventually manage to smuggle hundreds of Thompsons into Ireland and into the hands of the remaining anti-treaty IRA brigades after the army split over partition. McGarrity's Thompsons would be the most valuable weapons in the IRA's arsenal during the ensuing decades, keeping them involved in armed conflict.

But by 1970, that historic effort was seen as the high-water mark of Irish-American gun trafficking. McGarrity's network had decayed after his death in 1940, especially as the IRA's waning presence in Ireland made it harder for supporters in the States to justify such risks. Instead, across the 1950s and 1960s, the effort to funnel weapons toward the cause had been left to an ad hoc, loosely connected group of expat IRA veterans — men like Conlon.

This web of IRA gunrunners periodically helped move small hauls of American weapons to Northern Ireland, usually on passenger ships like the Cunard Line's *Queen Elizabeth II* or smuggled onto planes. But the network's efforts were constrained by its modest size and unorganized structure: Conlon in Philadelphia, a man named George Harrison in New York, a few others scattered between Chicago and Boston. But the group didn't work with the kind of large-scale gun shipments that McGarrity had; in Philadelphia, for instance, Conlon maintained relationships with only a few gun dealers from whom he procured the odd rifle, often sending them over in small, smuggled shipments with connections on airplanes.

Conlon's efforts worked well enough, especially during the quieter years following the failed border campaign in which both he and O'Connell had served. But following the British Army's deployment into Northern Ireland in 1969, many in the Provisionals knew the trickle of American guns would never be enough to sustain the IRA in an all-out war.

The situation in Belfast and Derry had grown increasingly dangerous in the months after the IRA's acrimonious split. The Provisionals were no longer just fighting against Loyalist gangs and the British Army; now they were at odds with their onetime partners in the Official IRA. Following the split, the IRA's two branches had become wholly separate, sometimes violently opposed groups. The Provos derogatorily referred to the Officials as the "Stickies" or "Sticks," a tongue-in-cheek nod to the Easter Lily pins that the old guard was known to sport on their lapels, a performative gesture the Provisionals considered a symbol for their larger issues with the Officials. But now, what began as an ideological divide had morphed into an urgent tactical competition.

There was plenty for the two warring IRA factions to fight over, but the most pressing was guns. The backbone of the IRA's arsenal had been McGarrity's aging Thompsons, but even before the IRA split there were hardly enough left to sustain one army. Even faced with the violence of 1969, Goulding refused to break out what few gun stores the Officials still had; the Provos, meanwhile, couldn't steal the Officials' guns without risking an even more deadly feud. Instead, the Provos resorted to training their men with whatever old, rusty guns they could find, busing volunteers to farms in the middle of the night so they could familiarize themselves by passing the outdated rifles around a table. Rarely was a gun ever fired outside an active engagement; ammunition was just too difficult to come by. So, as they sought to become the preeminent fighting force of nationalist Ireland, the Provos' biggest priority — and their first mission — was finding proper weapons for their soldiers. Forty years after Joe McGarrity first outfitted the IRA, it was time, once again, for the army to look toward Philadelphia.

O'Connell's mission to America wasn't the first mounted on behalf of the Provos. In the winter of 1969, a month before the formal IRA split, a small contingent of Provo-aligned IRA men secretly traveled to the States with a proposal for Vince Conlon and Clan-na-Gael.

The Provo delegation included Sean Keenan, a Derry man who, in a last-ditch effort to mend ties between the Officials and the Provos, had gone so far as to approach Conlon's old friend Cathal Goulding in Dublin before he set off. Keenan had proposed the trip to America as a joint mission, one that could patch up the relationship between the Provos and the Officials and restock the IRA's dwindling armory. But Goulding had unceremoniously rebuffed Keenan's suggestion. Sensing that the group would soon split, Keenan set off anyway. He was joined by Joe Cahill, who would become the commander of the Provos' Belfast brigade.

The pair visited a handful of East Coast cities and made public appearances at various Irish Clubs to speak about the unrest in Northern Ireland. But the true purpose of their visit was not meant for public consumption. Sean Keenan and Joe Cahill had arrived to set up a secret American gunrunning network modeled after Joe McGarrity's, and they needed Vince Conlon and Clan-na-Gael to help do it.

Keenan and Cahill's presentation to Conlon, his fellow Clan leader Neil Byrne, and the rest of the group's Philadelphia members was simple: the Provos needed the Clan's loyalty, and they needed guns. McGarrity's Thompsons were now the old stock of the firearms world, and if the Provos were to survive against the well-heeled British security forces, they would need something more contemporary, and more effective.

Enter the ArmaLite rifle.

The ArmaLite AR-180 — the semiautomatic, commercial version of the standard ArmaLite AR-18 — was lightweight and magazine-fed. Streamlined and easy to use, it was foldable, transportable, and simple to clean and take apart. At twenty-seven inches long and only eight pounds, it was a compact long gun, and its gas-operated system was capable of firing off twenty rounds at a time without reloading — and when it did need reloading, users didn't have to feed the bullets into the gun by themselves, a groundbreaking change from the clunky hand-loaded rifles many IRA combatants were used to. Further still, the gun was capable of being individualized with extra features: flash suppressor, scopes, and grenade launchers could be attached.

Perhaps its most formidable feature, though, was just how rapidly the ArmaLite could shoot. The gun could eat through three twenty-round cartridges in a minute — sixty bullets fired in as many seconds. It could shoot constantly for four minutes before it would overheat, and even then it could be back in action not long after. It was accurate from up to eleven city blocks away, and could penetrate a British Army helmet. That range, in a claustrophobic place like Belfast, was mind-boggling. It was a weapon unlike any that came before, built for the sort of urban guerrilla warfare that was coming to define the Troubles.

Deemed "America's rifle" by the National Rifle Association, the ArmaLite was also a distinctly American gun — developed by a former marine, inspired

An ArmaLite AR-180

by the US military's M16 rifle, and initially produced out of a plant in Costa Mesa, California. It was why, when the IRA decided it wanted ArmaLites, there was only one place to go.

Keenan and Cahill's 1969 visit sent the Official IRA into a tailspin. Goulding arrived in Philadelphia not long after to attempt to discredit the two men and their mission, but it was of little use; by 1969, Conlon's relationship with the Official IRA and Goulding had so soured that he was already threatening to leave Clan-na-Gael altogether and go rogue. Instead, in Keenan and Cahill's proposal lay Vince Conlon's long-awaited opportunity. When it came to the IRA's future, Conlon believed, the Provisionals were the way to go — and if they needed ArmaLites, he was the man to get them.

But Vince Conlon wouldn't be able to do it alone. That was what had brought Dave O'Connell to America, just a few months later.

Despite his long list of revolutionary accomplishments, the first thing most folks noticed about Mike Flannery was his hair. Pompadoured and curled around his forehead, by 1970 it was one of his most recognizable traits — that, and a long IRA résumé.

Flannery was an eccentric character in the universe of New York City's Irish, a devout Catholic and teetotaler who attended mass every day at 8 a.m. His path to America had been similar to Conlon's, though he had come a generation earlier. Both were experienced IRA veterans who had fled to the States under duress: Conlon after having escaped jail time, Flannery after having aligned with the losing, anti-treaty side of Ireland's civil war. And like Conlon, Flannery had once harnessed the power of Irish America, first getting involved with Joseph McGarrity's Clan-na-Gael in the period following the 1920s and the partition of the island. Flannery eventually assumed leadership of the entire organization — just as Conlon would go on to do — and established the group as a haven for expat IRA men. But by 1970, the days of Flannery's frontline service were behind him.

Still, he was no pacifist. When it came to the Irish struggle, Flannery was unequivocal in his support for militant nationalism: "The sword," he said, "is the only means of getting peace." But he was also a member of polite society in a city with one of the biggest Irish populations outside of the island. Indeed, by the time Derry and Belfast were at war, Flannery had slipped into the Irish-American mainstream, having spent decades establishing himself as a well-respected personality among the broader community: among other endeavors, Flannery helped manage Irish social clubs in New York and was involved in the city's Gaelic Athletic Association, the popular group that organized Irish football and hurling leagues. His new network made fomenting illicit revolutions more difficult, but it gave him valuable credibility among the diaspora.

This was why Mike Flannery was one of the first people Dave O'Connell visited after arriving on the East Coast in 1970. The preceding months had made something very clear: the IRA was about to have a new moment, and so too could Irish America, as the main source of support for the cause outside of Ireland. Wars, after all, were expensive, and not just because the Provos needed to buy guns; the conflict would further tax Northern Ireland's under-resourced Irish Catholics. Dave O'Connell and the Provo leadership knew this. Further, the coming months would bring a near-constant cull of IRA volunteers, lost to prison and otherwise — men whose absence would prove a financial burden on their families. This looming toll was underscored by the IRA's own policies, which aligned with those of more traditional armies: since the 1920s, the organization had sought to financially support the families of volunteers who were captured or killed in action. It was a modest kindness, one that was more easily managed during the quieter years of the 1950s and '60s — but, O'Connell predicted, that was about to change. The Provisional IRA was likely to soon be confronted with an unprecedented wave of fatherless children and widowed spouses who would need money. And Flannery, as the former head of Clan-na-Gael turned duke of the East Coast diaspora, knew how to find it.

O'Connell had a road map in mind. A defunct group called the Friends of Irish Freedom had collected financial support for the IRA from Irish-Americans during the War of Independence in the 1920s. Perhaps, O'Connell thought, a similar group could be stood up under Flannery, who had already established the sorts of contacts and social heft that would be needed to legitimize such an effort.

What the Provisional IRA needed, if it was to succeed, was a fundraising mechanism that would tug at the hearts and purse strings of the Irish diaspora in America, without directly linking the money to the IRA. After all, while many in America were sympathetic to the cause, few were so bold or bellicose that they would knowingly fund arms purchases for the IRA. Irish Americans needed an organization that they would feel inclined to support but that could not be traced back to the illicit maneuverings Conlon and his colleagues were pursuing. In other words, they needed to maintain plausible deniability, in case anyone tried to connect the organization's money to guns.

This was why O'Connell had so eagerly sought out Mike Flannery, who was well placed to shepherd the more anodyne fundraising activities of the Provos' American strategy. Still, fundraising would be complicated; Irish-American politics tended to be much more moderate than those of Irish-born rebels like O'Connell and the Belfast brigade, who were significantly left of center. Flannery and his collaborators would have to tamp down that rhetoric, lest they alienate the very donors they were seeking to court.

There were already troubling signs of such political schisms. In 1969, Bernadette Devlin, a staunch Irish nationalist and parliamentary representative from County Tyrone, had embarked on her own fundraising effort in America. Rather than drum up support for the cause, however, the tour had led to clashes with Irish Americans, who bristled at what they viewed as Devlin's radical stump speech: In visits to Irish cities like Chicago and Philadelphia, Devlin invoked Black liberation issues and voiced support for groups like the Black Panthers. She embodied the contemporary Irish Republican consciousness, which found common cause in those movements, but her worldview clashed sharply with the more conservative — and often racist — outlook of Irish Americans, who soured quickly on their guest from the homeland. Devlin chastised them for "narrow-mindedness"; in turn, the Irish Americans labeled her a communist.

It was a disastrous foray, and a cautionary tale — a mistake people like Flannery would avoid repeating. Political principles, it was clear, would have to be secondary to the practical needs of the Provos.

And so, when Flannery realized that Irish-American support would be critical to the already under-resourced Catholic communities in Northern Ireland, he and O'Connell were adamant that if the effort was to succeed, it needed to have mass appeal. That meant it needed to be free of any links to the IRA's violence. Unlike Clan-na-Gael, it simply could not be institutionally linked to the army; instead, the organization would exist solely under the vague humanitarian mission "to help and clothe the people of Northern Ireland."

But what to call this fundraising organization? Flannery, O'Connell, and two other veteran IRA men brainstormed in New York that spring, trying and failing to find the right moniker. "The Dependents Fund," a nod to the families of IRA prisoners, was considered but deemed too vague. Instead, the group settled on the Irish Northern Aid Committee, or NORAID. Headquartered in New York and led by Flannery, the organization would be linked with a Belfast-based group of the same name, to which it would send most of its proceeds.

The catchy acronym would soon be widely known, echoing up and down the East Coast, in Irish pubs and in community centers across America. And by the end of the year, it would be flying up and down the hallways of the FBI.

Initially, the schism between the Official and Provisional IRA confused Irish-American clubs, which often failed to differentiate between the factions and underestimated just how acrimonious the split had been. In some cases, clubs even continued inviting members from both IRA branches to speak, or sent money to both armies.

It was a confusing moment for a diaspora that until 1969, was mostly ambivalent toward the Northern Irish conflict or supportive of the politically pragmatic Official IRA, which was revolutionary enough for most Irish-American tastes. But the split of 1969 had sent the diaspora into its own dizzying spiral of feuds, conflicts, and divisions. Some Irish Americans quickly endorsed the violent tactics of the Provisional IRA. Others, while moved by the plight of Northern Ireland's Catholics, were less sure about the solution, viewing the Provos' militancy with deep unease. Still others balked at it entirely and continued to support the Officials.

NORAID would clarify the battle lines. Soon, the group was feuding with more conservative Irish Republican clubs that aligned with the Official IRA. Those who supported NORAID accused other clubs of being "communists," and the clubs, in turn, tarred NORAID as "green fascists." Fistfights broke out between NORAID picketers and members of Irish Republican Clubs at anti-British demonstrations, and NORAID members protested at Official-linked bars. Out of these scuffles, NORAID quickly established itself as the stronger, better-supported network, capitalizing on the general Irish-American outrage over happenings in Northern Ireland. In a field of antiquated social structures, NORAID offered a fresh, more contemporary outlet for Irish Americans to exercise their heritage and provided a means to engage with the Irish struggle in a way that more traditional clubs did not. NORAID emerged as clearly the most prominent of the Irish-American organizations.

Behind closed doors, Vince Conlon was managing a similar division within Clan-na-Gael. That split became urgent after Conlon accepted Keenan and Cahill's mission to arm the Provos. Not everyone within Clan-na-Gael agreed with that direction. Even among the more militant diaspora in Philadelphia, some members felt deeply loyal to Goulding and eschewed the Provisional strategy; chief among those voices was Brigid Makowski, the organizer from Derry who first pushed Clan-na-Gael to open its rolls to women members. (Coincidentally, it was Conlon's compatriot Neil Byrne who first endorsed Makowski's enrollment into the Clan.) Longtime friends, Makowski and Conlon had spent most of the 1960s as a united front, building up the Clan and establishing its base in Philadelphia. But when the moment came in 1969 to choose sides, Makowski remained loyal to Cathal Goulding. Although supportive of the IRA's campaign of violence, she was unconvinced that the Provos' politics could sustain lasting change — reservations that brought her into conflict with her old friends. It was a slow, bitter estrangement, but Makowski eventually returned to Ireland and pledged loyalty to the Officials (she would later grow disenchanted with the Officials and found her own, Provisional-adjacent political party, the Irish Republican Socialist Party). The debacle underscored how deeply the Provisional split had fractured Irish America.

Most of Philadelphia's Clan-na-Gael contingent, though, stayed with Conlon. Among them was his friend Neil Byrne, who moved into a new role within the Provisional IRA's American campaign, working closely with a group of coconspirators in New York. There, Sean Keenan had courted another ally for the IRA, a man who would come to work very closely with the Philadelphia cell. After all, in order to buy guns for the IRA, Vince Conlon and Neil Byrne needed money, and NORAID was about to have a lot of it. It was as simple as that.

NORAID took to Irish America like wildfire to dry prairie. Dozens of chapters exploded in all corners of the country, from Boston to Chicago to small enclaves in Montana and the rural West. They sprang up so quickly that NORAID leadership could hardly keep track of the group's scope. Thousands joined NORAID as members. There were one-man chapters in North Dakota and groups in Chicago and San Francisco that grew and grew. Its billing was simple: NORAID collected money and donations to send to Northern Ireland's Catholics, many of whom had lost their homes and belongings during the riots of 1969, and continued to face unemployment, threats of jail, and hostilities by British troops. O'Connell's prediction had been prescient: Irish Americans, long passionate about their roots, wanted a way to help. In NORAID they found it.

To be sure, America's Irish diaspora was large and varied, with tens of millions of Americans who could claim some degree of Irish heritage, and NORAID membership represented a relatively small proportion of that very large demographic. But while they may have been proportionally modest, NORAID members made up for it in enthusiasm. Among those who stayed engaged with their Irish roots, NORAID exploded in popularity. The group traded in small donations, mostly in cash. The vast majority of NORAID's donations came from individuals who gave small bills and spare change. Some of the group's most lucrative fundraising drives were conducted with tin cans at Irish pubs, and at informal auctions, where organizers sold off handicrafts — often made of leather or matchsticks — that had been handmade by IRA prisoners and then smuggled into America. The convoluted cash flow was a convenient security measure, too, since it ensured that the money trail from NORAID to Belfast was difficult to track and almost impossible to tie back to a specific person or chapter. Flannery was no fool on this front. "With cash," he reflected later, "the government didn't know how much we sent."

NORAID contributions were collected from all corners of America, then combined and sent to Belfast. The disbursements were put into large checks and ferried discreetly across the Atlantic in an ad hoc courier system: trusted NORAID affiliates who planned to visit home were often asked if they'd be willing to "take a message" to Belfast on their travels. The message often included tens of thousands of dollars in bank checks, which the travelers were expected to hand-carry to the leadership of NORAID's primary beneficiary, the Northern Aid Committee in Belfast.

Whether the money went to guns, clothes, or familial support of prisoners was a question Flannery never sought to clearly answer, for reasons of plausible deniability. NORAID, he said, only maintained a relationship with its sister organization in Belfast, and had no direct connection to the IRA.

But the circles of NORAID, Clan-na-Gael, and the IRA overlapped, early and often. The truth was that NORAID was born of a very specific need, and when Flannery and his cofounders first established the group, they also created a shadow hierarchy inside it. Known as "the inner circle," it included a small network of NORAID members whose proclivities went beyond the benevolent, many of whom also happened to be members of Clan-na-Gael. It would make it much easier to skim some of NORAID's funds and slip them toward the efforts of people like Conlon.

The members of NORAID's inner circle were drawn from a handful of locales, usually places with radical tendencies and strong, historic ties to Irish Republicanism. Philadelphia, of course, was one of them and quickly became one of the organization's strongholds, with chapters in all corners of the city — Philadelphia was second only to New York in terms of NORAID membership rolls and contributions. Given the city's passion for the IRA — *and* its historically Northern Irish makeup — NORAID leadership carefully staffed Philadelphia's various chapters with people who could oversee both NORAID's fundraising and its lethal freelancing. They were handpicked by Vince Conlon and Hugh Breen, the founding members of Philadelphia NORAID.

Neil Byrne, Conlon's friend in Clan-na-Gael, was an obvious choice for one of these positions. Byrne would lead NORAID's Bucks County chapter, covering the territory immediately to the city's north, in close cooperation with Breen, the IRA veteran who owned Breen's Café, a pub in Northeast Philadelphia. But there was a gap in the city that needed filling: many of its Irish had spread to southwestern suburbs like Delaware County, a working-class, Irish area whose politics aligned with the more radical bent of Breen's and Byrne's. There, too, NORAID needed a member of the inner circle.

The job of finding such a man fell to Breen, whose pub was quickly becoming a staging ground for these sorts of illicit operations. To lead such a group in Delaware County, the NORAID inner circle needed someone both discreet and reputable, someone who was already known within the city's Irish circles — but not someone as well known as Conlon, who was already associated with the IRA.

Breen knew just such a man: a quiet, intense carpenter who had settled in Delaware County after emigrating to Philadelphia from Cork in the 1950s. Breen was spending time with him recently and was impressed. A decorated American Army veteran with his own business, the man was well respected and well liked, inside the Irish community and beyond it. He was exactly the kind of man they needed to handle NORAID's business — kosher and otherwise.

CHAPTER 5

"UNTIL IRELAND IS FREE OR UNTIL I DRAW MY LAST BREATH"

LATE ONE NIGHT at Bridge and the Boulevard, Hughie Breen's tavern was at its usual hum when one of the regulars raised himself from the bar. He motioned to a young laborer nearby; there was an errand that the older man needed to run, and he wanted company.

Tall and bookish with thick glasses, dark eyes, and a swath of curly, black hair, Daniel Cahalane was well known among Philadelphia's Irish, easily spotted by the green work van that he drove all over the city. He had been a mainstay in the Irish community for years, but in recent months he had taken on a new, more serious role — one that only a chosen few knew about.

Cahalane directed the young laborer out onto the dark street and into the passenger seat of his van. They glided silently eastward on Roosevelt Boulevard toward the New Jersey Turnpike, the busy highway that connected New York City to Philadelphia.

The younger man glanced around nervously. He had heard rumors about what might be going on during these evening drives, and having just discreetly arrived in Philadelphia himself from Northern Ireland, he had enough trouble, and wasn't eager to court more. But Danny Cahalane was respected and trusted. Even on this secretive errand, he seemed calm behind the wheel.

Cahalane finally swung the van into a darkened rest stop on the side of the interstate. He parked, turned off the ignition, and got out of the van; the anxious young man followed suit. Wordlessly, the pair walked through rows of cars until Cahalane motioned for the boy to join him in a different truck. He started the vehicle and they drove back to Philadelphia, leaving his own van in the dark lot.

A few days later, Cahalane was driving his green work van around Philadelphia again. No one ever quite explained to his young accomplice what happened on that dark turnpike, why Cahalane seemingly abandoned the van — and whatever else might've been left at the rest stop while the two of them had driven in silence, back home.

Until 1970, nothing about Danny Cahalane suggested a tendency toward fanaticism, of the Irish ilk or otherwise. Tall and quiet, often smoking a pipe, he was equal parts magnetic and mysterious in the small Irish community he came to call home. He was a particular man, prone to wearing pressed suits and ties even among gatherings of friends, of which he kept a tight circle. But there was a part of Danny Cahalane that was enigmatic, as if there was a side of him that no one, not even his closest friends, could really know.

Cahalane's path to suburban Philadelphia from rural Cork, a county along the southern coast of the Republic of Ireland, had followed a common script at the time. Far removed from the bustle of Dublin, County Cork was mostly rural, mostly poor, and plagued with unemployment and scarce resources, isolated on the rocky shore of Ireland's most southwestern corner. Facing few prospects, Cahalane had looked to America for the same reasons many immigrants did: it was the land of opportunity, and in Cork he had none. At twenty-four, he traveled to Dublin, walked into the American consulate, and applied for a visa, telling the official that he had family in Philadelphia who would help him get on his feet; his aunt and uncle lived there. And so, lured by the promise of work and a soft landing, Cahalane set out, in the winter of 1949, for the States.

He missed Ireland and returned periodically to visit family; but from the moment Cahalane set foot on US soil, he was enchanted by the country's promises of freedom and equality. He embraced American culture in ways large and small, coaching little league and putting on neighborhood movie nights.

Not long after first emigrating, Cahalane enlisted in the American army and served in the Korean War, a path taken by many immigrants at the time who sought a faster path to US citizenship. It was a brief deployment — Cahalane was discharged before 1951 was over — but he returned from the assignment decorated, receiving a Purple Heart for injuries sustained at the front. For whatever pride he may have had in the honor, he never spoke of it. By 1970, Korea was a ghost in Cahalane's past, but for the persistent hearing loss that would plague him for the rest of his life. All he said of the peninsula was that it was both the hottest and coldest place on earth.

Korea was Cahalane's only brush with conflict, despite his origins in the heart of so-called Rebel Cork, a region with deep ties to Irish rebellion. Cork was the scene of some of Ireland's most brutal fighting in the 1920s, when the Irish Republican Army first came to be. The region would see a disproportionate number of raids by the Black and Tans, a British-backed policing group that harassed and abused Irish residents of the occupied island (the same mercenaries who brutalized the New York gunrunner George Harrison and his family in County Mayo, farther north).

But most of those battles were long over by the time Cahalane was a boy. With the end of Ireland's war for independence and the birth of a free Irish state in 1921, the British left Cork, and so did the fighting. Cahalane was born deep in the quiet fishing village of Glandore, hundreds of miles away from the contested Northern Irish border, where the remaining clashes were concentrated. He never joined the IRA and never seemed to regret it, and by 1970 he landed something of a first-generation American dream.

By most measures, Cahalane was a classic mid-century suburban dad, and a self-made immigrant. He found it all in Philadelphia: family, friends, a successful business. Compared to Ireland's gray, Philadelphia was a riot of color and opportunity. Cahalane met a Philadelphia girl, Jane McCloskey, and the pair married on Thanksgiving weekend, 1952. They first settled in Northeast Philly, the same neighborhood where Vince Conlon and Hughie Breen held court. There, Cahalane quickly established himself as a skilled contractor, and by 1970 he owned his own business, zipping around the city and its suburbs in the green work van with which he came to be synonymous. When he and Jane started a family, they moved out of the city to the suburb of Newtown Square, in Delaware County, just outside the city limits of West Philadelphia. There, Cahalane and their friends had built his and Jane's family home with their own hands.

Danny and Jane were comfortable and happy, raising three children — Mary Jane, Connie, and the youngest, Danny Jr. — among friends. Despite his reserved demeanor, Cahalane was a gentle man, never known to raise his voice. Some things, though, he never let go: no matter how long he was in the States, he held onto his Cork accent, a dialect so thick that words could be indistinguishable when spoken quickly.

But quietly, in 1970, Cahalane had started to radicalize. In a strange way, he was closer to Ireland's turmoil in Philadelphia, with its disproportionately large Northern population, than he ever was in Cork.

Fortune and success in America had tempered some of the diaspora's politics, even in a more radical city like Philadelphia: many of the city's second- and third-generation immigrants had gone on to become successful businessmen and women, teachers, doctors, and lawyers, and few in that company had the stomach for hard-line politics like Conlon's or Breen's. Their convictions had softened — and as disturbed as they may have been by the behavior of British security forces in Belfast and Derry, they stopped short of full-throated endorsement of the IRA. Philadelphia's diaspora was thus fractured into increasingly isolated segments, both politically and geographically: the more moderate Irish Americans stayed in the city's center and its affluent suburbs, known as the Main Line, while the blue-collar crowd, the ones like Cahalane, remained where they had landed, in Mayfair, Olney, and later, Delaware County. The older Irish-American generation might've grown soft, but these new arrivals hadn't, and they were alert for any sign of trouble back home.

Left:
A young Danny Cahalane, around the time he emigrated to Philadelphia in 1949

Right:
Danny and Jane Cahalane met in Philadelphia and wed in 1952.

Even for people like Cahalane, who never seemed inclined toward the harder edge of Irish Republican politics, 1969 changed things. Whatever indecision had existed before, such ambivalence was untenable now. Everyone around Cahalane knew it. Things were different. *He* was different.

And, he wasn't alone. Breen's Café, too, had changed. For years it was a favored watering hole for Danny and men like him, who could relax in the quiet bar among like kind. But ever since riots had spilled across Northern Ireland, the place had taken on its own foreboding pallor. The pub was in Mayfair, but some days it might as well have been Derry or Belfast. Hushed conversations were murmured across its bartop, and men shuffled in and out of the attic for secret gatherings. It had never been the sort of place that catered to outsiders anyway, but by 1970 every stranger who walked through Breen's door had started to feel like a threat.

Cahalane's best friend grew up in Armagh, the same border county as Vince Conlon. Gruff and towering, sandy-haired with a crooked smile, Bill Corry's bottom jaw seemed permanently set forward, like a bulldog primed for a fight. It was a posture that served Corry well — unlike Cahalane, he had been raised in the Irish Republican tradition. His father was involved in the IRA during the 1920s and spent most of Corry's childhood a hunted man, chased by the British. Corry was a famously indulgent storyteller, known to recount memories of his dad punching through the thatched roof of Corry's childhood home, and slipping through the straw to escape soldiers at the door.

Like many men his age from the divided North, Corry had encountered the brutality of Northern Ireland at close range and joined the IRA's Armagh brigade. But Corry had left before he could see service in the poorly imagined border campaign of the late 1950s. Instead, after bouncing around work in Belfast, he fled to America in 1949, the same year Cahalane had.

It was perhaps fated that Corry and Cahalane's paths would collide, as they did in the 1950s. Among Philadelphia's insular community of Irish laborers, the two men quickly became inseparable. They were an odd couple — the brash, muscled Corry with rolled-up work sleeves and a loose collar; and the slight, rigid Cahalane who socialized in a carefully pressed suit. The pair spent free nights driving Cahalane's van around Philadelphia or hunting rabbits. By the time 1970 rolled around, both men were raising young families in the city's outskirts, where they had helped build each other's homes.

Corry was a workhorse, a born and bred union man who knew everyone and could find a way to build, fix, or jerryrig just about everything. That enterprising streak translated just as well to politics as it did carpentry: everyone on Philadelphia's docks knew Corry, and every Irishman who needed to get a union card and a bed, fast, knew where to find him. Corry was tied in with them all — John McCullough's roofers' union, the dockworkers' union, the electricians' union. The outfits were great for jobs, and great for the working man, but they were also great for the Irish, especially when tensions back home started sending hordes of them on the run. If a man needed a fake name and a job, Corry knew how to find him one. The walls of his home were plastered with photographs of Irish revolutionaries, and by 1970 a rotating cast of characters — strangers with thick brogues, introduced only with a first name — routinely appeared for a few days at the Corry home in suburban Philadelphia. His children grew accustomed to the strange rhythm of the house, their dinner tables populated with new faces. The rule was simple: be kind and don't ask questions.

By the early 1950s, Corry was entrenched in the city's network of Irish radicals, and he was well connected with one in particular: Vince Conlon, with whom he had been close since the pair had met on the border, in Armagh. They had worked together with Clan-na-Gael through the 1960s and even bought property together on Philadelphia's outskirts. Corry had earned a reputation among Conlon's circle as a bold but astute operator, with the right mix of caution and confidence. It was perhaps no surprise that by 1970, Corry, Conlon, and Cahalane had become fast friends — and coconspirators.

Nearly a dozen NORAID units would spring up around Philadelphia, and many operated just as Mike Flannery had intended, at least outwardly: they were humanitarian organizations that collected charitable donations for the North.

But Danny Cahalane's mission was different. As the head of the Delaware County NORAID unit in 1970, he was part of the group's clandestine inner circle. Confronted with this enormous task, he excelled. Churches, dinner halls, community centers, speeches and rallies and protests — if there was something going on in the city that concerned Ireland, Dan Cahalane was there.

The responsibility transformed the otherwise understated Cahalane, who had generally shirked attention and was unmoved by much — aside from the plight of the country he had left behind. To be sure, he remained characteristically low-key — that nighttime mission with the young laborer was proof. But underneath that calm exterior, he was nursing a radical bent.

"I promise to work for it until Ireland is free or until I draw my last breath," he would later say during a speech at a NORAID event. He tacked on an ominous addition: "Whichever comes first."

PART II

THE INNER CIRCLE

CHAPTER 6

JEKYLL AND HYDE

THE FATHER WAS dressed as dark as the night, his frock hardly visible against the flat black of the dockyard. Silently, he slipped among the shipping crates. He was alone, a one-man operation in a city of shadows. That was how they had to work, though. Any additional person was a liability, and with the way things seemed to be going with the FBI, they couldn't afford any.

The Father set his sights ahead and trod casually along, or as casually as he could with his clunky cargo: two heavy boxes, far too heavy for a normal man to lift. But he was no normal man — sturdy and tall, his hands were as big as paddles. He shifted the weight of the crates easily.

The boxes had undergone a long journey, hand-carted from one apartment to another, transferred between car trunks, up and down the Eastern Seaboard until finally they landed in a small Bronx apartment. There, they were packed full of everything that the group of NORAID men had collected over the previous weeks. The Father had labeled the boxes as plumbing supplies, stenciling an Irish address haphazardly on the side — no one on the docks would know the difference anyway.

It was more than a year since that first fateful visit by the Provos, when Sean Keenan and Joe Cahill came to America and asked for help. Philadelphia wasn't the only city the IRA men had visited, nor was Vince Conlon the only gunrunner they'd propositioned. Keenan and Cahill had courted a new network, and they worked together now, all of them. Here, on this New York dock — this was the system NORAID's inner circle had established. The whole machine was reliably unpredictable. Patterns, after all, were dangerous. Patterns were clues, and those had to be avoided. The boxes were rarely picked up by the same man twice, and were rarely dropped at the same apartments or even at the same time of day.

The operation was one of constant false starts, plans that worked for a while and then didn't. Improvisation turned into the only way. They were able to cart things over on the *Queen Elizabeth II,* the luxury ocean liner, their contraband secreted across the sea in the luggage of sympathizers. And the Philly boys had a good connection with air freight for a while, sneaking guns over via amenable pilots. But that, too, became riskier the more the situation in Belfast spiraled. These days, they were back to using ships. It was silly, really, that they hadn't thought of it sooner — New York's Irish laborers were all over the city's docks and container industries, which meant the inner circle could sneak illicit cargo into and out of shipping lanes with relative ease. More than that, a handful of friends in border patrol made sure the crates left the country undisturbed. If they needed a container left alone, or an extra box scratched off the itinerary, that was easy enough.

The cargo came from everywhere, but it was the Philadelphia cell that had recently hit their stride, sending a steady flow of stock up to New York, where it could be forwarded to Ireland expeditiously through the docks. They were pushing significant numbers. If the FBI or Scotland Yard had any idea how much firepower was moving up and down the New Jersey Turnpike on any given weekend, they would be dumbfounded, even more so if they knew who was behind it. An entire guerrilla war was being propped up by a strange collection of suburban fathers with brogues — and some faith, still, in a united Ireland.

Satisfied, the Father left the boxes at the docks. They would get where they needed to, he was sure of that for now: to the front lines of a war in which there were few other choices. Eventually, the man shed his disguise. Robust and boy-faced, he was unassuming enough; no one really knew who he was, and he liked it that way. And he was no priest; Marty Lyons was an Irishman and a plumber, friendly with Sean Keenan and Vince Conlon going all the way back to the border campaign. And these days, he also happened to be the chairman of the Irish Northern Aid Committee.

If Irish America needed any further encouragement to sit up and pay attention to Northern Ireland, 1970 had brought it. The worst fears of the region's

Catholics were realized with the arrival of British troops. Rather than serve as arbiters between them and Unionists, the soldiers' operations seemed designed to further target nationalist neighborhoods. The same script would play out time and time again: British troops would descend on Catholic ghettos, barging through front doors and ransacking homes in a hunt for guns and men. The raids quickly scuttled any goodwill between Catholic Belfast and British soldiers. One incident in particular became infamous: the Falls Road Curfew.

It started innocuously enough on July 3, 1970, when a British Army brigade arrived to a small group of houses on the Lower Falls. The soldiers had their sights on a cluster of homes where they believed a store of IRA guns and men were hidden, but even that supposedly simple mission was misguided: the soldiers, armed with bad, outdated intelligence, were targeting homes run by the Official IRA, not the Provos, despite the fact that it was the latter group who had emerged as the clear purveyor of violence in Belfast and elsewhere.

As the troops began to leave the neighborhood after their initial, unsuccessful operation, they were pelted with stones by bitter locals along the Falls Road. A small group of soldiers became trapped, and backup was summoned. That straightforward maneuver quickly spiraled into a panicked escalation. The trickle of military reinforcements became a tidal wave. Soon some three thousand soldiers were occupying the neighborhood's claustrophobic streets.

It was, essentially, an invasion of the Lower Falls, which responded with the fury of a people under siege. So disproportionate was the British response to the incident that even Falls Road residents who were not originally aligned with the Provos joined in the fight, hurling petrol bombs and stones, and sheltering IRA men and their guns. As the fighting raged on, a British Army helicopter descended over the Lower Falls and declared a weekend curfew. Anyone found on the streets, its loudspeaker screeched, would be shot, essentially restricting twenty thousand residents to their homes. There, they were forced to wait as British troops went door to door, kicking their way into Catholic homes in the search for IRA members and their guns.

For three days, the Lower Falls was ransacked. Tearing through homes, bars, and businesses, soldiers confiscated around a hundred weapons, but at a steep price: four residents with no IRA connections were killed — three shot by British troops, a fourth crushed by an army vehicle. And the full cost of the curfew would be felt for years to come. For most in the Lower Falls, the weekend erased any hope that the British troops might be a mediator between nationalists and Unionists. Instead, the weekend turned much of Catholic Belfast toward the fledgling Provisional IRA, which seemed to be the only organization with any chance of striking back against Unionists, Loyalists, or British troops.

As the curfew was lifted, the people of the Lower Falls flooded the streets, Provisional fighters concealed within the crowd. Everyone, it seemed — women, children, grandmothers — had united behind the Provos, shielding the volunteers from view and hiding their guns, sometimes in baby strollers. A new era of solidarity had dawned, and it favored the Provos over their factional rivals in the Official IRA, whose diplomatic tactics now seemed gravely miscalculated. There was no more ambivalence, at least not among the residents of the Lower Falls, who had now seen just how brutal life under occupation would be.

Incidents like the Falls Curfew helped turn the fledgling NORAID into a household name at most Irish-American dinner tables, and a regular part of the diaspora's lexicon. Flannery was right: plenty of Irish Americans wanted to show solidarity with the Irish people, especially as they dealt with such hostilities. Irish communities had always boasted a robust social structure of clubs and social organizations, but few had such urgent political postures. In NORAID Flannery filled a gap, and it had come at exactly the right time. The group became the de facto cultural center for huge swaths of Irish America, and its political edge provided something most Irish organizations didn't: a chance to engage earnestly with the Irish conflict. The horrific images beamed across the ocean from Belfast and Derry had agitated an entire segment of Irish America — people who may not have considered themselves hardcore, militant Irish Republicans, but who still wanted to express their outrage. NORAID became the principal way for them to do so.

It's hard to know how much NORAID's rank and file knew — or chose to ignore — as far as the group's connection with the Provos. By 1971, even among more conservative Irish Americans, violent incidents like the Falls Curfew far overshadowed concerns over NORAID's loose affiliations with — or tacit endorsement of — the Provos. Plausible deniability was the order of the day, both for NORAID's leadership and for the group in general. And, it grew so quickly, and spread so fast, it was easy to claim ignorance, attributing NORAID's shadowy IRA links to a few bad apples rather than to the organization itself.

Indeed, NORAID remained almost elementary in its simplicity: The group would take any amount of money, anytime, from anyone. Plied by promises that the donations were helping their countrymen in Northern Ireland — like those who had just had their homes ransacked by British soldiers — members emptied their pockets. In its first year of fundraising disclosures to the US government, the organization claimed to have sent more than $130,000 to Northern Ireland.

Trade unions like John McCullough's roofers' union, in Philadelphia, were also dependable NORAID supporters, thanks to their heavily Irish membership rolls. Not only did the group cut checks, but McCullough made sure there were always bodies around to bolster protests, or help organize events: "If we told John [McCullough] we needed five hundred people tomorrow morning at nine o'clock," one union leader and NORAID member said, "he'd have six hundred."

It was incidents like the Falls Curfew that added legitimacy to NORAID's public-facing cause. Indeed, there was an urgent need to support the Catholic families of Northern Ireland, especially those in cities like Belfast and Derry, who were increasingly being forced from their homes, their belongings destroyed, left with nothing. The inner circle may have had its own illicit purpose, but NORAID's outward mission — humanitarian support for Northern Ireland's disenfranchised Catholics — was entirely legitimate in light of the abuses that group was suffering.

In Philadelphia, Dan Cahalane led marches and protests, rallying dozens outside the city's British consulate. There were regular trips to New York to demonstrate on Fifth Avenue with NORAID chapters from across the country. Overnight, it seemed, the group became bound up in the fabric of daily life in Irish America. Community centers hosted meetings, churches hosted auctions, and anybody with a room big enough hosted dances and dinners. NORAID wasn't just a club; in cities like New York and Philadelphia, it became a ubiquitous part of daily life.

Leaders like Mike Flannery, who had fought in Ireland's War of Independence, were a big reason why NORAID found such an eager base of members. The IRA heroes of the 1920s resonated deeply with Irish Americans, who often gravitated toward less complicated, more sentimental versions of Irish Republicanism. Flannery and his colleagues acted as figureheads around whom NORAID members could rally. He was a good personality to be running the group, and the right name to get Irish Americans interested and involved.

But Flannery's leadership position in NORAID masked a deceptive hierarchy. Flannery had meant what he said when he and Dave O'Connell first set up the group the year before: on its face, NORAID *had* to appear benevolent, free of ties to the IRA and all its violent trappings. But NORAID's purpose had been inherently linked to the Provos since its inception, back when Vince Conlon first agreed to be a gun smuggler for the Provos. Members of the inner circle, people like Danny Cahalane and Neil Byrne, were scattered throughout NORAID, keen to use some of its windfall for other, more lethal methods of support. But they needed someone to direct that clandestine effort — someone placed high up in NORAID who could facilitate the interface with Conlon's more militant Clan-na-Gael faction, which had openly associated with the IRA. This person couldn't be Flannery, who needed to maintain NORAID's benevolent façade. Instead, Flannery's Jekyll needed a Hyde. This is where the Father came in.

A sturdy man with a ruddy face and a brusque demeanor, Marty Lyons hailed from Galway, a wind-beaten, seaside county in the west of Ireland. He, too, was a veteran of the IRA, although a generation younger than Flannery; like Vince Conlon, Lyons had served in the 1950s border campaign and had emigrated to New York in 1960, not long after that fight had sputtered. Known simply as "the Boy," he had established a quiet life for himself in the Bronx, where he became a successful plumber and a leader in the industry's union, a powerful labor board that was one of many in the city run by the Irish. But unlike Flannery, who also courted such company, Lyons was an enigma in New York's insular Irish circles, preferring to keep a low profile.

Most history books would eventually pass over Marty Lyons's name when they covered NORAID and Irish America. But if Michael Flannery was the best-known personality in NORAID, Marty Lyons was the most powerful. He worked in the shadows, unknown even to most of the organization's members. And this was for the best, since Lyons was uninterested in the delicate politics required of an American-based humanitarian group. In short, he was the exact kind of muscle man Flannery needed to manage NORAID's secret endeavors — and to fulfill its illicit purpose.

"We took the older men from the '20s, who had gained tremendous respectability among the Irish community in New York and Chicago and California and everywhere else, and we put them out front," Lyons would say later

A NORAID pamphlet honoring Marty Lyons in the 1970s

Martin Lyons was born in Cashel Glenamaddy Co. Gal tendded St. Patrick's school Boyounagh and Glenamaddy,

of NORAID's structure. "Behind them were younger people with the new ideology." This arrangement, he mused, "worked very well."

Among the inner circle, at least, everyone knew who was actually in charge. When a member ran afoul of Flannery, a colleague assured the man: "Don't be concerned about him. He's not the number one boy. Martin Lyons is."

It was a fragile arrangement, having a public-facing organization as the front for a decidedly illegal transcontinental gun-smuggling operation. But that was what made Lyons the perfect fit. To run something clandestine, NORAID needed someone who wasn't that well known. Someone with discretion, someone with a face that was easy to forget.

"Who knew Martin Lyons that long ago?" Lyons once said of himself, coyly. "Nobody."

One person, though, did know who Marty Lyons was, and in early 1971, he had set out across an ocean to find him.

Brendan Hughes, a scrappy fighter with the IRA's Belfast brigade, wasn't the kind of person you'd normally send on a high-stakes negotiating mission. He was a fighter, full stop — not a fundraiser, not a diplomat, and certainly not a politician. Dark-haired with a bushy mustache, Hughes was a young merchant mariner from West Belfast when he first fell in with the Provos. He was home on a brief break from the sea during the Clonard Street riots in 1969. It was a formative experience for Hughes, who would enlist with the IRA and never return to the shipyard. By the spring of 1971, he had emerged as one of the Provisionals' key soldiers, closely aligned with Gerry Adams, one of the leading young voices in the Provos. During incidents like the Falls Curfew, Hughes solidified himself as a close ally of Adams and one of the IRA's most daring and capable fighters, fatally elusive and nicknamed "the Dark."

Hughes liked guns, but in the early days of the Provos, he didn't get to use them much, especially as the young IRA faction struggled against the more efficient weapons of the British Army; back then, neither the Officials nor the Provos had much of an arsenal to speak of, let alone anything that could compete with imperial firepower.

"You had this sort of conflict going on, the Official IRA trying to hold onto the weapons that they had, and the Provisional IRA trying to get a hold of them," Hughes said.

The situation that followed was emblematic of the early organizational problems with the Provos and their nascent efforts to solidify inroads in America. In those formative, chaotic days of 1970 and 1971, there were dozens of small alliances and groups, factions of the Provisional IRA and factions of Irish America, who variously worked together or against each other, depending on the day and nature of the effort. Put simply, the transatlantic right hand didn't always know what the left was doing; and more than that, there were various hands in the mix. Further complicating matters was the fact that the Provisional IRA was rather decentralized in its early days. Communication between brigades in Derry and Belfast was haphazard, and many of the newer, younger Provisionals didn't maintain connections to border campaign veterans like Vince Conlon or Dave O'Connell, who had quickly risen to the fore of the new Provisional army. Mild tension even simmered between the two generational factions, with the older, more polished veterans warning the younger Belfast contingent to shape up.

So it was that as the conflict dragged into the 1970s, Gerry Adams and Brendan Hughes reached the same conclusion that Sean Keenan and Joe Cahill had reached years before in 1969, when Keenan and Cahill sought the help of Vince Conlon: the Provos needed to get their own guns, and they needed something far better than the aging weapons the Officials had.

There is little indication that Hughes or Adams knew of Keenan's and Cahill's previous trip to the States, or the various arrangements it had inspired.

As the story goes, while Keenan and Cahill had gotten their introduction to the ArmaLite via Vince Conlon in Philly, Adams, Hughes, and the Belfast brigade had gotten theirs from a small pamphlet that arrived in the winter of 1970, having made its way across the Atlantic in the hands of a sympathetic deckhand on the *Queen Elizabeth II*. It advertised the ArmaLite as a new American rifle, versatile and fatally efficient.

Hughes and Adams knew immediately that a gun like this could completely change the strategic reality for the Provos. Armed with their unreliable arsenal of World War II–era weapons — most of them McGarrity's aging Thompson submachine guns, along with M-1 carbine and M-1 Garand rifles — the army was on borrowed time, but if there was a way to get those American rifles into the hands of the IRA's growing corps of volunteers, it could be a different war. Indeed, this was the exact sentiment that had separately sent Keenan and Cahill to Conlon the winter before.

Among the Belfast brigade, huddled in a safe house, the verdict was unequivocal: they needed to get ArmaLites, they needed them fast, and the path to them lay in America. So that spring, Hughes picked up a fake passport and a plane ticket and set off for New York.

By early 1971, when Hughes first struck out on a mission to America for ArmaLites, the Provisional IRA, NORAID, and Clan-na-Gael were already well on their way to establishing the ArmaLite trafficking operation that Hughes and Adams were seeking. It was a discreet mission, handled mostly at high levels between border campaign veterans like Dave O'Connell, Joe Cahill, and Sean Keenan in Northern Ireland, and Vince Conlon, Clan-na-Gael, Marty Lyons, and NORAID's inner circle in America. Newer Provo infantry like Hughes — however well regarded — were hardly privy to such arrangements.

Still, for Hughes, Adams, and West Belfast, the situation was desperate. The Falls Curfew had prompted a significant population shift in the city. Places like the Falls, which sat adjacent to Loyalist neighborhoods, were doomed to be powder kegs for the foreseeable future; faced with that reality, many began fleeing the front line. Of the eighteen hundred Belfast families that relocated just in the aftermath of the 1969 riots, fifteen hundred were Catholic, many of whom had been burned out of their homes entirely. Some went south, seeking safety and shelter in military camps in the free Republic of Ireland, on the safer side of Northern Ireland's border. Others pushed deeper into West Belfast, resettling in housing projects (known as estates) that were popping up farther toward the city's outskirts.

Lenadoon, west of the Falls in the nationalist ghetto of Andersonstown, was one of them. Nestled in the shadow of Belfast's Black Mountain, the estate, owned by the Northern Ireland Housing Executive, had not even been completed when refugee Catholic families began pouring westward. Many would be temporarily housed in schools, emergency buildings, and half-constructed homes.

Andersonstown may have historically been a nationalist neighborhood, but until 1970, Lenadoon, within it, was a mixed-religion estate. Catholic and Protestant residents lived there, and despite its location in nationalist West Belfast, Lenadoon's Catholics were actually the minority. This made the neighborhood predictably tense. Even the geography of Lenadoon seemed designed to court sectarian tensions; as a 1970 survey noted, "the physical layout in itself seems to discourage the formulation of an integrated community." Indeed, as floods of Catholic families poured in, the increasingly outnumbered Protestant residents grew more and more on edge, and most would eventually flee the neighborhood.

This population shift would change plenty for the Belfast city. But it also marked a significant strategic change for the Provisional IRA. Lenadoon and Andersonstown were now strongholds, with a deep network of supporters and prospective volunteers. Gerry Adams, who was well familiar with Andersonstown's streets, knew this. In the desperate dispatch of Brendan Hughes was an effort — however clumsy — to get them guns.

Brendan Hughes took a seat at the conference table, its formality a stark contrast to the chaos of Belfast. Back home, Hughes had lived on the edge, slipping between borders and rarely spending more than a few nights in the same place. He and Adams were under constant surveillance, never far from the threat of imprisonment or worse. But here he was, seated inside a meeting room in New York City, feeling more out of place than perhaps he'd ever felt in his life.

Hughes had arrived to America with only one contact: a Vietnam veteran referred to only as Bob, with whom he connected as soon as he landed. Bob's links to NORAID remain unclear, but together he and Hughes decided unilaterally to approach the organization, a group with which Hughes was familiar

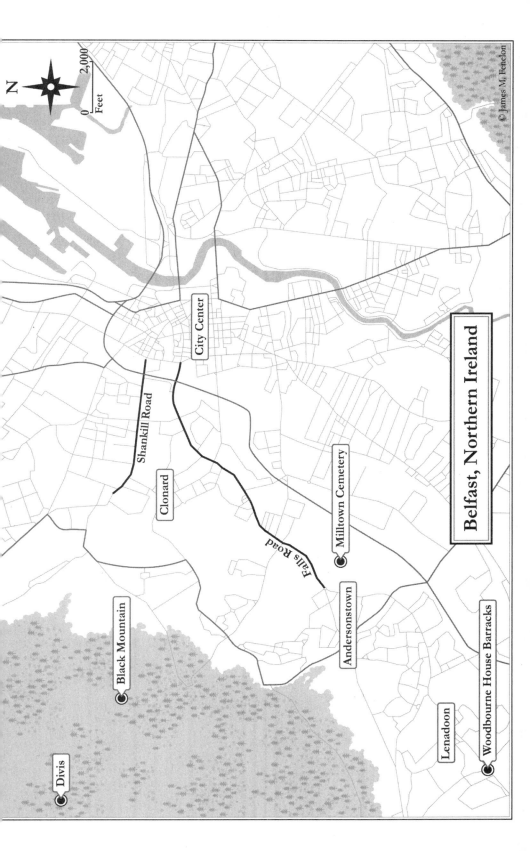

Belfast, Northern Ireland

but with whom he and Adams had little direct contact; after all, the organization proclaimed itself to be separate from the Provos, a ruse that was believable if one wasn't briefed on the inner circle. Still, NORAID was publicly sympathetic to the plight of Northern Ireland, and Hughes sensed that it could be an ally in obtaining ArmaLites in America. It was what had led him to that conference table in the Bronx, where he got an audience with Marty Lyons. But the meeting was not going well.

Lyons was unimpressed with the ragged fighter before him; indeed, all he saw in Hughes was an insubordinate loose end with a dangerous lack of discretion. Hughes had arrived in the States unannounced, and he appeared to be freelancing: he certainly hadn't come under the auspices of the Provisional leaders with whom Lyons was communicating regularly. Joe Cahill, for one — the man to whom NORAID sent its checks, and who had helped organize Vince Conlon's initial cooperation — had heard about Hughes and Adams's rogue mission, and had shared his displeasure with Lyons.

So Lyons began the meeting by toying with Hughes. *ArmaLites?* "We were told by Dublin that you want Garands and M-1 carbines," Lyons said coyly, referring to the exact same guns that Hughes was seeking to replace.

"Listen," Hughes said, irritated, "I come from Belfast, and we're fighting the war there. We want ArmaLites."

It was a nonstarter, and the meeting devolved from there. Lyons, miffed at Hughes's break in protocol, ordered him out of New York. Go back to Belfast, he instructed, and go empty-handed.

"I'm not fucking going," Hughes growled, "without the ArmaLites."

But Lyons was unfazed, and the meeting ended with no agreement; the NORAID ArmaLites would never come — at least, not through Brendan Hughes.

The meeting would be Hughes's only encounter with NORAID. For the rest of his life, he would call them pacifist and out of touch.

"The NORAID people were so conservative," he would say decades later. "They had no understanding of what the war was like in Belfast."

Hughes, however, had misread Lyons and his organization. IRA brigades in Northern Ireland were about to receive some of the very ArmaLites that Hughes had come to New York seeking — care of Marty Lyons, NORAID's inner circle, and Vince Conlon's Clan-na-Gael.

CHAPTER 7

"NEW AND DRASTIC MEASURES"

Marjorie Palace's home was on the corner of a residential street in Morrisville, in Bucks County. It was just across the Delaware River from Trenton, New Jersey, and well north of Philadelphia's city limits — close to both cities, but far enough to be free from their more restrictive gun regulations.

Palace and her husband had built a small but well-regarded gun operation in Morrisville, run out of their modest home. They sold the standard fare — rifles, handguns, and ammunition — but over the years, the couple had earned a reputation for finding guns that other people couldn't. Friends and colleagues would come to her with challenging requests: Lugers, Lee-Enfields, ArmaLites — big, unique guns in large quantities that weren't readily available elsewhere. For the right customer, and for the right price, Palace could provide them. And depending on just how right the price was, she might even be able to arrange the sale without real names or addresses.

Harry Rutherford was another gun dealer in the community, an older man who mostly handled firearms repairs, but who had occasionally come to Palace when a buyer needed something he couldn't find. This was why he was standing in her office on an autumn morning in 1971 with a man Palace didn't know.

The stranger was tall and smart-looking, with a heavy brogue. His name was Vince Conlon, Rutherford explained, and he was one of Rutherford's regular customers. He had a reliable pay record, and the two of them had worked together for a long time.

What Rutherford didn't say was what had brought him and Conlon together in the first place. Rutherford had been part of Conlon's modest gun-smuggling network, across the 1960s, back when it was just a small group of them, running around New York and Philadelphia, carting guns into and out of basements. Rutherford was a reliable connection and friend, and had long been willing to help Conlon obtain the occasional gun to smuggle back to Northern Ireland. But things had changed in recent months. The group of them seemed to have a new stream of money, which had elevated Conlon's operation to a much more serious scale — and Rutherford couldn't keep up.

Conlon's orders, Rutherford explained, were becoming too much for his little shop to fill. Perhaps, he ventured, Palace would like to inherit Conlon's business.

Palace was intrigued. This client was a bit different from others to whom Rutherford had introduced her. He clearly wasn't a casual buyer, and this deal wouldn't be a one-off. The man wanted big orders, regularly — mostly rifles and ammunition. It sounded like the arms were used for target practice at a gun club, which explained the large quantities. That was enough for Palace. Having worked in the shadowy world of collectors and rare guns for a long time, she was never one to get overly concerned about details.

There was one catch to the deal, but it would serve all of them well: they needed to be discreet. Conlon would pay in cash, and pickups would be handled by a rotating cast of his associates.

If the caveats worried Palace, they didn't deter her. Conlon seemed legitimate enough, and this was shaping up to be a straightforward deal with few downsides for her — and plenty of plausible deniability. She agreed.

Not long after their first introduction, Conlon came back to Palace's gun shop with his friend Neil Byrne. The two men each put in an initial order — a test to see how quickly and efficiently Palace could operate. Conlon's order was relatively simple: ten Lee-Enfields, a standard-issue British military rifle that was easy enough to come by in the United States. Byrne, by contrast, ordered thousands of rounds of armor-piercing ammunition, an unusual amount for one man, and a particularly hard ask given that the supply in the United States was drying up.

The two orders totaled nearly a thousand dollars, but the men saw signs of promise right away: Palace took down the order without asking questions. Conlon and Byrne, pleased and hopeful, even signed their real names on the federal forms that Palace was required to keep, for each gun sale. She filed them away in her logbook.

While he may have seemed eager, Vince Conlon did not take such endeavors lightly. Although a veteran IRA fighter who was hungry for the front lines — and who now fully backed the Provos — Conlon understood that violence was the last resort. The Troubles, it was now clear, would bring a merciless guerrilla war to Northern Ireland, and such strange theaters did not have the same kinds of standards as a traditional conflict. Brutality would be the order of the day, and it didn't always sit well with Conlon. He had occasional qualms with the conduct of IRA fighters back home, sometimes challenging IRA leadership, raging in letters against comrades who behaved carelessly while fighting, or targeted civilians. Such senseless violence was inexcusable, Conlon thought, and ought to be condemned.

Indeed, although the IRA had tacit and spiritual support among Northern Ireland's Catholics, many nationalists across the region — even in strongholds like Derry and Belfast — were wary of the army and its increasingly violent ends. Though they cultivated strong networks of support and recruits in places like West Belfast, the Provos also very often bolstered their control of nationalist ghettos through intimidation and codes of silence, menacing those who refused to participate and attacking those who were rumored to be cavorting with the IRA's various enemies.

Still, for many like Conlon, the army's less kosher means were justified by its ends. Conlon's conviction derived less from religion or national identity than simple logic: entire segments of the Catholic population in Northern Ireland had been marginalized and oppressed for years. What other choice did they have?

And in keeping with Conlon's leonine temperament, the more things heated up back home, the more he and his wife, Marina, thought about returning. After years as a generally toothless army, the Provisional IRA would soon have serious guns, serious numbers, and would be capable of holding its own against British troops. The goal to drive the British from Northern Ireland seemed possible in a way it hadn't in decades. Conlon couldn't look away.

Each day, he returned home from work and, at 7 p.m., shut himself in his family's basement to listen to the BBC World Service news on a small shortwave radio. "New and drastic measures may have to be taken," a broadcaster announced in February 1971, amid scenes of burning homes in Belfast; seven people had been killed in the previous days, the bulletin said, and a five-year-old girl was crushed by a British Army vehicle. In another broadcast, Protestant pipe and drum bands celebrated the election of Ian Paisley, a firebrand Loyalist minister, to the Stormont Parliament. And in October 1971, the news broadcast the funerals of two young sisters — volunteers in the IRA's women's auxiliary — who had been shot and killed by British soldiers. Such official dispatches were buttressed by Conlon's own, personal string of updates, contained in letters from friends that came regularly from the border. And there were regular in-person accounts from people who'd seen the fighting firsthand; as the Troubles raged on in Northern Ireland, more and more people were turning up on American shores.

Along with managing the joint Clan-NORAID gun-smuggling operation in Philadelphia, Conlon had also taken on the busy job of coordinating IRA fugitives' arrivals in and out of the States. He often helped his old comrades sneak into the country, and then ferried them around for publicity tours with NORAID, which would quietly advertise speeches and talks with IRA volunteers from the front lines. Irish Americans loved the proximity to Provo fighters, and each event reliably brought a flurry of donations.

Marina, too, had found her own place in the movement. She was from sectarian Armagh, but unlike her husband, she had not grown up in the Republican tradition. It was through Vince that she had been introduced to — and ultimately embraced — the IRA's mission. Busy with raising their family and keeping the house, she stayed away from the front, or any of her husband's more lethal dealings. But in Philadelphia, she had found her own way to contribute to the cause.

Marina was close with Brigid Makowski, Conlon's friend and fellow Clan-na-Gael member, before the group fractured over the Provos, and together the women would travel around to local shops, putting BOYCOTT BRITISH GOODS stickers on English products. Even after Makowski returned to Ireland, Marina continued to adapt her domestic routines to the needs of the IRA: she hosted army visitors to the Conlon house, where dances and local Irish rebel bands frequently provided entertainment in their living room.

The family were glad to be able to provide a home away from home for Irish visitors, but Vince and Marina both missed home themselves. Each had their own reasons: Vince, for his part, had never quite shaken the tendencies that had earned him that reputation so long ago, pacing the attics of safe houses along the border; the caged lion didn't like being so far from the fight. But his and Marina's desire to return to Ireland stemmed from more primal longings, too. They had both left family and friends back in Ireland, and most of their children were too young to remember much of life there. No matter how robust and supportive Philadelphia's Irish community might have been, it couldn't substitute for Ireland itself.

The burnout didn't help. The year 1971 was an exhilarating but exhausting year. The Philadelphia chapters soon emerged as some of NORAID's most productive, punching well above their weight in financial donations; the city collected about $10,000 a month, a contribution second only to New York. Donors in Philadelphia received a receipt, with two lines:

Though the strife of the North fill poor Erin with care,
There are hearts true and trusted toward Erin so fair.

It seemed every day there was something to do, somewhere in the city to be: a dinner, a dance, an auction. NORAID sparked a cultural renaissance of sorts in Philadelphia's Irish community. For so long, it had only been Conlon, Neil Byrne, and Bill Corry holding things together in the city. Now, though — now everyone seemed engaged in the Irish struggle. Conlon's old friend George Harrison was working with them in New York, and Marty Lyons had an efficient operation running through the docks. Even those who shied away from full-throated endorsement of the IRA seemed to at least empathize with the army's plight, so moved were they over the treatment of Catholics in Northern Ireland. And NORAID was reaping the rewards of all this enthusiasm.

The small-scale gun-smuggling operation that Conlon had managed for so long had quickly grown to rival Joe McGarrity's. Finally a structure was in place to move large numbers of weapons, and there were people around Conlon willing and able to help. He and his accomplices in the Clan, and their partners in NORAID, were taking full advantage.

Bill Corry had friends in Syracuse who were working to find guns, and he and his pal Danny Cahalane had long since proven themselves to be capable leaders in Philadelphia. The two of them were always running somewhere, trading something, selling something, picking something up.

Conlon was impressed; Cahalane, who was more than a decade his senior, had embraced the work, and had made his NORAID chapter, the Delaware

County group, the center of Philadelphia's gun smuggling; they had even started referring to his chapter as "the Cahalane Unit." He had become a critical member of NORAID's inner circle, too, as keen for a public dinner as he was for a nighttime errand; Cahalane had even welded a false bottom onto his green work van so that he, Byrne, and Conlon could easily cart around rifles and bullets without the risk of being seen. The three of them had taken to gathering at Hughie Breen's pub on Roosevelt Boulevard, roughly equidistant to their various suburban homes — and a convenient meeting point, if any of them were planning to take a late-night drive to Marty Lyons's apartment or the nearby NORAID headquarters, in the Bronx.

New York, though, was starting to get uncomfortable. As the group expanded, NORAID's increasing popularity was a liability. Too many people wanted to start their own chapter, form their own council, find a way to send their own money. It had started eliciting uncomfortable questions at NORAID's headquarters, where curious members of the group were inquiring about its finances. As far as the inner circle was concerned, those were questions that were better left unasked.

CHAPTER 8

THE FEDS

THE FBI AGENT wouldn't have looked entirely out of place as he made his way through the West Bronx. A dense expanse of tenements and row houses, the borough was — and is — one of New York's most diverse and dynamic, reinventing itself regularly as a haven for the city's immigrant communities. Beginning in the early 1900s, it was where many of New York's Irish émigrés had settled.

At last, the special agent arrived at NORAID's modest headquarters on East 194th Street and stepped inside. It was August 4, 1970, not long after the group was first founded. Wedged between newsagents and cafés, the organization's new office was innocuous enough; there was Irish Republican literature, information on protests and demonstrations, and copies of *An Phoblacht,* the IRA's affiliated newspaper, printed in Dublin. (Copies were flown into New York regularly by Irish International Airlines, and Marty Lyons picked them up to distribute.)

The organization had been on the radar of the FBI essentially since NORAID's founding, thanks to its intentional visibility and its connection to the Irish Republican cause. But to judge by the evidence in its West Bronx headquarters, NORAID was hardly a threatening outfit; and based on the agent's observations, the FBI filed a memo saying as much.

In the months following the agent's visit, the FBI kept its investigation of NORAID low-key, leaving the case open but assigning it a "pending inactive" status. The bureau would go on to describe NORAID's leadership, including

Mike Flannery, as "conservative" and "responsible" in an internal law enforcement memo. The group's Janus-faced strategy was working.

NORAID had further strengthened its cover story by registering with the American federal government almost immediately upon its formation. This registration was legally required under the Foreign Agents Registration Act, or FARA — a 1938 statute that compelled individuals or organizations working on behalf of a foreign entity to register with the United States attorney general, and which required, among other things, that the filing party declare the nature and depth of its allegiances: it had to disclose the foreign entity with which it was affiliated, and file regular financial reports with the Justice Department outlining how much money it had collected from donors, how much it had sent overseas, and to whom. NORAID identified itself as a representative of the near-indistinguishably named Northern Aid Committee in Belfast, which was advertised as a sister humanitarian group. By willingly subjecting itself to this level of scrutiny and by appearing to adhere to US law, Flannery bolstered the case that NORAID wasn't a threat.

But as the Troubles raged on, political winds began shifting, and they were not in NORAID's favor. In a meeting in 1971, the same year that NORAID registered under FARA, President Richard Nixon and British prime minister Edward Heath discussed the connection between America and Northern Ireland — namely, British concern over the positive sentiment that Irish Americans appeared to harbor for the Provisional IRA. Organizations like NORAID had grown rapidly popular, and the group's disclosures showed it was collecting reams of cash. Where was all that money going?

It was but one instance in what was fast becoming a troubling trend for NORAID. Bolstered by months of the group's financial disclosures, British officials began raising the issue regularly on visits to the US, expressing concern about Irish-American support for the Provos. Even though NORAID claimed to stay at arm's length from the IRA, the group certainly didn't condemn it; moreover, NORAID often seemed to implicitly promote the Provos' cause, pushing Irish reunification and amplifying grievances against British soldiers and the RUC. The US government, having warily avoided the Irish conflict as long as possible, began quietly ramping up its investigation of NORAID.

Federal agents, of course, had long kept an eye on Irish-American networks in the United States. FBI investigators had been following Vince Conlon around nearly since he first arrived in America, and the bureau had opened a case file on Clan-na-Gael as early as the 1950s. But American officials generally treated Northern Ireland as Great Britain's problem, and there was little political incentive for Washington to intervene; after all, to have supported Irish reunification would alienate the British, a key ally, and to support the British would risk enraging America's powerful Irish-American voting bloc. Hence, the modest trickle of American guns supplied by Conlon and George Harrison's network to Irish nationalists had never quite been enough to rouse a bona fide investigative effort, and given the IRA's weak status in the 1960s, the Brits had not forced the American hand.

But things were different in the 1970s, when the rising influence of NORAID introduced a new variable to this political calculus. Unlike Clan-na-Gael, the group boasted far-flung support and was overflowing with American dollars, and pressure from British officials was mounting. Any investigation, though, would be a tricky maneuver; by Michael Flannery and Dave O'Connell's design, NORAID was on its face a political fundraising organization, and its activities in the US were protected by the American Constitution. Such protections were very much in the public consciousness, and there was heightened awareness around any law enforcement action that might trample them — at the time NORAID rose to the fore, the FBI was weathering its own public bruising stemming from abuses by its outgoing, mercurial director, J. Edgar Hoover, who used the agency to surveil and infiltrate progressive groups, blackmail his political enemies, and widely spy on American citizens. There was little appetite to court such controversy again.

But in its own government filings, NORAID unintentionally gave investigators an easy excuse to surveil them. Flannery might have claimed that NORAID was merely the US agent of a Belfast-based humanitarian group with the same name — and that NORAID supported the Irish people, rather than the Irish Republican Army — but he had been lax in maintaining that pretense.

When NORAID sent its contributions to the Northern Aid Committee in Belfast, the checks were made out to the organization's president: Joe Cahill, the man who first arranged the ArmaLite smuggling operation with Conlon — and who also happened to be the chief of staff of the Provisional IRA.

Nearly as soon as NORAID's links to Cahill and the Provos were declared, British and Northern Irish authorities made sure that those links were highlighted regularly in public discourse about the organization. And they pressured their American counterparts to do the same. In communiqués across the ocean, officials urged American media and government officers to play up the violent nature of the IRA, linking its brutalities to NORAID. All the while, British and Northern Irish officials internally debated how best to promote the line that Irish America was enabling grotesque acts of war, pushing American newspapers to parrot such points. It was a prescient strategy that targeted NORAID's Achilles' heel, one that Mike Flannery and Dave O'Connell had long sought to protect. The Irish-American mainstream might not look as kindly on NORAID if the supposedly nonviolent group was accused of gunrunning and terrorism.

"The greatest joke is they wouldn't dare bring any real Provos over here," an American friend of Conlon's would later grouse to a newspaper reporter. "All the Irish cops would hear one word out of their mouths and that would be the end of the contributions."

The British government's sudden sense of urgency about shutting down NORAID stemmed from practical — and lethal — concerns. On the streets of Belfast and Derry, the fledgling Provos were no longer struggling to find weapons. Instead, it was the British who seemed to be getting outgunned. One doctor noticed something particularly chilling: gunshot wounds coming from West Belfast and Derry were no longer the moderately traumatic result of antiquated weapons. Instead, emergency wards were seeing severe injuries, indicative of high-velocity guns whose bullets tore through their targets with explosive force.

The reason for this ballistic escalation, too, had become clear. More and more often, as British soldiers and policemen raided homes and searched for guns, they were finding not rusty, World War II–era weapons, but well-oiled, new ArmaLites.

These discoveries, ultimately, were what explained the fact that in 1970, security forces in Northern Ireland and law enforcement in the United States commenced a cautious, transatlantic dialogue. There wasn't an identifiable fire — yet. But between America, Northern Ireland, and the Irish diaspora, there seemed to be a lot of smoke.

CHAPTER 9

"DON'T MAKE ANY MISTAKES"

JOHN CASEY'S CAR slipped through the crowded streets of the Bronx toward Somerville Place, a residential street in Yonkers. The drive was just a few miles north from the West Bronx, the neighborhood where Casey, a journeyman plumber, spent most of his time these days. He had made countless trips like this before. But tonight Casey was stressed.

The man's story mirrored that of so many Irish Americans, and especially those of his colleagues in the plumbers' union. Casey's great-grandfather had emigrated from Ireland, and the ancestral connection had given Casey a passing interest in the island's politics. In the early 1970s, however, as Ireland had featured more and more prominently in the news, Casey had found himself increasingly engaged in the goings-on in his ancestral home.

Casey's colleagues in the union had noticed. One, Frank Grady, told him about NORAID, an organization headed by some men in their union, dedicated to raising money to help Catholics in the North. Intrigued, Casey had tagged along with some of his coworkers one evening to a pub in the Bronx. No sooner had he entered than he was rushed into the back room of the bar, where he was seated at a table with four other men who were sorting large stacks of bills — hundreds if not thousands of dollars in cash.

"Receipts," one of the men explained, gruffly, "from an Irish Northern Aid Committee dinner-dance."

That was a year earlier. Casey sometimes looked back, bewildered at how it had gone so far — from a simple interest in his grandfather, to this.

Not long after that strange night at the bar, Grady asked Casey to take on a larger role: officer for NORAID's Yonkers chapter. Situated just north of the Bronx in a heavily Irish area, the Yonkers group — like Philadelphia's Delaware County — kept a far more radical bent than most of NORAID. There were moments when Grady and his boss, the gruff ringleader Marty Lyons, seemed like they were speaking of a completely different organization than the NORAID they talked about in pamphlets, the NORAID that first caught Casey's interest. Somehow, in Yonkers, Casey had found himself a member of the group's militant inner circle.

Still, he came to terms with the role. Embraced it, even. The news from Ireland had enraged Casey, there was no denying that. He felt compelled to do something about it — and even if he had never pictured himself as an international gun smuggler, it felt good to help. It felt important. Plus, he had some sense of what he was getting into: not long after he was first recruited into NORAID, Casey stumbled on a box of handguns in a closet in Marty Lyons's house.

Casey's indoctrination started with a cryptic task, not long after that initial backroom meeting. He still remembered every detail. He was dispatched to a hardware store in Yonkers, a small place known as the J&J bait shop, where a NORAID member had arranged for a large shipment of guns; they just needed men to handle the pickup. It turned into Casey's first test. He tagged along to the shop as arrangements were finalized, lingering as his NORAID colleagues chatted with the shop's owner. One man produced a thick wad of cash and passed it across the counter. A week later, Casey returned to the shop with Frank Grady. Little was said — the owner, the same man who had seen him before, knew Casey was no customer. He produced a book and indicated where Casey needed to sign, and Casey nervously moved to fill in the first blank space he saw. The owner abruptly pushed his hand away.

"Pay attention," Grady hissed. "Don't make any mistakes."

Casey approached the book again and signed, carefully, and the rest of the operation went off without incident. A few days later, Casey was handed gun transfer receipts from Marty Lyons, with the names of dead Irishmen; hold on to the paper, Lyons told him, in case he was ever questioned about the guns. The group had falsified paperwork to show that the weapons Casey signed for had been transferred to the men on the receipts — no one need know they were actually dead.

Casey's first operation was a resounding success, proving his worth to Lyons and NORAID's inner circle. He started making regular outings for the group — errands such as the one that had brought him to Somerville Place that night in the autumn of 1971.

The car finally came to a stop in a dark alley behind a modest family home, indistinguishable from the houses that line the streets of Yonkers. Casey walked up to the front door and rang the bell; the man who answered was a stranger, but still, Casey was waved inside and led down to the basement. Plywood, two-by-fours, and tools were scattered everywhere, and on the floor, Casey could see the bones of a large crate, which the man went back to hammering. When they were satisfied the makeshift box was sturdy enough, they began filling it with armloads of carbines and ammunition. Together they carried the box to the car and loaded it into the trunk. By the evening, the crate would be delivered to Lyons, who would take it wherever it needed to go next.

Did Casey feel guilty? Sometimes, sure. People were joining NORAID and giving money, most believing it was going to help destitute families and needy children in Northern Ireland. Some of it, perhaps, did. But the rest of it? Well, now Casey knew where it went.

The dishonesty of it — that's all that really bothered him. Rumors about gunrunning were beginning to swirl among the Irish-American community, and members naturally began asking Casey how their money was being used. Whether what they'd been hearing about NORAID — that it was a front for guns, for the IRA — was true.

For Lyons, such matters of conscience were a luxury. It was easy to have moral debates from an ocean away — NORAID's public-facing policy, after all, was that funds would not go toward direct, lethal support to the IRA. But to Lyons, it made no sense to draw that line in the sand, to say you supported Northern Ireland's Catholics, but not their army. If NORAID members weren't willing to do both, Lyons believed, they could take their money elsewhere.

"People are questioning us, as to where the funds are going," Casey said to Lyons one day, cautiously broaching the subject. "We don't know what to tell people."

"Change the policy," Lyons snapped, in a frustrated outburst. "If the people over there want to use it for guns and weapons, that's okay. That's the new policy."

The group's public position, of course, remained unchanged; NORAID's true purpose would remain hidden. But for Casey, Lyons's tantrum left one thing unambiguous: once you were in NORAID's inner circle, there was no easy way out.

CHAPTER 10

"WHAT OTHER MEASURES COULD BE TAKEN?"

THE GUNS FROM Philadelphia started arriving in 1971, leaving a bloody trail across West Belfast and Derry. The year began with a march of violent incidents, pressing Northern Ireland more definitively into war. In February, the first soldier to be shot and killed by the IRA died in North Belfast. That same evening, the first IRA man to be shot and killed by the British Army died, too, also in North Belfast. That same month, five civilian men were killed as they serviced a BBC transmitter, blown apart by an IRA bomb meant for the British Army. Elsewhere, two RUC policemen were shot and killed by the IRA.

In March, in an incident still remembered for its brutality, three British soldiers were taken to a quiet road outside Belfast and executed by the IRA. Two of the dead — aged seventeen and eighteen — were brothers. To be sure, these were hardly the first soldiers to be killed in Northern Ireland's tumult. But they were the first who had been targeted while off duty, plied with booze, and then lured out of a pub.

It was a harbinger, perhaps, of what was to come, a small taste of the intimate horror that comes with unconventional wars. The deaths of the brothers and their comrades brought the terrifying stakes of the conflict into focus for British authorities, prompting rallies, protest marches, and outrage from Unionists in Northern Ireland.

While the IRA had grown out of a clear need for nationalist Belfast to defend itself against Unionist and Loyalist threats, it was also earning a reputation as one of the most vicious guerrilla outfits of the twentieth century. Its ruthless tactics — car bombs, executions, killings, and disfigurements, as public warning — muddied what might otherwise have been considered a morally superior mission in Northern Ireland. The IRA's targets were not limited to Unionist and Loyalist factions, either; the Provos policed their own territories, in some cases killing and maiming their own neighbors to spread fear or intimidate uninvolved civilians to support the army. Some suspected informers were kneecapped, others executed and disappeared, or left to be discovered, as darkly cautionary tales. These tactics hurt the IRA in the war for public opinion and almost certainly cost them some measure of support within nationalist communities in Northern Ireland. And yet the IRA continued to draw on deep wells of solidarity in ghettos like Andersonstown, which tended to back the army unconditionally.

As the Provos gained power, one thing became clear to the British government and their Unionist cohort: something serious needed to be done about the situation in Northern Ireland. And rather than come up with a new solution, they decided to dust off an old playbook.

The practice of internment — indefinite imprisonment without trial — was used periodically by the British during its occupation of Ireland. In 1920, as Great Britain sought to counter the uprising of Ireland's War of Independence, thousands of suspected IRA men were thrown into prison camps and jails without charge or trial, subject to brutal conditions and maltreatment; five internees would die and three were shot across that period. Later, during the 1950s border campaign, Unionist officials instituted internment in coordination with authorities in the Republic of Ireland, where membership in the IRA remained illegal — the same policy under which Conlon was imprisoned in the Curragh prison camp, outside Dublin. Both instances were seen as successes by British and Unionist officials, which may explain why, following 1971's summer of violence, Unionists were eager to reinstate internment in Northern Ireland.

But it would be a risky maneuver — perhaps riskier than even the British government first realized. By the time the Troubles exploded in full force, the Provos were composed mostly of new recruits, young men and women without criminal records. Meanwhile, British intelligence pertaining to the IRA was decades old. Whatever rudimentary intelligence existed was mostly contained in notebooks that soldiers kept in their pockets while on patrol, full of blurry pictures of alleged IRA volunteers. With so little to go on, accurately targeting those men for internment would be exceptionally difficult, if not impossible; it was far likelier that the security forces would miscalculate and imprison the wrong people.

"No one could be certain what would be the consequences," the British home secretary, Reginald Maudling, said years later. It was Maudling who grudgingly approved Unionists' desires to reinstate internment, fearing inaction from Westminster would enrage Loyalist factions in Northern Ireland. "The question was simply this: what other measures could be taken?"

On a quiet morning in August 1971, the British commenced a large-scale arrest operation called Operation Demetrius. They began in nationalist neighborhoods of Belfast, where thousands of police officers and British soldiers flooded into fortified areas like the Falls Road, Andersonstown, and Lenadoon. Indiscriminately rounding up hundreds of men and boys, the troops treated their detainees with "casual brutality," in the words of two journalists who examined the debacle decades later.

It quickly became clear that the British government had gravely overestimated its own intelligence: many of the Provos it sought had caught wind of the operation and preemptively snuck to safety across the southern border. Perhaps inevitably, British troops stormed the wrong houses and arrested the wrong men. In one instance, the soldiers attempted to arrest a man who had been dead for four years. In others, they confused the names of fathers and sons, arresting one when they were meant to be after the other.

Many of the people detained during the first sweep of Operation Demetrius were held for hours or even days, despite the fact that they were clearly innocent. Some were subject to brutal interrogation tactics — placed in stress positions, subject to sensory deprivation, denied food and water — that history would later deplore as torture. In the first six months of the policy, 2,400 people were arrested. The vast majority were eventually released without trial.

It is difficult to overstate how consequential this instance of mass internment was for the Troubles, and for Northern Ireland. The reintroduction of this draconian practice — and its shocking application — was proof to Irish civilians that British and Northern Irish authorities intended to wage a full-scale assault against Catholic communities in the North. And while the practice was billed as a security measure, nationalists saw it as inherently political: each internment order was personally signed by Northern Ireland's Unionist prime minister, Brian Faulkner. That conclusion was only bolstered by the fact that Loyalist neighborhoods were almost entirely spared from raids and imprisonments, even though they had produced their own paramilitary groups, one of which would soon perpetrate one of the most heinous acts of violence in the span of the Troubles: the bombing of McGurk's bar, a popular nationalist pub in Belfast where a bomb planted by Loyalist paramilitaries killed fifteen people, including two children.

Internment also had another effect, one that British and Northern Irish authorities certainly hadn't intended: an entire generation of Irish civilians, witnessing the everyday traumas of West Belfast and the incursion of British troops into daily life, would be pushed toward the IRA. The more that British troops lashed out blindly at the Provos, the angrier the Irish public became — and the harder the Provos were able to strike back. The British Army, it turned out, had become the IRA's best recruiting tool.

"If they keep going like this," one senior IRA volunteer said at the time, "we can't lose."

The Catholic ghettos of Belfast were turning into war zones. Barricades went up in nationalist neighborhoods like Andersonstown and Lenadoon, which quickly became no-go areas for the security forces, too dangerous for the RUC or British soldiers to even enter.

Meanwhile, Belfast's infrastructure crumbled. Public transit broke down and the city's public services were regularly suspended. Buses were hijacked and cars were yanked from showrooms to use in barricades. The very pavement of the streets was chipped apart, tossed onto blockades to further fortify Catholic neighborhoods against British authorities. Milk vans were stolen, the bottles used to make petrol bombs. The clattering of trash-can lids echoed across the city — the residents' system for warning each other that British soldiers were coming.

Following internment, Northern Ireland erupted. From the policy's introduction in August 1971 to the end of the year, five times as many people were killed than had died in the entire eight months before. Explosive, too, was the shift in political sentiment. Operation Demetrius proved what previous centuries' instances of internment had already demonstrated: rather than dismantling extremist networks, the practice radicalized the communities it targeted, making sympathizers of people who had originally been lukewarm toward, or even against, the IRA.

This was especially true of Republicans in the south, who up to 1971 had been relatively ambivalent and wary of intervening in Northern Ireland. That changed after Operation Demetrius — families from Catholic ghettos like the Falls Road and Derry's Creggan and Bogside had already begun moving south, but after internment thousands of refugees fled to the Republic for safety, bringing with them tales of the British Army's brutality and Loyalist paramilitaries' impunity. Such stories inflamed Republicans in Ireland's south, who shifted gears, ideologically and tactically. Almost immediately after internment was introduced, once-sleepy IRA units in the Republic were called up to the Northern border to prepare to enter the embattled territory, a desperate effort to backfill the IRA's ranks in the event more Provos became interned. (Such dilution also aided in the ongoing erasure of difference between the Provisional and Official IRA, which, since the split, was slowly being absorbed by the Provos anyway.)

The fabric of Northern Ireland's Catholics, once a loose weave of civilians, political organizations, and the IRA, was becoming cinched more tightly than ever thanks to the Unionist and British governments. Even the staunchest proponents of internment would later acknowledge the move had been disastrous, effectively spelling the end of any chance at a peaceful, politically negotiated end to the Troubles. And it meant, among other things, that the IRA's need for support — lethal and otherwise — was only going to grow.

Michael Flannery and Dave O'Connell had initially pitched NORAID as a provider of humanitarian aid for families in Northern Ireland, including the families of prisoners — and as the arrests swept through West Belfast and Derry, NORAID was ready. Days after internment was introduced, the group organized large-scale demonstrations at British consulates in the United States. In New York, NORAID demonstrators carried a coffin draped with the Irish tricolor. Leadership organized American tours for released internees, who, much like the Catholic refugees in the Republic, brought tales of British brutality directly to eager Irish-American ears.

To capitalize on the circumstances, NORAID arranged a four-week American fundraising tour for Joe Cahill, the Provo leader who was also NORAID's beneficiary at the Belfast Northern Aid Committee. But as he landed in

America from Ireland, Cahill was stopped upon entry at New York's JFK Airport and slated for deportation; unbeknownst to him or his NORAID handlers, Cahill's visa had been canceled midair by US officials, who had been pressured to do so by their British allies. Cahill would eventually agree to be deported, but rather than neuter NORAID's fundraising ambitions, the debacle became a cause célèbre for Irish Americans, who saw it as proof that their own government was cooperating with British authorities in the North. This impression was further underscored by the fact that weeks before Cahill's deportation, a British official had visited the US and defended the British Army, railing against the IRA. In the eyes of Irish America, Washington had shown its cards: it was censoring the Irish perspective, while protecting and amplifying the British one.

The introduction of internment and all that followed led to an immediate increase in financial support to NORAID: In the four months following, the group reported nearly $130,000 in donations being sent to Ireland, a sum worth nearly a million dollars today. It was a significant increase from the previous half of the year, and proved what NORAID and Dave O'Connell had known all along: Irish Americans were not only paying attention to the North, but they were also ready to help — even if that meant setting aside questions about how, exactly, their money was being used.

Along with activating financial networks in America and tactical networks in Ireland, the large-scale imprisonment of innocent Northern Irish citizens also galvanized civil rights groups in Derry and Belfast, whose 1969 marches had first sparked the Troubles.

In Lenadoon, mass demonstrations took place against internment. The events led to violent clashes between Catholic residents and British security forces, who brutally intervened to shut down such displays — at one Lenadoon march, a fourteen-year-old boy was shot and killed by the British Parachute Regiment, a special forces unit that had been deployed to Northern Ireland. In the second half of 1971, 150 people were killed; almost half were Catholic civilians, twenty-nine of whom were killed by British soldiers. The public outrage over these deaths grew when British authorities falsely claimed that many of the victims were armed. Such instances only served to strengthen the resolve of civil rights organizers, and history would often show that many of these victims had actually not been carrying weapons at all.

It was against such a backdrop that the Northern Ireland Civil Rights Association scheduled a march in Derry for January 30, 1972. A large group of peaceful demonstrators would proceed through the Catholic ghetto of Creggan into Derry's center, an act that would be in direct violation of a military order that forbade parades in Northern Ireland — a policy that seemed selectively enforced against Catholic demonstrators. The people of Derry, though, were determined to carry on peacefully.

"Sunday is a make-or-break day for the cause of civil rights," said one organizer, amid reports that the British Army was sending reinforcements to Derry in preparation. If any violence or clashes were to occur, the organizer said, it would be the British Army — not the protesters — who perpetrated it.

CHAPTER 11

THE MASSACRE

IT WAS LATE on the night of January 30, 1972, in the middle of a frigid Pennsylvania winter, and Dan Duffy was behind the wheel of his car, agitated. The nighttime drive home from Philadelphia was a regular pilgrimage: on a near-weekly basis, Duffy and his wife would pack their children into the back seat, drive from Delaware County into the city, and walk a NORAID protest line as a family — sometimes at the British consulate, sometimes at events that involved British-linked acts or musical groups. That evening, Duffy had taken his children to the Spectrum, one of the city's largest indoor arenas, to protest a performance by the Black Watch, a pipe and drum band affiliated with the British military. Now, the Duffys were on their way back to the suburbs, and to bed.

It had been a long winter in a long year, and Dan Duffy had felt every month of it. He understood, perhaps more than most, just how grave things had become in the North. Derry was where Duffy had been born, where he had been raised, where he had left his family and friends. He cherished those roots, but an ocean separated him from them now, and his sporadic trips back weren't enough.

Duffy had grown up in the nationalist heart of Derry, in the Catholic ghetto of the Bogside, wedged between Derry's medieval walls and the hills of Donegal to the west. It was right on the edge of the city's border with Ireland's other twenty-six counties, and for Catholic residents like Duffy, the proximity only made the Republic seem farther than ever.

If there was a place that crystallized the Northern Irish conflict, Derry, and Bogside within, was it. The very name of the place — Derry, or Londonderry — carried a dark political weight, laden with centuries of meaning. Your chosen descriptor revealed your own loyalties: Derry, if you were Irish: Londonderry, if you were Unionist. It was a tough place to grow up, and a tough place to stay in, and Duffy hadn't, as much as he'd wanted to. The city was defined by oppression, and for Duffy and his Irish Catholic neighbors, this meant fewer jobs, flimsy housing, and the constant threat of Unionist police forces and the Loyalist gangs they tacitly encouraged.

Duffy had tried, though. He was a skilled mechanic, and despite the odds, he had found a comfortable living in his youth at a Derry auto shop. It had worked out for years, until suddenly it hadn't: in the 1950s, amid Northern Ireland's seemingly endless, cyclical tensions, the owner of the shop said he was sorry but Duffy couldn't work there anymore; Duffy was Catholic, and the man was being harassed for employing him. Left with no prospects, Duffy headed for the softest landing — his aunt and uncle's place in Philadelphia. It was where he started over, and where, on that January night, he flicked on the car's radio.

A dedicated newshound, Duffy listened to the local news radio station, KYW, religiously — and true to form, it was murmuring in the background as he drove his family home from Philadelphia that January night. He was known to be a hothead, easily agitated by any news that had to do with Northern Ireland, especially his hometown. But now, as unbelievable, tragic news crackled out of his car's speakers, something darker settled over him.

Duffy gripped the wheel and listened, stricken, as the radio anchor described the day's events in Derry. The anti-internment march organized by the Northern Ireland Civil Rights Association had devolved into a bloody massacre at the hands of British soldiers, who had opened fire on the unarmed marchers, right down the street from where Duffy was born. The scenes seemed straight out of a horror film: priests waving white kerchiefs, desperate for safe passage; limp bodies carted through the residential streets; women and children huddled behind cars and walls, seeking shelter.

The day would become known as Bloody Sunday, and out of an ultimate twenty-five years of brutal conflict, it still stands as one of the Trouble's darkest moments. By the end of it, thirteen civilians were dead, their bodies riddled with British bullets; a fourteenth man would succumb to his injuries months later.

In a different moment, with different choices, Duffy might have been one of the dead. He had joined NORAID the year before, in what seemed like a natural, rightful step to staying engaged with the struggle back home. He and his family were part of a chapter based out of Philadelphia's Irish Center, which was located just outside Jenkintown and the MacSwiney Club. It was far more moderate than the Delaware County or Northeast Philly groups, and until that January night, Duffy had generally been content with that status quo. Theirs had been exactly the sort of involvement that NORAID promoted: support for a benevolent, community-based organization, work that curtailed the more lethal rumors that trailed NORAID. But Duffy had heard the whispers. He knew there were groups of them elsewhere in the city — Mayfair, Delaware County, Jenkintown — who dabbled in other, more illicit business.

Up until this point, Duffy had mostly steered clear of that sort of stuff. But in the claustrophobia of the car, with his children anxiously watching, something seemed to shift. For years, he had spouted off about the IRA to friends and colleagues. Perhaps it was time to put some muscle behind those words.

The next morning did little to alleviate the tension; the phone rang early, delivering news from home. It was an old friend of Duffy's. Times had grown dire, the friend said. After the events of January 30, it seemed impossible to maintain any kind of neutrality. It would be impossible for any self-respecting Irish man or woman to stand by. Duffy, safely in America, was in a unique position.

"They're killing us," Duffy's friend said, pleadingly, over the line. "We need help."

Balding with a heavy, dark brow and sharp nose, Daniel Duffy was the kind of man who never seemed to sit still. He had a turbulent personality, always agitated and full of consternation, even on days that didn't bring particularly bad news from home. Whenever there was a microphone, a journalist's recorder, or just a willing — or unwilling — ear in front of him, Duffy would talk about the plight of Catholics in the North. This was the burden of leaving such a troubled place. You were never really gone.

Still, the life that the Duffys had built for themselves in suburban Philadelphia was a world away from the troubles of Derry. At the dawn of 1972, Duffy was living with his wife and three children in Upper Darby, a small community in Delaware County, and had landed a full-time job as a mechanic at Rudy

Daniel Duffy holds an Irish flag during a march in Philadelphia.

Valentino Ford, a family-run dealership in the same township where he had climbed through the ranks and served as a union steward. Their evenings and weekends were filled with community events at the Commodore John Barry Cultural Center, the Irish community center in Jenkintown. Life had reached a satisfying, middle-class stability.

Duffy had joined NORAID in its early days, enlisting in the Irish Center chapter, a convenient location, as it was where many of the Irish community's gatherings happened. The group kept a packed schedule, organizing clothing drives and fundraisers. Duffy told friends he was raising money to build a glass factory in Northern Ireland, hopefully to employ Catholics.

But it was hard to live in such comfort while the people he loved were in a fight for their lives back home. He felt it all deeply. In the garage, friends knew to steer clear of Duffy whenever Northern Ireland was in the news; anything about the place seemed to send Duffy into a tailspin. He would rage about the British Army, lamenting that he wasn't back in Ireland and able to join the IRA. He once brought a heavy rubber bullet into the shop, showing his fellow mechanics what kind of projectile the British Army was using against the people of Derry. He would ask colleagues — jokingly, or so it seemed — if anyone knew how to get guns.

"I love Ireland like my mother," Duffy would growl. "Homes with the plaster kicked in. People dragged out of their beds in the middle of the night. You can't just sit by three thousand miles away and say 'Let it happen.'"

To most of Duffy's colleagues, the words were just that: empty talk. One of those coworkers was Jeffrey Reh, a new arrival at the Ford dealership. Duffy sat one desk down from him and, as the local union steward, was in charge of orienting new employees to the garage. It was Duffy who'd trained him for the job. Reh had heard Duffy's chatter but stopped short of ever taking it too seriously. Duffy liked to sound off, but Reh had found him to be collegial and helpful enough, otherwise. The pair had a cordial relationship. But while Reh was careful to stay on good terms with his new colleague, he also kept his distance. There were moments when Duffy's flashes of aggression seemed to hint at something dangerous — a tendency underscored by an unpredictable temper. Reh saw it firsthand. Not long after the pair met, they had a minor run-in over a botched repair at work; Duffy threatened to break Reh's neck.

Particularly egregious abuses of the Irish Catholic population in Northern Ireland, such as the Falls Curfew or internment, had the effect of galvanizing the Irish-American community in the years leading up to 1972. But those episodes paled next to Bloody Sunday, which dramatically and immediately changed how Americans viewed Northern Ireland's plight. For the first time in the long history of Ireland's various wars of resistance, images and photographs of the carnage were thrusting the issue of Northern Ireland into the US mainstream, as thousands of Americans watched the horrific images on their televisions and listened to the chaotic aftermath on their radios. No longer was support of the Irish cause limited to those who shared a heritage and birthright. Even those who didn't identify as Irish American felt moved by the abuses they were seeing. NORAID, which welcomed everyone, regardless of ancestry, ushered them in.

The surge of interest that followed Bloody Sunday would pay dividends to NORAID for years to come. Flannery later called the tragedy the group's "first big publicity break." In the six months following Bloody Sunday, NORAID's checks back to Belfast nearly doubled, topping more than $300,000. And this was only what was acknowledged in government filings; the actual amount was likely far greater.

The moment also injected a new sense of urgency into Irish America, especially in Philadelphia, where Donegal and Derry had an outsized presence among the city's Irish diaspora. For the first time, in public forums, private chats, and newspaper pages, the tide of opinion was turning against the British government, long shielded from criticism and seen by the vast majority of Americans as a critical, long-term ally. It was difficult to see the images from Derry and *not* notice a brutal power imbalance — one that echoed the images from Selma, Birmingham, and other cities of the American South that had so shocked the country's conscience in the previous decade. Coincidentally but significantly, the infamous 1965 attack on Black civil rights demonstrators as they marched across the Edmund Pettus Bridge, in Selma, Alabama, had become known, too, as Bloody Sunday.

Duffy had his own complicated history with the cause. Though he had grown up in the Bogside, a hotbed of Republican ideology and a prime recruiting ground for the IRA in Derry, he had stopped short of heeding the call, even while he may have talked a big game. He not only steered clear of Vincent Conlon's Clan-na-Gael, but he actively questioned their direction. He was familiar with Conlon and Neil Byrne as early as the 1960s, when they were just starting to build their network, and his wariness appeared to hew closely to broader skepticism among the more conservative Irish Americans, who saw Conlon's radical politics as akin to communism and a potential threat to the Irish cause.

Bloody Sunday changed that. Political skepticism was shelved in the wake of the horrors that occurred in Derry that January day. More people than ever before flocked to NORAID gatherings, outraged by what they had seen on their own television screens. NORAID meetings across the country were full of new faces. Depending on your perspective, it was either an encouraging show of support or a concerning liability — after all, with all the new members, it was now easy for anyone who was curious about NORAID to slip in, unnoticed, and take a look at the group from the inside.

CHAPTER 12

MONTGOMERY LOAN COMPANY

THE GUNS STARTED turning up in November of 1971, seized by the British Army during their scorched-earth offensive against the Provisionals. It started as a trickle but soon became a flood. The rifles seemed to be everywhere: in abandoned yards, hidden in cars, or stashed in empty safe houses. How had they gotten there, in a country that was increasingly flooded with security forces, its borders policed and its neighborhoods locked down?

Investigators with Northern Ireland's Royal Ulster Constabulary pored over their growing arsenal, searching for clues about the weapons' origins. And they didn't have to look very hard: on many of the rifles — ArmaLites, Lee-Enfields, M-1 carbines — there were serial numbers etched onto the guns' cold, hard metal. Whoever supplied the weapons to the Provos, it seemed, had been so careless — or perhaps, so bold — that they never bothered to file the identifiers off.

If it had been difficult for Vince Conlon to stay away from Ireland before, it was doubly so after the horrors of Bloody Sunday. Even before that horrific day in Derry, Conlon had been wrestling urges to return home, for reasons both personal and principled. Among other things, it would help fill a gap that was emerging as internment thinned the ranks of his IRA comrades in the North. But to return home in 1972 would be complicated, far more than it had been in the 1950s, when Conlon had enjoyed relatively free movement between Ireland and America. He had been a young man then, with few obligations. Now he was more than a revolutionary — he was also a father and husband, three things that could be difficult to balance.

Still, as deeply as the Conlons had sunk their roots into Philadelphia, it wasn't Ireland. Vince, Marina, and the children — five of them now, including boys who were nearing their teenage years — had spent most of their lives far from their families. And after Bloody Sunday, Vince's longing for home grew and festered. The degrees of separation between him and the casualties were small: one of the day's victims was a close friend of Brigid Makowski, Conlon's former colleague in Philadelphia's Clan-na-Gael. Makowski herself, who had since returned to Ireland and was living in Limerick, had planned to be in Derry that fateful day; her salvation, ironically, had come from the Irish authorities, who jailed her on suspicion of IRA membership, which remained illegal in the Republic.

After more than a decade away, Vince and Marina resolved to move back to the island. Wary of the risks of returning to Armagh and the North, the Conlons instead turned their eyes to Monaghan, a county just across the border from Armagh, in the relative safety of the Irish Republic. Conlon had a lead on property there, a quiet parcel of land in the countryside, owned by the family of Fergal O'Hanlon, Conlon's fallen IRA comrade from the Brookeborough border raid in the 1950s. More importantly, Conlon had a post lined up with his old IRA unit, with whom he had maintained regular contact. His sons would be raised in a Republican house. He and Marina made the decision together, and in the weeks after Bloody Sunday, they hastily made arrangements.

But there was something that Conlon needed to sort out before he could leave.

Neil Byrne would remain behind in Philadelphia, tending to the illicit gun-trafficking network the pair of them had built. But Byrne couldn't manage the operation alone. Conlon needed to bring someone else into the fold — someone with a reputation for leadership, who wouldn't be turned away by the IRA's violent means. Someone trustworthy and serious, capable of shouldering the monumental task that Conlon had handled for years. Conlon, after all, would be giving this person the key to the IRA's American gun network: his successor would be ushered into a secret world of allies and connections, late-night drops and early-morning meetings. There would be regular trips to

New York, regular communication with the network outside Philadelphia, and the constant threat of arrest or worse.

In other words, before he could leave in good conscience, Vince Conlon needed a protégé. He had someone in mind.

The three men stood shoulder to shoulder at the counter of the Montgomery Loan Company, relaxed and unconcerned. Conlon and Byrne had been at the gun shop many times before, but these visits were new for Danny Cahalane, whose success in Delaware County had long earned Conlon's respect.

The shop, a modest pawnbroker, was a regular stop for Conlon, part of the loose network of gun dealers he used to collect rifles and bullets. He had a standing relationship with the owner, a man named Charles Shulberg. Conlon had often bought ArmaLites and bullets there, paying in cash. Conlon got on well enough with the shopkeeper, and no one hassled him, not even the shop's clerk — a particular woman, tasked with filling out the federal firearms forms. Under her watchful eye, Conlon and Byrne had purchased dozens of guns from the shop in recent years. If the woman had any misgivings, she didn't voice them, although she often seemed suspicious of their frequent orders.

The energy that winter afternoon was palpable. After all, that day's visit was more important than the rest. It was the first and last time they would all be together at this shop, on this shared mission.

The three men stood at the counter, looking at the pile of guns laid before them: twenty-five sleek, brand-new ArmaLite AR-180s. On the streets of Belfast, they would be priceless.

Unlike Marty Lyons's operatives in New York, none of them bothered using a fake name; the sale was legal enough, and it was over quickly. Conlon was pleased. He, Byrne, and Cahalane handed over a pile of cash, said their goodbyes, and carted the rifles to the car.

It was the last time Vince Conlon would buy an American ArmaLite for a very long time, but he knew: those guns, just like him, would make it home.

Like the rest of the Philadelphia guns, the weapons from the Montgomery Loan Company would wind their way to Northern Ireland through a delicate, time-tested script. The Philadelphia men would collect their guns and move them to New York, where they would be transferred to Marty Lyons's group and held at a warehouse in the Bronx. There, the guns would be boxed up and mislabeled as plumbing material or other household supplies. Sometimes, the New York men would strip down furniture — cupboards, mattresses, sofas — and fill the frames with guns, carefully concealing them within the upholstery before shipping the items overseas. They used connections in the longshoremans' union, which handled heavy freight on the city's docks, to sneak the crates and furniture onto shipping containers bound for Ireland. Sympathetic customs officials in New York and Ireland would coordinate, ensuring that the clandestine shipments reached their destinations without issue. Many of the guns were brought onto the island through the Republic via the Dublin docks, then secretly smuggled up north and hidden in towns just south of the border, sometimes in trees and shrubs. IRA fighters would then make their way to the arms dumps in rented, borrowed, or perhaps stolen cars and gradually ferry the weapons into Northern Ireland, often opting to sneak them across in cars with women and children, on a weekend, when security checkpoints were more lax. Eventually, late-night phone calls would direct IRA couriers in Belfast and Derry to collect the weapons, which would then be distributed to various quartermasters — the keepers of the IRA's guns — and used by IRA brigades in West Belfast and Derry.

It was a convoluted chain, difficult to trace and even harder to stop. But for the men in Philly, evidence of their success was clear: by 1972, the IRA was no longer on its heels. Instead, it was fending off the full weight of the British Army.

However militant he could be, Conlon was a diplomat at heart. It was part of what made him such an effective operative for the IRA in America, capable of uniting warring factions of the country's Irish diaspora and nudging them in the same direction. But this also made him an anomaly among more extreme Provisionals: in addition to being an avowed IRA man, he had never abandoned hope in politics, the source of so much strife and division within the movement. Even as the conflict raged, Conlon urged regular dialogue with Unionists, hopeful that they might eventually see the value of a united island. If prompted, he would call himself a realist: if there was a fair way forward, he would compromise. He abhorred religious tribalism and hated the conflation of Loyalism with Protestantism. To Conlon, the fight for Irish autonomy was never about religion; it was about respect and agency.

Sinn Fein, the IRA's political wing, had gone through its own series of acrimonious splits over the years, and the political party had itself eventually separated into an Official and Provisional wing not long after the 1969 split of the IRA. Conlon had been a member of Official Sinn Fein for years, even as the party limped along, weakened by neglect. But the Belfast Provos had reincarnated Sinn Fein and were attempting to turn it into something more influential. Conlon, a popular figure and a capable leader, was being recruited as a candidate, to help facilitate the strange go-between of the IRA and its forward-facing political arm. It was early days, in the Provos' play for political legitimacy, but Conlon hoped to be in on the ground floor. He had hitched his political cart to the Sinn Fein Belfast boys.

The end to the conflict, Conlon knew, would require more than guns and bullets, and a key step would be legitimizing Provisional Sinn Fein as a serious political outfit, not just a front for the IRA. It would be a challenging maneuver. To settle Northern Ireland, or at least reach a fragile détente, would take a hearty dose of compromise that the hard-liners among them would never accept. Sinn Fein would be the means by which to negotiate it. Conlon knew: politics, not blood, would be what ultimately ended the war.

For extreme supporters of militant Irish Republicanism, this was unacceptable. For them, there was no solution short of a united, thirty-two-county Republic, an Ireland that is entirely itself and free from British rule. Negotiation for anything less was seen as a grave betrayal, punishable by exile or worse. Michael Collins, hailed as an IRA hero of the 1920s, was assassinated by the dissident, hard-line, anti-treaty faction of the IRA, after he negotiated the partition of Northern Ireland, which ended the War for Independence in 1921. Attitudes among some Republicans had hardly softened in the decades since. Indeed, this difference of opinion was what initially caused the split between the militant Provisionals and the Official IRA, who increasingly looked toward politics as a solution for the Northern problem.

The politics, though, were complicated — and still are — when it comes to Irish Republicanism. Today, Sinn Fein is the main Republican and nationalist political party in Ireland, but historically it was the political vehicle of the IRA, which is technically a military rather than a political entity. The relationship between Sinn Fein and the IRA has always been convoluted, not least because Sinn Fein eventually became — and remains — a legal, public entity, and the Provisional IRA was an outlawed, illegal guerrilla force. Although the party was banned in the United Kingdom until 1974, it eventually became permissible to publicly pledge allegiance to Sinn Fein; the same could not be said of the IRA. Sinn Fein, then, was the outward-facing arm of nationalist, Republican politics. Its association with the IRA has always been obviously, uncomfortably close, so much so that for years, many legitimate political parties around the world refused to engage with Sinn Fein, lest they be accused of negotiating with the IRA.

It was why, as the Provisional IRA began to dabble in politics, people like Vince Conlon were palatable choices to put forward as candidates: older, uninvolved on the Troubles' front lines, and respected among the Provos' younger volunteers. It was yet another reason for Conlon to return home; there was an opportunity for him there. Provisional Sinn Fein, which had emerged as the preeminent Republican political party of the Troubles, wanted to begin entering local elections in the Republic of Ireland, where the party was unrestricted, building a network of political support in order to elevate the movement and propel it to legitimacy in the North, too. Conlon, who had been away from Ireland for years and therefore didn't carry much recent baggage, was a good man for the job.

Conlon answered the phone in Philadelphia for the last time in early 1972, a familiar ritual that Cahalane would soon take over: anytime Conlon picked up guns, it was carefully coordinated with New York. Conlon called Lyons, who called his contacts in the labor unions, who arranged the drop-offs. A squirrelly man named Eugene Marley, whose cousin owned a plumbing warehouse in the Bronx, was also involved, and had become an important link in the chain. This game of phone tag played out nearly the same way every time, in a series of cryptic, brief calls discussing the transfer of "stuffing" or "clothing," the code words the group had settled on for guns and bullets, fearful of speaking plainly lest their phones be tapped.

The posture of American law enforcement toward Irish America was increasingly hostile. Some days, it seemed like it was only a matter of time before authorities closed in. In a strange paradox, though, the men still didn't file off the serial numbers of the rifles before sending them off. Perhaps they believed someone else further down the chain would do it, or that the guns would be scrubbed once they reached Ireland; at any rate, as careful as the group may have been, they left the most valuable clue in plain sight.

Conlon should have been more cautious. As he made his final phone call from America, alerting NORAID to his last haul of ArmaLite rifles from the Montgomery Loan Company, his communications were not as private as he might have hoped.

PART III

THE
BOYS
IN
PHILLY

CHAPTER 13

GHOSTS

THE HILLS OF Donegal's Inishowen peninsula had always felt unsettled. A rugged strip of land jutting out from the island's northwest coast, the peninsula — Ireland's largest — is connected to the Republic's mainland only via a small passage skirting the Northern Irish border, across which lies Derry and its Catholic ghettos. Small, insular towns dotted its sparse mountain landscape, offering sanctuary from Derry — and from the British Army.

By the early 1970s, the Inishowen had become the nearest safe haven for IRA men fleeing the Bogside, a place to recover and regroup before heading back across the border, into the front lines. Because of this, it had also become a vital logistical hub: the peninsula's coastal hills hid IRA training camps and gun stores, stockpiled arsenals of the latest weapons, smuggled in from across the ocean.

Burnfoot, a small village on the peninsula, was the last real town before the border, and since the start of Northern Ireland's war, its sleepy two-lane main street had been transformed into a wartime boundary. A few miles east of the town limits, near the Northern Irish border, the British Army established a checkpoint in the early 1970s, fortifying the crossing with tanks and guns. It was one of only twenty official routes along the 310-mile border between Northern Ireland and the Republic, the rest having been destroyed or blockaded by the security forces. At these secure checkpoints, soldiers quizzed people who were crossing between the two countries, stopping cars, and throwing occupants against the pavement, forcing them to open their trunks.

These brass-knuckle tactics were meant to ensure that IRA fighters weren't slipping between the two territories, but in 1972 there was also an urgent new piece of intel: the Donegal-Derry border had become a critical smuggling route for guns making the final leg of their long, clandestine journey. If the British wanted to stop the IRA, they would have to stop the guns. Seizing them from car trunks was one thing. What they really needed was to stop whoever was sending them there in the first place.

Raids were a part of daily life on the Inishowen, but one morning rumors started to ricochet around the peninsula about a bizarre search that the Garda Síochána — the Irish police force — had conducted the day before, at the house of one of their own.

The role of the Garda was a complicated one in the Troubles, especially in places like the Inishowen, so close to the Northern Irish border. At the time, the Garda had a division based in Dublin, called the Special Branch, which dealt with IRA-related investigations. Individual members of the Garda, however, often turned a blind eye when wanted men fled across the border and into the Republic; in return, the IRA initially upheld their end of a long-standing gentleman's agreement not to target the Irish police.

In other parts of the Republic, it was easy enough for the Irish police to feign ignorance as to what was going on at the border. But in claustrophobic places like the Inishowen and Burnfoot, where Irish police and British security forces frequently ran up against each other, looking the other way was difficult, especially as the Troubles brought security headaches to both sides of the border.

The day before, the rumors went, Irish police had descended on a house near Burnfoot's outer limits, part of their sweeping effort to confiscate the IRA's guns. The home's resident — a uniformed member of the Garda Síochána — was a strange man, known to keep to himself. More concerning was the officer's fascination with weaponry, a trait that had raised red flags given the Inishowen's reputation as a key gun-smuggling channel.

When officials showed up to search the man's home, they found piles of arms: crossbows, pistols, rifles. One weapon in particular, though, stood out: a long gun, light and easily maneuvered, one of the newer ArmaLites that was being used all over the streets of Belfast and Derry. It couldn't have come from Ireland, and it certainly didn't belong to the police or the Army.

How the gun had made its way to the policeman wasn't clear; he didn't seem to have ties to the local Provisional brigade. It was likelier that he was not the gun's intended recipient, and had instead picked it off of a Provo at a car stop or house search and kept it for himself. Regardless, the officer was quietly let go from the force. His arrest and subsequent dismissal never hit the local papers, and he largely disappeared from the public eye.

That, though, was little bother to Northern Irish and English authorities. The significance of the raid lay not with the disgraced officer, but on his ArmaLite: chiseled into the metal was a serial number, an addition to the dozens they had uncovered over the past year.

Clues such as these had been mounting in evidence files since 1971, but attempts to trace the serial numbers were frustrating, and often fruitless. The rifles were usually ghosts, bought under fake names, spirited away through a horde of unidentifiable middlemen.

This time, though, the serial number turned up a hit almost immediately. The ArmaLite had been bought on March 10, 1972, at a small pawn shop outside Philadelphia. The store was called the Montgomery Loan Company. The man who purchased the rifle went by the name of Daniel Cahalane.

In a circle of muted characters, Neil Byrne stood out as an eccentric. A sharply dressed, bespectacled bachelor who worked as a grocery store clerk in a Philadelphia suburb, Byrne was a solitary man whose pastimes included writing effusive columns in local Irish-American papers. Byrne had first arrived in the city in the 1950s, hailing from a small fishing village in Donegal called Glencolmcille — the same village from which Dave O'Connell, Vince Conlon's old friend, had commanded the county's IRA brigade in the years after the border campaign. Like Cahalane, Byrne enlisted in the US Army and served in Korea before returning to Philly and linking up with Conlon, who at the time was only just reestablishing Clan-na-Gael. He proved a capable sidekick as Conlon worked Clan networks up and down the East Coast, and in time Byrne became one of the Philadelphia Clan's key figures, a dedicated believer and a key point of contact for IRA leaders in Dublin as the army pivoted toward its 1969 split.

Partnering with Byrne had been smart planning by Conlon, who perhaps even then knew he wouldn't be in Philly forever. Byrne was unique in the inner circle; he had a hand in both Clan-na-Gael and NORAID — no small feat in Irish Philly, where feuds and rivalries often split the various clubs' loyalties. He took to the MacSwiney Club, owned by a Clan member named Matt Regan, and the bar became the organization's headquarters. The small Jenkintown clubhouse, nestled in Philadelphia's outskirts, was a members-only space, its rolls full of Clan members.

Meanwhile, Danny Cahalane, Conlon's anointed successor in the gun-running scheme, exceeded even Byrne's and Conlon's greatest expectations. The months following Conlon's departure saw Cahalane take on his inherited role with vigor. He had always been a dedicated leader for NORAID, present everywhere and at everything. But after Vince Conlon left, Dan Cahalane took on this new, clandestine directive with equal dedication. The responsibility awoke something in him: behind a NORAID podium, the otherwise unemotional Cahalane was a man transformed. In fiery speeches, he roused his fellow expats to give money and get involved. Nearly every day, he attended an event at Breen's or other pubs across the city. He embarked on endless visits and house calls, his energy convincing even the less sympathetic to throw a few dollars into the NORAID tin can. On weekends, he and Bill Corry packed Cahalane's green work van with beer and soda, drove it to the Gaelic Athletic Association grounds in the city's northeast, and sold refreshments during hurling and football matches; the money, of course, went straight into NORAID's coffers.

It was a family affair. Cahalane often carted his young son along with him on strange errands deep in Pennsylvania. His other children flitted in and out of NORAID dinner dances. On Sundays, he drove around to the local parishes with them, hawking copies of *The Irish People,* NORAID's affiliated newspaper; they could hardly leave the house without Cahalane shoving stacks of the paper into their arms.

The transformation was stunning and obvious, especially to his teenage daughter and his wife, Jane. The roots of this radicalism, though, were a mystery, even to those closest to him. Cahalane had never spoken about any particular incident with British troops back in Ireland, never shared any personal experience with the British Army's brutal behavior. Had he been radicalized by his friendship with Bill Corry, and this newfound fervor stemmed from personal loyalty? Or was it due to his proximity to Conlon, a persuasive, impassioned leader in the Irish community? Either way, by 1972 — two years after first being named head of the Delaware County chapter of NORAID — Dan Cahalane was one of the IRA's most successful international gunrunners.

Cahalane never discussed his illicit proclivities with Jane, but it was impossible to hide everything. She noticed the cars outside the house, noted Cahalane's bizarre hours, clocked the strange men who moved in and out of their quiet cul-de-sac. The children noticed, too. They were young but sharp, their imaginations running wild as unmarked cars zipped in and out of the dead-end residential road on which they lived.

If any of it bothered Cahalane, he didn't show it. On the contrary, the scrutiny seemed to embolden him. He slept soundly at night, sure he and Byrne were on the right side of history.

Some three years on from the Clonard Street riots that had kicked off the Troubles, one thing had become clear to British and Northern Irish investigators: the IRA was getting a lot of guns, and most of them were coming from America. Incidents like the Burnfoot raid, moreover, were yielding clues about precisely which Americans were sending them. Sifting through their growing pile of seized guns, investigators in Belfast started sharing the weapons' serial numbers with their American counterparts, who were tracing many of them to purchases in the same two US cities: New York and Philadelphia. This circumstantial evidence forced the US Justice Department to abandon its initial assessment, established after the FBI first visited NORAID headquarters back in 1970: that NORAID, an organization that after all had deep roots in both of these eastern US cities, was a responsible and politically moderate organization. Based on a growing list of evidence from Northern Ireland, that didn't seem to be the case.

As the FBI dusted off its investigation into NORAID, their interest was primarily in a clerical issue, one with big implications. NORAID had legally filed under FARA as a representative for the supposedly innocuous Northern Aid Committee in Belfast, an organization with which it essentially shared a name, and to which it sent its checks. Federal investigators came to suspect that this was a ruse. After all, the head of that committee in Belfast was Joe Cahill, a well-known, high-ranking figure in the Provos who was already suspected of smuggling guns over from the States. NORAID's true foreign principal, federal investigators suspected, was not the Northern Aid Committee but rather the Provisional IRA.

The potential FARA violation was the basis of the FBI's investigation into NORAID, and investigators hoped to force NORAID to publicly declare its links to the Provos. Meanwhile, probing NORAID's gun smuggling fell to a different law-enforcement agency, a newer organization specifically tasked with investigating gun crimes. The Bureau of Alcohol, Tobacco, and Firearms, or ATF, had joined the hunt.

At the time, the ATF was a small federal agency mostly known for its work policing contraband cigarettes and chasing bootleggers during Prohibition. In the 1930s, with the passage of the National and Federal Firearms Acts, the ATF also inherited oversight of the gun industry. For years it remained a division of the Internal Revenue Service and was therefore limited in its jurisdiction. But in 1972, in the wake of gun-control legislation passed in the 1960s, the ATF became its own agency, tasked with reporting directly to the Treasury Department's Office of Enforcement. (The agency was renamed the Bureau of Alcohol, Tobacco, Firearms, and Explosives, as part of the Homeland Security Act of 2002, enacted in the aftermath of the 9/11 terrorist attacks.)

Practically overnight, the ATF became a serious law enforcement agency. While it still had to fight for respect and influence, often getting muscled out of large criminal cases by the FBI and other, better-resourced agencies, the ATF had an opportunity in NORAID — and a mounting file of evidence from Great Britain — that could change all that.

That winter felt like a prelude to war.

The inner circle's gunrunning operation had never been running more smoothly. In Philadelphia, the departed Vince Conlon had passed on a promising new source for guns in Marjorie Palace. In Syracuse, where Bill Corry's friends were hard at work procuring weapons from their own sources, there was talk of a new supplier of rocket launchers. And in New York City, Marty Lyons and his gang were making sure the supplies kept moving through the docks.

The risks, though, were becoming clearer. John Casey knew it; Marty Lyons, the NORAID chairman, knew it. They all did.

In the earliest days of the operation, they took guns from anywhere and sent them over to Ireland however they could. But now, paranoia was starting to set in. As the boys in Belfast were fighting the British Army, the boys in NORAID were barreling toward their own confrontation, with the US Department of Justice.

To be sure, the IRA's secret gunrunners had been ducking American law enforcement for decades. But it had been easier when the group was small — when they weren't moving all that many guns, and it was easy to keep track of who was trustworthy and who might flip. Now, though, the network had grown, and the number of shipments — and with it the pool of potential informants — had expanded along with it.

Public linkages to the IRA had worried Mike Flannery and Dave O'Connell ever since NORAID's founding. Faced with the threat of having to register as a representative of the Provisional IRA, Flannery enlisted the services of Paul O'Dwyer, an Irish lawyer long sympathetic to the cause, and his nephew, an enterprising, bullish attorney named Frank Durkan. O'Dwyer and Durkan helped NORAID register as a representative of the Northern Aid Committee in Belfast instead, but they weren't able to completely protect the organization: in early 1972, the FBI used the FARA statute to demand access to NORAID's books, leaving Flannery with no choice but to grudgingly turn them over through the attorneys.

If any of them were rattled, though, they didn't show it. Frank Grady, the man who had first brought Casey into the NORAID fold, was traveling everywhere these days. He had just returned from Texas, where he was picking up weapons. Lyons, meanwhile, was constantly on flights to and from Ireland, and had recently spent a weekend in Philadelphia. As a member of the inner circle, Casey was briefed on those endeavors.

He was just one link in a long chain, but Casey knew — and took pride in — where it led. One afternoon that winter, Casey and Grady were killing time, and Grady was thumbing through a copy of the New York *Daily News*. He stopped abruptly on a bold headline: INSIDE THE IRA. Splashed across the top of the page was a photograph of an explosion. In the foreground was the shadow of a man gripping the spindly outline of a long rifle.

Intrigued, Casey examined the newspaper. Grady grinned.

"That," he said, pointing at the picture, "is one of our guns."

The horrible events of Bloody Sunday unleashed a full-blown political crisis for the British government, and a surge of new recruits to the IRA. The anger from nationalist and Catholic residents was compounded when British authorities failed to acknowledge the wrongdoing of the soldiers who indiscriminately

fired into the civilian crowd that day; the furthest they would go was a conces-
sion that the troops' lethal behavior had "bordered on the reckless." To many of
Northern Ireland's Catholics, this was yet another sign that armed resistance
was the only viable option. One phrase became synonymous with the months
following the Derry massacre: "We are all IRA now."

The army was a completely different beast than it had been even a year
before. The Provos were a real, well-armed outfit now, and it had left the British
scrambling. Troops were turning Catholic ghettos inside out, and their raids
were uncovering more and more American guns. Though they claimed to be
targeting nationalist and Unionist ghettos equally, the operations were deeply
biased toward Catholic ghettos: in one representative month, December 1972,
108 nationalist homes were raided, compared to just two Loyalist homes. Still,
the soldiers weren't operating entirely without cause. The following month,
January 1973, the British Army seized thirty-seven rifles, sixteen pistols, and
five shotguns in Belfast's Andersonstown neighborhood alone. In a single raid,
police arrested a woman after finding five guns and fifteen hundred rounds of
ammunition in her house.

West Belfast had set itself firmly on a war footing ever since that horrid
Sunday in Derry. In the span of a week, one newspaper's daily crime blotter
reported multiple hijacked vans, eight bombs, and daily shoot-outs between soldiers and snipers in Lenadoon and elsewhere. The local post office was robbed
so many times — under the very nose of British soldiers, who were supposed to
be providing security — that Belfast's postal service threatened to shut down.

The year 1972 proved to be the deadliest in the twenty-five-year history of
the Troubles, so depraved and brutal that at times Northern Ireland seemed
beyond saving. The instability prompted a dangerous arms race between
warring Republican and Loyalist paramilitary groups. The IRA continued
to stockpile ArmaLites and other types of rifles from America and also —
under the direction of the Long Fella, Conlon's border campaign comrade,
NORAID founder, and now Provisional IRA chief of staff, Dave O'Connell —
introduced the car bomb, a sinister strategy that would become so synonymous
with the romanticism of the IRA that Irish America would later name a popular cocktail after it. Meanwhile, Loyalist paramilitaries like the Ulster Volunteer Force, or UVF, and the Ulster Defence Regiment, or UDR, also increased
their own arsenals, cognizant that the ongoing practice of internment was bolstering support for the IRA. Emboldened by all of this newfound firepower,

the UDR and the UVF targeted Catholics while IRA volunteers kidnapped Protestants.

Caught in the crossfire were Northern Ireland's civilians, on both sides of the region's divide. Newspaper articles cautioned parents to keep their children away from unfamiliar objects like abandoned bags or packages, lest they be disguised explosives. Bloody Friday — July 21, 1972, echoing the tragic weekend that had started that year — would become another of the conflict's dark colloquialisms, marking the day that the IRA set off a string of car bombs in Belfast's city center, killing nine and injuring more than one hundred. Overall, the month of July had seen the unthinkable rate of three deaths per day, a staggering toll considering Northern Ireland's population numbered only around 1.5 million.

Meanwhile, political panic erupted after Bloody Sunday. British and Unionist politicians, fearing a near-complete dissolution of civil order in Northern Ireland, considered repartitioning the territory into Catholic and Protestant districts, offering dual citizenship to the region's residents. They even privately dabbled with the idea of Irish unity — a possibility that would

An IRA fighter passes a magazine to a fellow combatant in Derry, 1972.

have surely enraged and incensed Loyalists had they known it was being considered. Among the proposals was a power-sharing arrangement that would guarantee a mixed cabinet and Catholic representation in governance — an idea that was soundly rejected by the prime minister of Northern Ireland, Unionist Brian Faulkner. Instead, he defended the status quo and even urged authorities to continue with internment, despite increasing evidence that the policy was helping — not hurting — the IRA's recruiting efforts.

Amid this political fracas, Stormont, the legislative body that had ruled Northern Ireland since its creation in 1921, was shut down, and local governance was suspended in favor of so-called direct rule by the British government. It was a development more important for its symbolism than any concrete political effect; after all, ever since the British Army first set foot on Northern Irish soil, officials from London had quietly shaped the day-to-day affairs of the territory. But in the dissolution of Stormont, Unionists in Northern Ireland lost their most direct cudgel against Irish nationalists. This bolstered the long-held paranoias of Loyalist factions, who feared that Great Britain, long wary of its political albatross, might abandon Northern Ireland entirely; in turn, Loyalists flocked to paramilitary organizations like the UVF and the UDR. With the collapse of Northern Ireland's homegrown parliament and the growing influence of extrajudicial paramilitary forces, the ruse of an autonomous, representative government in the region came to an end. And Northern Ireland would have to endure another quarter of a century of bloodshed before it could claim to rule itself once again.

CHAPTER 14

"SOMEONE ELSE IS LISTENING"

THAT SUMMER, AMERICAN and British investigators scored a coup in their hunt for the IRA's American gunrunners. And ironically enough, it was Joe Cahill — the Belfast IRA commander collecting NORAID's checks — who first led them there.

It started with the arrival of a group of suitcases on a dock in Cobh, a small harbor town in Cork: six of them, blue in color, left unclaimed after a stopover by the ocean liner *Queen Elizabeth II*. The luggage was heavy, much too difficult for a single man to lift. When customs agents at the port opened them, there were no clothes, souvenirs, or trappings of a luxurious transatlantic cruise. Instead, the suitcases were filled to the brim with American guns, ammunition, and grenades, carefully packaged with pages from the *New York Times*.

The spectacularly botched delivery was a subject of derision among the Provos. Joe Cahill, the man who coordinated much of the Provos' lethal American support, apparently forgot to make arrangements to have the suitcases picked up and transported to the border. This error was more than just a headache. The IRA had lost out on a new haul of guns, sure; but more critically, those six suitcases exposed the American network that had sent them there.

Indeed, in an increasingly desperate cat-and-mouse game, the six suitcases were a spectacular find for British and American investigators, who had been joining forces to neuter NORAID. Two of the *Queen Elizabeth II's* kitchen workers — both from Belfast — were arrested when the ship docked in

England; their fingerprints were found on and inside the suitcases. But those prints weren't the only evidence revealed by the guns; arguably, they were the least significant. By that summer, investigators found forensic breadcrumbs that connected the weapons, the United States, and the IRA. For the suitcases were connected to five New York men, all of them Irish immigrants. They weren't part of that insular inner circle, but all of them, it seemed, had ties to NORAID.

It was summer when the car tires crunched on the gravel outside the Montgomery Loan Company and a young federal agent stepped out. Robert L. Doyle was part of a growing cadre of ATF officials assigned to the NORAID investigation.

That probe stemmed from those six suitcases in Cobh, but it quickly spiraled into a much larger investigation, one that expanded far beyond New York. NORAID was now in the United States Justice Department's crosshairs, nationwide, and the guns from the smuggled luggage were but one strand in an increasingly tangled web. Now dozens of other gun recoveries in Northern Ireland were leading back to NORAID members, too.

Some members of the organization in Philadelphia were buying guns; that part was easy enough to figure out. After all, they usually signed their real names on the federal firearms forms when they bought their ArmaLite rifles. The question was what they were doing with the guns, which virtually disappeared after they were purchased.

The ATF finally had answers. Among them: two of the guns that were sold to the NORAID men by this little suburban gun shop bore serial numbers matching guns that turned up in Northern Ireland.

It had been nearly six months since that visit in March, when Daniel Cahalane, Vince Conlon, and Neil Byrne arrived together at the Montgomery Loan Company, signed their names, and walked away with that pile of twenty-five ArmaLites. Federal agents might not have realized it yet, but since that visit, Cahalane and Byrne had collected an arsenal of weapons. The two men returned regularly to the pawnbroker to order more ArmaLites. The owner never bothered them, and the nosy clerk left them alone.

That was all about to change. Agent Doyle strode into the Montgomery Loan Company and asked for Charles Shulberg, the shop's longtime owner. The clerk lingered for a moment after Shulberg appeared, but then sensed the weight of the conversation and hurried off.

The agent stopped short of telling Shulberg everything: there was no need, and he couldn't be too careful. And anyway the problem, as the agent explained it, was straightforward. The men to whom Shulberg had been selling guns were not the upstanding citizens they claimed to be, and the guns were not for their own personal use. Instead, he said, the guns had turned up in Northern Ireland.

Shulberg was engaged and seemed genuinely concerned. After all, he was well familiar with the customers about whom Agent Doyle was speaking. One in particular stood out: the man with horn-rimmed glasses and curly black hair. Danny Cahalane visited regularly and, Shulberg realized, had been in just the week before, to order another haul of guns: fifty ArmaLite rifles, of which Shulberg had already procured twenty-five directly from the ArmaLite company in California.

Agent Doyle left, satisfied that Shulberg understood the situation's seriousness — and that this source of guns, at least, had been shut down. His visit was an unambiguous warning, and Shulberg heeded it immediately. He canceled the order and never sold to Danny Cahalane again.

Cahalane was never told why that last order to Shulberg was canceled, but it didn't take too much imagination to figure it all out. A shadow was spreading over NORAID, from New York to Philadelphia. The counter at Breen's Café was frequented more and more often by strangers, dressed too sharply to be day laborers or construction workers. Occasionally, they slunk out of the pub, trailing NORAID members who had just left the premises. Cahalane began noticing strange clicks while he was speaking on the phone; so did his wife, Jane, who heard the noise while on calls with her own family. "Get off the line!" she would howl into the receiver.

Wary of being surreptitiously overheard, Cahalane, Byrne, and Corry began operating with more caution, opting for meeting in person at their homes, or in hotel bars and pubs. When they had to arrange something remotely, they did it via pay phone, speaking in code. Still, even though they grew more cautious, they did not slow the pace of their efforts. The guns kept coming.

Suspicion even followed Vince Conlon back to Ireland, where he had returned to the front. He and Marina had bought a country property in Monaghan; along the border, on a clear day, they could see Armagh out of the home's north-facing windows, close but so horribly, politically, painfully far.

Conlon had taken on a role as an intelligence officer with the Provos' local brigade. Meanwhile, Marina helped turn the family home into a border safe house. Through the Conlon doors was a rotating cast of men on the run. They stayed there as they bounced between farms and other sympathetic homes, just out of reach of British and Northern Irish authorities.

And so it was that even back among the comforts of home, the Conlons never quite relaxed. The local Garda Síochána kept a close eye on Conlon, starting nearly as soon as he arrived back to the island. Officers seemed to take any excuse to call by the house, or search the premises. And, he was sure, British intelligence was almost certainly watching him, tracking his movements and waiting for a reason to pounce. Confined to the Republic, Conlon left the family's Northern obligations to Marina, who traveled across the border regularly to see family. Mere miles from the land on which he had been raised, Conlon could see Armagh but didn't dare visit; it was too risky. When his mother died in his home parish, it was Marina who went to the funeral — and good thing, too, for the British Army had set up a checkpoint just feet from the Conlon family home in Armagh, in case Vince dared surface.

In a small closet where Conlon kept the telephone in their new home, he had scratched a warning into the wooden doorframe. It was a reminder to both himself and his children, who occasionally picked up the line.

"Be careful what you say," it read. "Someone else is listening."

CHAPTER 15

MAD DOG

THAT SUMMER OF 1972 brought sobering new developments, stemming from those five suitcases that had been intercepted at the Cobh docks. The five NORAID men to whom the luggage was traced — Thomas Laffey, Kenneth Tierney, Mathias Reilly, Daniel Crawford, and Paschal Morahan — were subpoenaed to appear before a grand jury, the first, it seemed, that had formally convened to investigate NORAID-linked gunrunning. No longer was the government's probe of NORAID a hypothetical, or in the abstract; there was now a real investigation, with real legal consequences.

Rather than trying the case in New York, prosecutors had convened a grand jury in Fort Worth, Texas, where the guns found in the suitcase had allegedly been purchased. The location was seen by NORAID supporters as uniquely punitive, for it forced the men to travel from New York and undergo the stress of the debacle far from their families and communities. These difficulties were compounded when the men refused to testify and were jailed in Texas for contempt of court.

In hard-line Irish cities like Philadelphia, the case was viewed as a severe injustice, akin to the extrajudicial procedures that were taking place across nationalist ghettos in places like West Belfast. Protests supporting the Fort Worth men spread across NORAID strongholds like Philly, where hundreds gathered in Independence Square. Supporters were encouraged to buy T-shirts with IRA lettering and symbols. One local Irish historian noted the garb soon became common outfitting at "work sites, ballfields, and boys' clubs all over the city."

It was a galvanizing moment for NORAID's true believers. But in the inner circle, perhaps, there was a dark sense of foreboding: Given the aggression of prosecutors in the Fort Worth case, it was almost certainly just the beginning. Who among them would be next?

The two prosecutors made an odd pair. Trial lawyers Robert W. Merkle Jr. and Brandon Alvey first met while working in the Justice Department's internal security office before being transferred to the department's powerful Criminal Division, which prosecuted all of the US government's main criminal cases. It was in such surroundings that the two men were given a strange assignment, with Alvey — the more senior attorney — as supervisor: a new, high-priority investigative effort within the Justice Department, one that was slowly taking shape around those six blue suitcases that authorities had seized on the Cork docks.

Hulking, tall, and built like a linebacker, Bob Merkle was fresh out of law school at Notre Dame, where he had played for the university's football team. A devout Catholic born and raised in America's South, Merkle had already established himself as a brawler in the courtroom. He was brash and proudly undiplomatic, traits that would eventually earn him the nickname "Mad Dog," and he operated with blind conviction in his own judgment. Few things, including facts, stood in the way of Bob Merkle, especially if he decided a certain case — or enemy — needed punishing.

Alvey, meanwhile, was twenty years' Merkle's senior, short and slight. With sad eyes and a long face, Alvey was darkly depressive, as crass as Merkle but with more vices and less charm. A British newspaper profile would one day describe him as having a "soft voice and an air of unassuming innocence," but those who knew Alvey knew this reserved surface hid a darkness. Tedious and particular, Alvey had been shot down in a bomber during World War II, lost part of his stomach, married his nurse, and, in the interim, developed a serious problem with alcohol. Colleagues knew not to try and have a conversation with him in the afternoons, when he would return from lunch flushed with booze.

The two prosecutors had little experience trying major gun-trafficking cases; Alvey was not regarded as especially talented or polished. But for whatever reason, the case against NORAID had landed on their desks. And unlike most gunrunning investigations, this was not a one-off case — the investigation into NORAID was a wide-ranging conspiracy, involving several different states. Those suitcases in Cork had initially led investigators to New York, it was true, but the city was far from their only target. Agents descended on NORAID chapters in Baltimore, San Francisco, and New Jersey, and were probing leads as far flung as Montana and Texas.

By the fall of 1972, Alvey and Merkle were overseeing a full-fledged investigation of Irish Philadelphia by the ATF. Via their British counterparts, the agency was tracking a growing pile of ArmaLites and other guns that were linking back to the same group of men who bought those two rifles, later recovered in Northern Ireland, from the Montgomery Loan Company. Philadelphia, it was clear, was supplying a significant portion of the Provos' ArmaLites.

Whether or not the Philadelphia men knew it, by that autumn agents had spent months burrowing into their personal lives. They had bugged NORAID phones and watched calls bounce between Vince Conlon, Marty Lyons, Eugene Marley, Bill Corry, Neil Byrne, and Danny Cahalane. One agent had scrubbed through Cahalane's finances; another had kept an eye on Byrne's highway toll records, watching how often he traveled between Philadelphia and New York. They noticed a change in phone call patterns after Conlon stopped calling Lyons and Cahalane started, his communiqués lining up suspiciously with their trips up the Turnpike to New York City. Other agents lurked at Breen's bar, trailed Bill Corry, or watched the Cahalane home, hidden in nearby bushes (one later lamented that while hiding in the brush, he was urinated on by an unsuspecting dog).

Still, NORAID's scattered bookkeeping had made it nearly impossible for investigators to draw a line directly between the group's money and specific weapons that ended up with the Provos. In internal documents, British and Northern Irish investigators lamented the difficulty of understanding NORAID's structure, and therefore of identifying the sorts of financial links that could build an airtight case against the group. "It has not yet been possible to link NORAID funds directly with arms purchases," one Northern Irish investigator wrote of the Philadelphia probe.

But clear links weren't necessary in waging the softer war of public perception. In newspaper interviews and speeches, British officials urged Irish Americans to be careful with their donations, implying heavily that NORAID was a front for supplying dangerous firearms to rebels. And while federal charges had yet to be brought, the organization was feeling the heat: just as Mike Flannery and Dave O'Connell had feared, the vast majority of Irish America did not want to be directly implicated in the IRA's brutal campaign, which — prompted by both American and British officials — the mainstream discourse had begun labeling as terrorism. The Fort Worth case validated the fears of Irish Americans whose loyalty to the Provos was lukewarm, making clear the dangers of associating with NORAID. In Portland, Oregon, a NORAID chapter folded after too many of its members fled the group, concerned about rumors of gunrunning. In New Jersey, another chapter thinned out severely after federal agents began questioning members about fundraising. Concerns among Irish-American members of NORAID were so great that one even offered to help the FBI "locate terrorists."

In truth, much of NORAID's fundraising likely *did* go to supporting disenfranchised Catholic families in Northern Ireland, including the widows and children of IRA volunteers who were in prison, killed, or wounded. But other facts were clear enough. Danny Cahalane, the chair of the Delaware County NORAID chapter, had single-handedly signed for 119 ArmaLites, and those guns weren't cheap. When ATF agents secretly subpoenaed Cahalane's bank statements, the numbers confirmed what Brandon Alvey and Bob "Mad Dog" Merkle already knew: Cahalane and the NORAID men, modestly employed, blue-collar laborers in Delaware County, couldn't afford to buy all those rifles by themselves.

CHAPTER 16

THE BINGHAMTON FIASCO

THE ATF'S VISIT to the Montgomery Loan Company had ended the relationship between the shop and the Philadelphia men, and it was a definite setback. For years, Shulberg had been one of Conlon's most reliable, discreet dealers; the group had ordered 160 guns from him — $20,000 worth — in the months before Conlon left, and all had expected the relationship to continue, even after Conlon's departure. The good news was, Cahalane and Byrne still had Marjorie Palace in Morrisville, who seemed to have more of a stomach than Shulberg did for suspicious purchases.

Legitimate gun dealers were more reliable than anyone they could find on the black market. But it was inevitable that the inner circle would eventually have to explore less lawful arrangements, and by the summer of 1972 its members had two leads that were particularly promising.

In secret meetings ranging from Chicago to Phoenix, Marty Lyons was vetting a potential source for rocket launchers. Meanwhile, Gene Marley, a longtime friend of Corry's and Conlon's with ties to Armagh, was working on a source of his own.

Marley had been a regular middleman for the inner circle through his cousin, Eugene Clancy, who owned Clancy & Cullen Moving and Storage — the company warehouse was where Marty Lyons and the New York crew stored the guns and packed them up as household and plumbing supplies. Marley had been included regularly in the games of phone tag that coordinated the drop-offs between the cities. And now, in an ambitious play to prove his worth, he found a potential weapons supplier in Syracuse, New York: a man who, if he came through, could give the IRA's secret American network perhaps their best source yet.

The phone rang that Sunday at Bill Corry's, at the same time it always did. Gene Marley was punctual, and stuck to their schedule: for years, he had called Corry on Sundays, keeping him apprised of what was going on in New York and at the warehouse. He was an odd guy, frenetic and aloof, with an air of professorial mania. But he and Corry went way back, and he had become a family friend.

However much he trusted Marley, however, Corry was wary as he picked up the phone. Things had been hard since Conlon had left, though for most who had known Vince, his eventual return to the front felt inevitable. They had managed well enough in his absence, but now there was a significant increase in pressure, as the threat of legal trouble mounted. Corry, Cahalane, and Byrne never had a quiet moment anymore, their days filled with endless errands: secret meetings at Breen's, nights in the attic of the MacSwiney Club, or appearances at some NORAID event. Most weekends, Cahalane would load his family into the green work van and arrive at Corry's unannounced, their children and wives left to socialize while the two men disappeared.

That Sunday, though, Corry was surprised to hear good news. His old friend Marley wasn't calling with a problem; he was calling with a solution. For months, he had been cultivating a new contact in Syracuse with surprising connections, a savvy arms dealer with a nose for cash and an appetite for risk. The man specialized in automatic weapons and rockets — exactly what the Philadelphia and NORAID networks had been trying to get their hands on for months. The dealer wanted to arrange something quickly, but Marley, wary of making a unilateral decision, held the man off for as long as he could. His wasn't a rogue operation, he explained to the gun dealer. He was part of something bigger, a network of IRA supporters in Philadelphia who worked as a group.

To buy the guns, Marley told the man, he would need approval from Philly, and it was no small ask: $6,000 for twenty launchers and fifty rockets.

But the weapons, as Corry knew, were exactly what the Provisional IRA needed to hold their own against the British tanks and armored police cars that were patrolling the streets. The inner circle had been searching for this kind of connection for months. Corry hung up cautiously optimistic.

Give the man $500 as a down payment, Corry instructed Marley, *and close the deal.*

It was nearing midnight at the Kirkwood Motel when the station wagon pulled in. A frantic Gene Marley cut the engine and raced toward Room 2. What had begun as a promising night — a promising arrangement — had gone horribly wrong.

The plan should have been simple: Marley, cleared by Bill Corry, arranged a transfer of rocket launchers with the arms dealer from Syracuse, and weeks of planning had led to this night. The man was supposed to call when he was fifteen minutes outside Binghamton, an industrial city along the New York–Pennsylvania border some seventy miles south of Syracuse. Marley would take care of the rest — he had an empty truck waiting, ready to load full of the weapons.

The promising operation had brought so much excitement to the network that NORAID's chairman, Marty Lyons himself, drove to Binghamton from the Bronx along with Connie Buckley, who, like Marley, was connected to the Clancy & Cullen Moving and Storage company, where the inner circle stored their weapons. Marley went off on his own that evening to wait for the call; as soon as he secured the launchers, he planned to meet Lyons and Buckley back at the Kirkwood, a nondescript roadside motel with lots of through traffic. It was there that Lyons and Buckley were waiting, as the hours ticked by.

But midnight got closer and Marley's phone remained silent. Anxious and alone, he faced an unsettling realization: the arms dealer wasn't calling, and chances were slim that it was a miscommunication. Something was wrong, and Marley would have no explanation for Lyons, who, as the head of NORAID, had cleared the money. Marley had bungled the operation hugely, and he would have to face the consequences.

Marley's failure went much further than the loss of $500 and a few guns. American prosecutors weren't publicly saying the purpose of their investigation in Fort Worth. But Lyons and his inner circle all knew: the US was now investigating American gunrunning to the IRA. There were too many strangers asking questions these days, too many new faces. Now Marley had exposed them to a stranger. Where had the dealer disappeared to? Who was he in the first place? To make matters worse, Marley had hardly been careful. Foolishly, he had treated the stranger like a member of NORAID's inner circle. He had let slip crucial details about the network in Philadelphia, and the broader shadow operation behind the ArmaLites that had moved across the Atlantic.

And so, the dealer, wherever he was — if he even was a dealer — had something even more dangerous than guns: he had information, enough to put most of the pieces together and connect them all to Philly.

Exhausted and frustrated, Marley, Lyons, and Buckley argued in the motel room until they couldn't fight anymore. There was no telling where the man had run off to, and who he might return with. The NORAID men needed to leave the Kirkwood, but they needed to do it casually. They slipped out of the room and loitered in the parking lot for a moment, Buckley and Lyons getting in their van, Marley in his. They drifted off into the night, heading in opposite directions.

The argument was an uncharacteristic eruption for the group of otherwise discreet men. But it was an intense moment in an intense year, and their frustration wasn't unreasonable. Still, it was inopportune. The ATF, after all, was in the room next door.

It was nearing dawn by the time Connie Buckley steered their van toward New York City, on the way home from the Kirkwood. The highway was quiet at that hour, late enough that the nightbirds had gone home, but too early for the morning commuters. It was a peaceful drive after a chaotic night, but the coming day would bring another round of questions and uncertainties for which he and Lyons had no answers.

How much longer would the operation be able to carry on? The Justice Department was already burrowed into NORAID's books, which had been turned over early that year. And the pressure to register properly under FARA had trickled all the way down to individual NORAID chapters like Philadelphia, where all of the men were registering under the statute in an effort to placate the FBI.

All of this hung over Lyons and Buckley in the small morning hours. It was hanging there, still, as the pair neared the George Washington Bridge and police lights flickered on behind them.

Buckley steered the van to the shoulder and waited obediently behind the wheel as the state police officer approached and asked for the car's registration and the men's licenses. But after a brief wait, the officer returned with the documents and motioned for them to drive on. It was almost as if the only thing he'd wanted was to see who was in the car.

CHAPTER 17

"WE'RE WORKING FOR THE IRA"

A MONTH AFTER Marley's mistake in Binghamton, New York's inner circle squeezed into the small living room of an apartment off Grand Avenue in the West Bronx. The place was stuffy in the July heat, crowded by large men with brogues. One of those men was John Casey, the plumber with the Yonkers NORAID chapter. Another was Connie Buckley, who had driven to and from Binghamton with Marty Lyons that botched night. Commanding them all was the Galwegian, Lyons himself.

There was a new face in the room, too: a man named Bill Kelly. And the air was thick not just with the summer heat, but also with suspicion.

Plans for the gathering had begun months before in Phoenix, when Marty Lyons had arranged a clandestine meeting between a member of the inner circle and Kelly, who had been communicating with the group's conspirators in Chicago. The inner circle was hoping to expand its arsenal, and was after major arms like bazookas, rockets, and grenade launchers. Kelly, an experienced professional, had offered to get them. The initial introduction in Phoenix had gone well, and the group, hoping to secure a new supplier, made arrangements for a meeting in New York.

Despite the optimism that followed the Arizona meeting with Kelly, there was a wariness in the room as Lyons probed the man's credentials. After all, it hadn't been long since the debacle with Marley, when they were burned on an arrangement that looked an awful lot like this one. More and more often these small interactions seemed to carry dark implications. It was hard to tell who could be trusted, who was a grifter, and who could be something else entirely — an informant, perhaps, or even an undercover agent. Still, they hardly had the luxury of choice.

Kelly's interest in the IRA's cause, they learned, stemmed from his Irish grandfather. What began as a purely genealogical interest had led Kelly to grapple with the morality of the conflict; he had grown concerned enough over the British behavior in Northern Ireland that he even discussed the issue with his parish priest.

"Well, you know the problems we're having over there," Lyons started carefully. The British Army was starting to enter IRA strongholds like Andersonstown in armored cars and tanks. "They can come in with those and just shoot us up." Light weapons such as the ArmaLite were useless against targets like that.

Kelly was genuine and curious, which loosened some of the tension in the room. Further, he had been in the mix for a while and was clearly invested in the relationship; he had traveled all the way to Phoenix, after all, and then to New York with no guaranteed payoff. Encouraged by Kelly's good faith, Marty Lyons and the group seemed to breathe a sigh of relief.

"We're working for the IRA," one of them finally said.

The revelation wasn't a surprise. Kelly had suspected as much; why else would a group of Irishmen in the Bronx be interested in bazookas and rocket launchers? Still, despite the tentative demonstrations of trust, both sides of the living room remained equally skeptical of the arrangement's logistics — Kelly, the gun dealer, unsure if the IRA men actually had money; and the men, unsure if Kelly actually had guns. Lyons in particular was wary of scams and false starts; rocket launchers the group had bought before had turned out to be useless duds with no power. If the group committed to Kelly, they needed to know the weapons worked.

Kelly was prepared. He showed off pictures of bazookas, ready to be dropped off as soon as the cash showed up. He even offered to let them test the weapons. But, he said, he wouldn't arrange for a delivery until he knew they had the money. He wasn't certain the NORAID men had deep enough pockets.

Fearing a stalemate, one of the men disappeared into a bedroom, emerging not long after with a black folder. He handed it to Lyons, who pulled out a thick wad of cash.

"This will be enough to pay for the first shipment," Lyons said.

Intrigued, Kelly peeled away the bills, which came mostly in hundreds and fifties. When he finished counting, he said, they were $300 short. The order, for ten bazookas and a hundred grenade launchers, was worth $11,300.

"There's $11,300," Lyons said, agitated. Together, they laid the cash out on the floor of the apartment. It turned out Lyons was right — Kelly miscounted. It was all there.

Satisfied, Kelly said the weapons were hidden in a panel truck, stacked in pieces inside shoeboxes, ready for delivery. The transfer would be simple enough; the whole thing could be done in less than twenty minutes.

"Connie and myself will take the truck and we will go, and we will return the truck within twenty minutes, and give you the keys back," Lyons said. "You can leave town."

Lyons didn't say it directly, but the whole room knew where the guns would end up. The storage warehouse wasn't far, and it was where they could keep the guns until they were ready to ship. They even had hoists and lifts to use if the boxes were too heavy, Lyons said to Kelly. All they needed was for the truck to arrive to them before 9:30 p.m. — any later than that, an arrival to the warehouse would rouse suspicion.

Finally, the men had a deal. More than that, though, Lyons's interest was piqued. It was the first business arrangement he had pursued with Kelly, but the supplier seemed to have access to big machinery. It was more and more apparent that the Belfast brigade was in dire need of something that could stand up to British tanks — and here could be their answer. As Kelly prepared to leave, Lyons stopped him.

Might he consider, perhaps, a regular role with the inner circle? The logistics could be negotiated, Lyons added, and depending on how well things worked out, and how much merchandise Kelly was able to procure, there was a chance their organization could use him full-time — not just here, but nationwide. The operation was headquartered out of New York, Lyons explained, but there were cells of men like him around the country.

Kelly said he was interested but would have to check with his business partner. And it would have to be worth their while. He certainly had the connections to meet their demand; he had a friend in the US National Guard who was able to procure pretty much anything they could want. But the deal would be more palatable, Kelly suggested, if the group expanded their shopping list. Might they be interested in semiautomatic rifles? ArmaLites?

Lyons cut him off.

THE NEXT ONE IS FOR YOU

"We have people that are buying submachine guns for us," Lyons said. "We have got a good price…better than the price you offered us."

Kelly would slink out of the apartment not long after, never quite sure to whom Lyons was referring. But everyone else knew who was sourcing the ArmaLites to Belfast and Derry. Lyons himself had said as much, after a NORAID colleague wandered in on him one day, looking more chuffed than usual.

"The boys in Philly," Lyons had cryptically explained, "really came through for us."

The man known as Bill Kelly left the Bronx that night with more than he could have possibly hoped for. It had been nearly a year since he first started following the group of men, piecing together their insular network and earning their trust. Now he had proof that Marty Lyons and his NORAID cohort had mountains of cash and were working for the IRA. The men themselves had told him so.

The truth was that Marty Lyons would have done well to heed his own misgivings. Bill Kelly, it turned out, was never after his business. The man Marty Lyons met with that night — the one to whom he had passed a wad of cash, with whom he arranged a clandestine gun purchase — had no intention of giving the men so much as a pistol, let alone a truckload of grenade launchers and bazookas. In fact, his real name wasn't even Bill Kelly. His name was William Kavanagh, and he was an undercover agent for the ATF.

CHAPTER 18

"THE HEAT IS ON"

JEFFREY REH SAW it play out again and again at Rudy Valentino Ford. Something about Northern Ireland would be in the news, and Dan Duffy would be mad. Reliable as clockwork. And when Duffy got mad, he talked big—about guns, about war, about the IRA.

Duffy could be an intimidating man when he was angry, but Reh, like most of their colleagues, always assumed he was just blowing off steam. After Bloody Sunday, though, it was clear that something had changed. No longer was Duffy speaking in hypotheticals; he wanted to get into specifics.

"Have you ever used M16s?" Duffy asked Reh, a US Army reservist, one day. What kind of ammunition? Duffy also asked. What else could they shoot out of M16s, and how accurate were the ones Reh had used as a soldier? Were the bullets armor-piercing, and could they be outfitted to penetrate a tank? What about rocket launchers, or hand grenades? How much did that kind of stuff cost? Did Reh think he might be able to sneak some out of Army storehouses in Philadelphia? The questions went on and on.

Dan Duffy harbored misgivings about Vince Conlon and Neil Byrne, but those feelings paled in comparison to the outrage and grief he felt over Bloody Sunday. The tragedy was six months behind them now but the situation in Northern Ireland was not getting any better. There was simply no more time for talk or petty gripes. He had watched from afar as old friends and family suffered under increasingly violent British troops. The NORAID chapter that he had joined, at the Commodore Barry club, had expanded in the months after Bloody Sunday, and he was constantly running around on clothing drives or fundraisers. Duffy even went so far as to get his aging mother out of Derry, bringing her to safer ground in Philadelphia. But that wasn't enough.

After the massacre, Duffy began inquiring about deeper involvement with NORAID. The proclivities of its inner circle were well-known among Philadelphia's Irish, and Duffy — with his deep ties to Derry, and his bold streak — could be a valuable addition to their operation. A known entity in Philly's Irish community, he was brought in slowly, procuring a few guns from black-market circles associated with the mechanic's shop, or buying them under false names, using the fake IDs of dead Irishmen. But by the fall of 1972, he was eager to make more of an impact. He even started taking visiting IRA delegations to a nearby state park, setting up shooting practice with spare flak jackets that were meant to represent British soldiers.

Duffy's initial proposal to Reh — that they steal guns from the military — wasn't totally unrealistic. For years, a network had existed through George Harrison, Conlon's old comrade in New York, that had procured black-market weapons from two military bases in North Carolina, Camp Lejeune and Fort Bragg. There, sympathetic marines had snuck guns out to black-market dealers who then got them into Harrison's hands. A United States Navy report would later find nearly seven thousand guns and 1.2 million rounds of ammo were stolen between 1971 and 1974, much of it presumably secreted to Northern Ireland.

Reh was familiar enough with the scene — and not just because of his knowledge of the military and his awareness of their leaky arsenals. He also knew his fair share of characters around Philadelphia. He didn't have to guess what Duffy was after. The US Army paid around $212 apiece for the M16s, Reh told Duffy one day, but buyers wouldn't be able to get them through normal channels. If Duffy wanted to get his hands on a lot of semiautomatic rifles, he could find them on the black market for around $350 each.

Duffy had hardly balked at such a steep price — "Money is not an object," he told Reh. It made Reh wonder who, exactly, Duffy was working for.

"Are you a member of the IRA?" Reh asked, finally.

It seemed the obvious question; Duffy was far too invested and far too interested in procuring guns to be a passing hobbyist. And he had started taking regular trips to New York, periodically showing up late to work, frazzled and unkempt.

"No," Duffy replied, cryptically. "You have to live in Ireland to be a member."

Instead, Duffy explained, he was part of an auxiliary army in America that was sending guns over to Belfast and his native Derry.

Reh was starting to believe Duffy's bona fides, but he wasn't keen to risk his own neck. An all-American kind of guy often compared to a Boy Scout, Reh had no interest in stealing guns from the US Army — among other hesitations he harbored, it seemed an inevitable, stupid way for them all to get caught. Eager to put some distance between himself and Duffy, Reh offered to introduce Duffy to an old school friend who worked in the black market.

It was exactly the sort of connection that Duffy was looking for, and exactly the sort his network in Philadelphia needed. And for Reh it was an easy way to get Dan Duffy off his back. After all, the man had taken a dark turn in the months since Bloody Sunday, and whoever he was working for seemed dangerous.

"They're tough," Duffy later told Reh, of the IRA. "And anyone that crosses them is going to be found in the river."

John Nigro was the kind of urban hustler that federal indictments are made of. Part restaurant worker, part barman, part arms dealer, Nigro had fallen in and out of trouble with the law for years before landing at the Back Street Restaurant in Doylestown, a working-class suburb outside Philly. His life was defined by transience; people and friends fell in, fell out, and then disappeared. Mobsters, washouts, petty criminals, coworkers — Nigro didn't particularly care who was in his circle, as long as they came with opportunity and a payout. There was no job too big or too small, no deal worth ignoring. So when Jeff Reh, an old acquaintance, surfaced at the end of September 1972, Nigro quickly returned the call.

The pair had attended the same high school in Philadelphia, but Reh had gotten his life together, landing a steady job and settling down with his wife in Delaware County. Nigro, though, had never found such stable ground. So when Reh sought to pawn Duffy off, it was Nigro that he called.

Wary of saying too much on the phone, the old friends instead arranged a meeting at the King of Prussia Mall, a large shopping complex about twenty minutes from Jenkintown. The two men reunited there one weekend in late

September. They hadn't seen each other in years, but there was little time for small talk.

"I've got a fella that works with me who's interested in obtaining weapons," Reh said. "And money is apparently no object."

That was enough for John Nigro. He told Reh to give Duffy his phone number. Satisfied, the pair parted ways. Dan Duffy was not Jeff Reh's problem — not anymore.

"I'm a friend of Jeff Reh, you know, that works at Rudy Valentino Ford. I wanted to use his name because he was telling me that you might have some stuff I wanted to be buying."

Dan Duffy's voice crackled across the phone line. He didn't know much about this Nigro character, but the man had come on Reh's recommendation and he seemed promising and well connected.

Nigro, meanwhile, had hoped for this ever since he had heard of the potential business opportunity. He had been in and out of the game for a while, but to hear it from Jeff Reh, Duffy seemed like a potentially lucrative business partner — and, most important for Nigro, leverageable.

"What did you really have in mind?" Nigro asked Duffy, hungry for the details.

"Well, he said that I don't..." Duffy paused. This was uncharted territory and he needed to be careful. "I don't want to say too much on the telephone."

Among Cahalane, Conlon, and Byrne, Duffy was perhaps the most cautious, a point that made him an outlier, and worried him as the months wore on. He had deep misgivings about the way they all carried on. The other men seemed either oblivious or arrogantly dismissive of the danger to which they were exposing themselves, and before Conlon left for Ireland, he and Duffy had a run-in over Conlon's habit of signing his real name for gun purchases. The weapons were often shipped off with the serial numbers still intact, a damning trail that worried Duffy greatly. He always took care to cover his tracks.

Wary of saying too much on the phone with Nigro, Duffy inched forward.

"Did he mention to you about some stuff, you know, arms and stuff?" Duffy asked, curious how much Reh had already divulged.

In the months since Duffy had taken up this mission, there had already been so many false starts, so much money lost to nameless, faceless men who promised a lot but disappeared and delivered nothing. Marley had skidded out in Syracuse, and the strange incident with Bill Kelly, the disappearing gunrunner from Phoenix, was still fresh in NORAID's mind. Duffy wasn't going to make any such amateur mistakes; he wanted to *see* the guns before he would commit to buying them, he said, as he didn't trust that Nigro actually had them. And if *he* was skeptical, the higher-ups — the people with the real authority to approve a purchase — certainly would be too. They all needed proof that the weapons were real before they handed over cash, and they needed to see that the arms were in working order.

Perhaps he was being paranoid, but the opportunity seemed too good to be true. If things with Nigro worked out, Duffy knew they could be looking at a reliable, large-scale, long-term arms deal in Philadelphia. The arrangement would be palatable for Nigro too; the group had an efficient operation in place, one that made certain the guns were boxed up and shipped off before anyone realized, so the risk to suppliers was low.

"It's leaving the country, you know. It's no possibility of, you know..." Duffy trailed off.

"It's gone within a week or ten days," he said, finally.

Nigro was intrigued. Rarely did these arrangements seem so straightforward, and rarely did someone talk as freely as Duffy. Nigro hadn't even asked for the particulars, but Duffy had offered them anyway.

"I'm a member of the Northern Aid Society," Duffy said. "I'm working for the IRA."

The Rudy Valentino Ford dealership, where Duffy worked as a mechanic, was located in his town of Upper Darby, just off the West Chester Pike, which connected Delaware County to Philadelphia. It was the sort of business establishment that felt slightly off-kilter, the kind outsiders might suspect was a front. The owner himself seemed to have his own off-the-books arrangements — rumors abounded of his connection to the Mafia, and every now and then a car would mysteriously go under, or a repair wouldn't work correctly. Given the apparent proclivities of his boss, Duffy brought John Nigro to Rudy Valentino's not long after their first conversation, thinking it would be a safe place to meet.

What they wanted was straightforward, Duffy told Nigro. ArmaLites. Colt AR-15s. Rifles that would penetrate a British flak vest. And, Duffy said, they were also interested in "heavy" stuff: rocket launchers and mortars that could be used to attack British tanks and armored cars.

If Nigro was the real deal — and Duffy was growing to believe that he was — then the timing was optimal. The group was finishing up a massive clothing drive, and one of the higher-ups in the organization would be in Philadelphia soon to pick things up. Known as "the general," the man would have a final say on whether the guns could be purchased. It wasn't an issue of money, Duffy said; there were definitely funds available through NORAID. And for Nigro, at least, there was little risk of getting caught, Duffy explained. They had previously used air freight to get the guns to Ireland quickly, but customs officials had grown more strict in recent months and it was no longer safe to sneak the guns over on planes. Instead, Duffy explained, they were now moving all of the guns to New York and putting them on ships, which went directly to Ireland, with far less chance of being intercepted.

Still, the group had to be vigilant. "We have to be very, very careful," Duffy explained. British investigators seemed to be cooperating with the FBI, he told Nigro, and they all knew what was going on in New York and Fort Worth. The pair parted with plans to reconvene during the clothing drive, so Nigro could meet the NORAID officer. But in the meantime, Duffy warned, they had to be very careful.

"The heat," he said, "is on."

The suburb of Jenkintown sits just outside Philadelphia's city limits in neighboring Montgomery County, adjacent to Mayfair and accessible from the busy Roosevelt Boulevard that connected Hughie Breen's tavern to Philadelphia and the New Jersey Turnpike. Brick row houses were stacked next to mansion-size homes with wraparound porches, and the neighborhood was a mixture of blue-collar and middle-class families. It was an important place, too, for Irish Philly; Jenkintown was the site of the MacSwiney Club, where Conlon and Byrne had headquartered Clan-na-Gael, and the bar's secret attic had served as the meeting room for Philadelphia-based gunrunners since the McGarrity years, in the 1930s and 1940s — the door even had a peephole, allowing those inside to see who might be lurking nearby. And when the day arrived, Jenkintown was a sensible place for another secret meeting between Nigro and Philadelphia's more contemporary IRA contingent.

It hadn't taken much time at all for Nigro to convince Duffy and the Philadelphia men that he was worth talking to, that he actually had access to the guns he was promising. Now he was en route to their first official meeting. It would be a discreet introduction, arranged in the parking lot of a popular shopping center. The man Duffy was bringing would have veto power over any deal, and if Nigro played his cards right, Duffy said, the man would approve the weapons purchase on the spot.

Nigro came prepared for such potential. In his pocket was a small stack of Polaroids, showing three submachine guns, the exact kind of weapons he was offering to Duffy. As far as Duffy and his IRA colleague were concerned, the guns in Nigro's photographs could be theirs within the day.

It was nearing dusk. Nigro slipped into the anonymous thrum of suburban traffic and wound his car through Jenkintown's residential streets, eventually landing at the Ben Fox Pavilion, a large, mid-century structure with a collection of scattered buildings and hidden corners. It was the perfect place to meet someone discreetly.

Nigro drove through the lot and parked in the front row, as instructed. Not long after, a car pulled up next to him, and Dan Duffy got out. He said nothing, only slid into the passenger seat next to Nigro. Around eight o'clock, a dark-green car pulled in next to them. Duffy moved into Nigro's back seat, motioning for the new arrival to join them.

"The man you're about to talk to," Duffy whispered to Nigro, "is a very high-ranking member of the IRA."

Neil Byrne was never supposed to be the one meeting John Nigro that day. It was meant to be someone from New York, someone like Marty Lyons. But something had come up and so, it was Byrne who pulled into the Ben Fox Pavilion, tasked with vetting Dan Duffy's new gun connection. Duffy was excited, that was clear, and his lead with Nigro *sounded* good — but Byrne was not so eager. There had been too many false starts as of late, and they had all stopped short of getting too excited about anything anymore.

But things overseas were growing urgent. The IRA had an endless supply of good men but the efforts of British soldiers were having an impact: the Provos were losing a lot of guns and ammunition. Raids and house-to-house searches were constant. Now, just as the British were bleeding the IRA's wells

THE NEXT ONE IS FOR YOU

dry, Philadelphia — its most reliable fount — was suddenly having trouble refilling them.

"Do you have them with you?" Byrne asked Nigro, skipping the pleasantries.

No, Nigro said, but he had photographs. He pulled out the pictures of the automatic weapons. Byrne sifted through the stack, intrigued.

"How much do you want for them?"

"$224 apiece."

"Good price."

"What other types of weapons are you interested in?" Nigro asked.

This, Byrne knew, was where things always got disappointing. There was the initial promise, but when they asked for more, their growing demands eventually exposed the shortcomings of small-time hustlers like John Nigro. Too many people had led them on; too many people claimed to have weapons they didn't. Many supposed "arms dealers" were only trading guns they had brought back from old wars.

The mission, Byrne told Nigro, was simple. He wanted anything that could penetrate British flak vests; it had gotten much more difficult for them to find armor-piercing ammunition over the previous months.

It wasn't really about money, Byrne added, but he wouldn't pay a penny over fair market price for a gun. He said $50,000 was earmarked in New York to be used for weapons and could be approved at a moment's notice, as soon as it was confirmed that Nigro really had something to sell. And the guns were sent directly to Ireland through New York.

There was something important, too, that Byrne stressed to Nigro: they were trying to stay above the law as much as possible. Ironically, it was why they were looking for rifles and other long guns. There was an important loophole in America: Handguns were governed by stringent rules around purchasing, carrying, and selling. But long guns, semiautomatic and otherwise — the ones that could really do damage — were hardly restricted at all. It's how the men were able to buy dozens at a time, legally. By buying long guns like ArmaLites, Byrne explained, "We would violate as few laws as possible."

Satisfied, Nigro said he'd get back to him within a few days to finalize a deal. Byrne left, but Duffy lingered; this had been his arrangement, and Duffy wanted to keep him on the hook. Nigro should call him tomorrow, he said, and they could talk more.

"How big are you in the firearms business?"

It was the day after the meeting in Jenkintown, and Nigro, as instructed, had called Dan Duffy to finalize the details.

"Big enough," Nigro said.

Duffy smelled potential in John Nigro, and not just for the occasional ArmaLite. He was a window into the city's black market, and Duffy had questions — just weeks before, the Philadelphia area was stunned when a quiet, nondescript police investigator was arrested with an unprecedented stockpile of weapons. George Fassnacht, an otherwise unassuming police clerk, was actually a CIA employee, and clearly had access to serious guns — but the Philadelphia men were as stunned as anyone to hear it. They had been asking around, trying to figure out Fassnacht's connections. There was a link to the US Army in Vietnam, apparently, and an implication in news reporting around the Fassnacht case that some of his weapons might have been smuggled to the IRA; the Philly conspirators had also heard a rumor that two other American officers were in on the plot, and were quietly funneling rifles from their own deployments to Ireland. If it was true, the Philadelphia men wanted to know. Nigro, Duffy realized, might have insight.

"Do you know anyone else in the area?" he asked. "Who are the partners of George Fassnacht?"

"I've heard of him," Nigro responded. "I'll try to find out."

Nigro was never able to nail down the answer, and the Fassnacht case quickly faded into history. Instead, the inquiry was one of the last times the two men spoke. Duffy rang Nigro at his office a few weeks later, agitated. *Where had he been?* Duffy hadn't heard a word from Nigro since the meeting with Neil Byrne, and the group was getting anxious. Nigro instructed him to wait, and more than that, to stop calling — if and when he located the guns Duffy wanted, he would give him a call.

Like so many other misadventures, Nigro's promises of guns were too good to be true, at least for Duffy. Such disappointments had, by then, become predictable. What they couldn't have foreseen, though, was that their collision with John Nigro would indeed turn out to be very significant — just not in the ways that any of them might have hoped.

CHAPTER 19

PALACE

THE ROAD FROM Newtown Square to Haverford winds across the edge of Pennsylvania's farmland, at the fault line where the Philadelphia suburbs turn into fields. Danny Cahalane could have driven the route with his eyes closed, his trek to Bill Corry's a well-worn path. It was a November afternoon in 1972 and, once again, Cahalane was headed there with a problem. It seemed there was nothing but problems anymore — in Philadelphia, in Belfast, in the Bronx.

Dan Duffy's endeavor had ended like most other things that year: big promises, big guns, and no delivery. It had thrust a hard truth in front of Cahalane, Corry, and Byrne: they were running out of options. John Nigro, the man with the submachine guns, had seemed so full of potential. But then that line, like so many others, had gone dead.

A group had gathered at Cahalane's house earlier that afternoon, their vehicles jammed into the small suburban driveway. It was a risky place to meet. They all knew they were being watched, but recently Cahalane had noticed a change: the agents were bolder now, as if they knew something, or were preparing to escalate. Strange cars were parking outside the house, the same ones every night. They followed him everywhere — to work, to Corry's place, to church. Unfamiliar men would walk through Newtown Square and loiter in the neighbors' yards, watching.

The rumor — among the neighborhood kids, at least — had always been that a Mafia man lived somewhere in the area. Cahalane, though, knew better. The agents were watching him. This fact seemed increasingly unavoidable. He had tried to shield his children, but he couldn't hide everything. Danny

Jr. was too young to notice, but Connie was old enough to figure it out, or at least notice the cars on their quiet suburban street. Danny Jr. was certainly old enough to sense his mother's nerves. And Mary Jane was a teenager now, with Jane's sharp eyes and her father's quiet curiosity. Not much escaped her. He didn't know how much she knew, but whatever it was, it was likely enough.

Danny Cahalane was immune to panic — and yet panic, in a moment like this, might have been adaptive. He had so far kept his cool even in the group's most intense moments, as government agents circled, appearing everywhere from Breen's bar to NORAID meetings, and every dinner and fundraiser. What they were up against was no mystery; the recent proceedings with the New York men in Fort Worth had made that clear. Still, even as the potential consequences played out, Cahalane — like the rest of the Philadelphia men — had hardly changed his routines. They had done little to account for the federal scrutiny, a posture that seemed equal parts arrogant and naive.

They had reasons, though, to feel secure. The FBI and ATF may have been chasing them, but the Philly boys seemed to always stay a step ahead; after all, the diaspora was wide-ranging. The ATF and FBI were stacked with Irish-American agents, but the Philadelphia men had their own network of allies in law enforcement, too; there were lots of men with badges who sympathized with the work that Byrne and Cahalane were doing, even if they didn't outwardly participate. The local courts and police departments were riddled with them. When a secret subpoena went through, or when the FBI or other federal organizations notified the local police that they would be in town (standard practice among law enforcement, to establish jurisdiction), Corry, Cahalane, and Byrne usually got a quiet phone call from the courthouse, as a warning.

Still, as Danny Cahalane steered toward Corry's house that day, he just couldn't understand why they, of all people, could possibly be in the government's crosshairs. He had never believed so much in something the way he believed in Ireland, and the moral rightness of what they were doing. Surely, the movement even shared DNA with his adopted country, which had fomented its own rebellion against British rule just a few miles east of Newtown Square.

Such parallels clearly had little bearing on their immediate predicament, though. Byrne was serious when he told Nigro of the IRA's dire arms shortage — in Belfast and Derry, British soldiers were decimating the IRA's ArmaLite stock, just as the Philadelphia arrangements were falling through and legal trouble circled. America's rebellion might've shared DNA with Ireland's, but that was centuries before. The state of play was far different now.

Few solutions seemed available, except for one, and Byrne and Cahalane were in a good position to pursue it: Marjorie Palace, the suburban Philadelphia gun dealer who had always been keen to work with Vince Conlon. She couldn't get them the hauls of black-market weapons that someone like John Nigro might have, but she could at least get them something, and the assurance of those guns was worth more than any notional business dealings that the group had in the works.

Cahalane meandered through the Pennsylvania countryside until he reached Bill Corry's home in Haverford, where he and his family so often turned up on weekends. Cahalane had a plan in mind. What he didn't seem to notice was the car that had been following him, all the way from Newtown Square. It rolled by as Danny pulled into Bill Corry's, the anonymous man inside peering out at the dark-green work van parked in the drive.

It was dusk by the time Danny Cahalane strode across the parking lot of the George Washington Motor Inn later that November, and the harsh glare of the motel's red neon sign pulled his dark frame out of the shadows. He was wearing a trench coat loose across his shoulders, and his black hair was combed neatly across his forehead. He slammed the heavy door of the Chrysler — an Imperial, a boat of a car that was far less convenient than his van — and walked swiftly to the lobby doors. He and Byrne were due for a trip up to New York, and, finally, it was for *good* news. Marjorie Palace, it seemed, was ready to take on a larger role in their operation. A new round of long guns would arrive shortly.

He and Byrne met at the bar of the hotel lounge, empty but for a few stragglers. A man brushed by them on the way to the bathroom, but they hardly noticed. After a brief exchange, the pair wandered to the parking lot; there was little time to waste. Marty Lyons was expecting them.

Tallying it up felt almost overwhelming. The year 1972 had started with a boon: fifty thousand rounds of standard rifle ammunition, and a thousand of armor piercing, packed, smuggled, and shipped to Northern Ireland by Cahalane, Byrne, and Conlon. Since Conlon's departure, Cahalane had made the purchases himself at a rapid clip: fifteen more ArmaLites in March, twenty-five more in June. Between Cahalane, Byrne, and Conlon, hundreds of rifles were moving from Philadelphia to Belfast and Derry.

Tonight wasn't for such pursuits, though. Cahalane steered the car quietly north, past the glowing lights of Lower Manhattan. An hour and a half after they had left the Motor Inn, he guided the car toward the George Washington Bridge and into the Bronx, where he and Byrne were due to see Marty Lyons. There was no reason for either of them to notice the car that had been silently following along behind them, all the way since they left the George Washington Motor Inn's parking lot. In the driver's seat was the same man who, hours before, had brushed by them at the bar, on his way to the bathroom.

Breen's Café sat on Roosevelt Boulevard between Mayfair and Olney, two of Northeast Philadelphia's Irish strongholds. Along with Cahalane's chapter in Delaware County, the two neighborhoods had produced one of the city's more militant NORAID divisions, and Breen was a central character. He was his own cult of personality, a gruff IRA veteran from the 1920s; it was he who first tapped Cahalane for more ambitious roles in NORAID, and, in the years since, he had emerged as a sort of patron saint for Philadelphia's various IRA envoys, providing rock-hard fortitude, authority, and a safe place to gather.

It was at Breen's counter that Danny Cahalane and Neil Byrne met on a winter evening, talking quietly with a familiar face. The man was the reason Cahalane and Byrne had made the trip to the bar in the bitter cold: Frank Grady, Marty Lyons's right-hand man from New York, had made the drive down the Turnpike. There was much to talk about. Finally, it seemed, there was good news.

Grady had his own endeavors running up in Yonkers, having secured standing orders for dozens of ArmaLites on a regular basis. And now, Cahalane and Byrne had found a new supplier in Marjorie Palace. All were eager to get the renewed relationship up and running. Such was the purpose for this joint meeting. After congregating at Breen's, the group of them made their way west, to the Commodore Barry Irish Center.

Unlike Breen's, the Irish Center was a less prickly gathering place, somewhere that welcomed strangers and curious passersby. Anyone could stop in and connect with Philadelphia's Irish. Tucked away on a small suburban street behind a railroad bridge, the nondescript complex looked a bit like a fire hall or a church. It was where the city's various NORAID chapters often came together, and where their various leaders frequently socialized. It welcomed visitors into a ceremonial foyer, draped with flags from the city's Irish benevolent clubs — the

Tyrone Society, the Donegal Society, the Friendly Sons of Saint Patrick. To the right was a bar, its counter playing host to debates and social gatherings. Beyond that was a large performance hall where dinners, dances, and traditional music were staged. It was a good place for a night out, and by December of 1972 it had become a setting for some of the city's most high-profile events and speakers around the Republican cause.

Father Sean McManus was among them. A priest from the border area of Kinawley, in County Fermanagh, McManus had made a name for himself as an advocate for the Republican cause, much to the chagrin of his church. "Whatever one may feel about the IRA, at least it has more right to operate in Ireland than the British Army has," McManus once said. A lightning rod for controversy, McManus was quietly sent out of Ireland "on loan" to a parish in Baltimore, for fear his rhetoric would embarrass the Catholic Church. Ironically, though, McManus found perhaps an even more willing audience in America: rather than keep him quiet, McManus's transfer saw him embraced wholeheartedly by NORAID, which elevated him as one of its transatlantic ambassadors. McManus responded in kind, with rousing endorsements: "In America, the Irish Northern Aid Committee is the only worthwhile organization," he once told a newspaper back in West Belfast. "They do tremendous work."

That winter evening McManus was due in Philadelphia. He was expected to bring new information from the border, where he had recently spent a week visiting imprisoned IRA leaders. Such billings drew a large crowd — good for NORAID donations, of course, and also convenient for the NORAID men, who could blend in easily among the large crowd.

They weren't the only ones. There was another man in attendance that night, a stranger who was at the Irish Center for one reason — and it wasn't to hear Father McManus speak. The man was there to tail Neil Byrne, who walked into the large auditorium around 10 p.m. with Frank Grady. Undercover agents had spotted Byrne and Grady at the counter of Breen's just a few hours before.

The stranger — an undercover ATF agent himself — passed easily among the faces at the Irish Center that evening, keeping an eye on Byrne. It was a relatively boring assignment, and his targets did little to arouse suspicion. The agent eventually landed at the Irish Center's bar, nursing a beer, waiting for something — anything — to happen. Midnight neared, and nothing did.

But as the crowd dispersed, Byrne and Grady disappeared. The ATF agent watched as they slipped into a back room toward the side of the auditorium's stage, a discreet place that made clear: whatever was happening inside wasn't fit for public ears.

It was a tantalizing lead, but the agent knew he couldn't feasibly wander into such an out-of-the-way gathering. Instead, he waited at the bar; the minutes ticked past. One hour, then two. Finally, as dawn inched closer, the group of men spilled out of their secret meeting, wasting little time for goodbyes or small talk. Instead, they brushed past the bar crowd, hurrying toward their cars outside.

Whatever had happened in that room might have been the key to the Philadelphia case. But the ATF was playing the long game, and that required time and discretion. The agent stayed put at the counter, glancing outside just in time to see his target, Neil Byrne, slipping into a car with New York plates and driving away.

Cahalane and Byrne returned to Breen's the next month, on a cold January afternoon. They sat with their backs to the street, huddled away from the rest of the pub's customers. The winter had been mild and mercifully free of snow, but the weather had turned sharply around Christmas. Breen's was hardly a busy bar, and it was even less so in the winter, when cold fronts from the Atlantic blew a bitter chill into Philadelphia, sending the city and its surrounding neighborhoods into hibernation. That day, a handful of patrons were gathered at the U-shaped counter, and there was a single man drinking alone, but otherwise the pub was quiet, and — most importantly — safe. Such things couldn't be taken for granted. It was difficult to blend in at Breen's if you weren't a regular; not that it was necessarily unwelcoming, but it was the sort of pub that stirred when an unfamiliar face stepped inside. That hadn't been a real issue until recently. More and more strangers seemed to be milling about the place every week, an unsettling change that had done little to quell fears over circling legal trouble.

"They're available," Byrne said, glancing around to ensure they weren't overheard.

Cahalane was intrigued.

"A hundred dollars apiece. Would take a thousand to buy ten."

It was promising news. Byrne, it seemed, had finally secured commitment from Palace for a large order. The pair of them finished their pints and wandered outside; they didn't make such large decisions on their own. They turned to the outdoor stairs and went up to Hughie Breen's apartment.

CHAPTER 20

THE STICKER

WHENEVER IT CAME time for Marjorie Palace to back up her reputation — to find rare guns, fast — she had a Rolodex of reliable options. John Rugg, a wholesale firearms dealer in Vermont, was one of them. She had ordered from Rugg for years, and had even used him to fill some of the large orders that Conlon had placed in the past. Rugg was an amenable business partner, happy to accommodate unique requests or fill last-minute orders. He had previously agreed to pack some of Palace's gun shipments in Cosmoline grease, a request that had surprised Rugg, but one that he had proceeded with anyway. Palace had justified it by saying the guns were wanted by collectors, but it was a thinly veiled lie; any reasonable dealer knew the Cosmoline was messy to deal with, and few legitimate collectors would want the hassle. Cosmoline grease suggested something else entirely — it was used when guns were getting shipped away, usually by boat, for long periods around salty air.

So, when the strange men from Philadelphia reemerged, it was Rugg that Palace called in the early days of 1973. Friends of Vince Conlon, her reliable old customer, needed thousands of rounds of ammunition — which Palace could handle — but they also needed twenty Lee-Enfield rifles, and fast.

"We're having a special sale," she explained to Rugg. Her shop was advertising in the local paper, and they were getting orders for more rifles than they could keep in stock. She needed the Lee-Enfields immediately, so immediately that she had to organize a sort of relay pickup to get them down south in time for her customer to pick them up. Instead of shipping the guns directly to Philly, which would take a while, she needed Rugg to drop them off at a middleman in the Philadelphia area.

Like Palace, Rugg had been in the firearms business for years and knew the quirks of the trade. This one, though, was beyond strange — it was worrying, and Palace's story wasn't adding up. Why would collectors want Lee-Enfields, and why the middleman? The rifles were a dime a dozen, having flooded the market after the World Wars, and they weren't collectors' items by any stretch. Palace's request to use an intermediary also disturbed Rugg; it would open them up to accusations of misconduct.

Rugg had always been particular about his own business dealings, and he didn't have the stomach for this kind of bizarre arrangement, especially coupled with Palace's track record. And so, his hackles raised, he refused to send the guns to anyone without a federal firearms license.

"We're kind of working together," Palace explained, of the middleman. "I received documents from his gun shop so I could ship the rifles."

Presented with the paperwork, Rugg no longer had a good reason to say no. But he could tell that something wasn't right. Rugg didn't like the notion of ratting out a fellow dealer, but he had a license to keep, and he didn't want to risk a visit from federal agents.

Instead, he decided to seek them out himself.

It was the call that Philadelphia's ATF division had been waiting for. *Fill the order as requested,* they told Rugg. *But do us a favor, and stick a very specific-looking red-and-white label on the boxes.*

Neil Byrne pulled his car into Danny Cahalane's driveway and walked inside the house on Horton Road. The two men's lifestyles couldn't have been more different: Cahalane lived in a comfortable home with a big yard and room for kids, in a leafy suburban development filled with families. Byrne, a bachelor, lived alone in a small, rented apartment in Philly's northern suburbs and worked as a grocery clerk at a local shop. He had few obligations besides keeping the Philadelphia network running, which he did for most waking moments of his life.

That, of course, was what had first linked the two men, what had brought Byrne to Cahalane's on this night in late January. The guns from Palace were on the way, but in the meantime Palace had hooked Byrne up with ten thousand rounds of armor-piercing ammunition, and Byrne had separately gotten his hands on a few other guns worth sending on. They would need to be ferried to New York, and Cahalane's van was built for such contraband errands, thanks to that false bottom he had welded onto the vehicle's frame.

The pair of them stood at the front door and peered out onto the quiet street, the only light a street lamp over Cahalane's garage. They looked left, then right, scanning for any sign of government cars or strange men. Satisfied that Horton Road was asleep, they crept outside.

Their cars were parked next to each other, and Byrne reached into his trunk and pulled out a large, rectangular artillery carton, so heavy he stumbled slightly while lifting it. Clutching it to his chest, he moved it to the back of Cahalane's van. It was the first of several packages; working quickly, the pair of them pulled three long rifles from Byrne's car and stuffed them in the other, next to the bullets. They were odds and ends, nothing like the large-scale orders they were waiting on from Palace; but a gun was a gun, and the group of them periodically got calls from friends and supporters who found antique guns in attics, or wanted to off-load older stuff left over from the wars. It was over in a moment, and the pair of them quickly got into the van and drove off, the guns and ammunition secured tightly among Cahalane's construction supplies. They didn't have time to off-load it; they were late for a social errand.

Did they know, then, that they were being watched? That a car was snaking its way behind them as they drove toward the city? If so, the men showed no urgency: in fact, they stopped to give two hunched, elderly women a lift, and the tailing agent left them there: carpooling two old ladies to a social outing, an arsenal just out of reach in the back seat.

Night was just falling in Morrisville when Danny Cahalane's car pulled into the driveway of Marjorie Palace's home. He and Neil Byrne had waited until nearly 9 p.m., for the full cover of darkness.

It was late February, nearly two months since they had first ordered the rifles from Palace. The weapons had gotten to her middleman on a bright afternoon, dropped off by a man in a station wagon with New York plates, who unloaded five long cardboard cartons. The ATF agents noticed a very distinct marking, the one they had been looking for ever since that phone call from John Rugg: a red-and-white sticker affixed below the label of each box. The

Palaces had picked the cartons up three days later, stashing them in the back of a bright-blue Thunderbird and carting them back to the Philadelphia suburbs.

Cahalane was thrilled to phone Lyons with the good news: the guns had finally arrived and were ready for pickup. Outside Palace's home, Cahalane and Byrne wrestled the long cardboard boxes into the car, stacking them in the trunk and back seat. It was over quickly, and the pair of them were back on the road not long after, headed to the George Washington Motor Inn. After a brief turn in the lounge, they parted ways, Byrne heading north, toward home, and Cahalane for the Turnpike, en route to Newtown Square.

There wasn't yet a clear plan on what to do with the guns, but that would come, in time. Cahalane was due to call Lyons the next day, and let him know all had gone well. Until then, it was just nice to have a win. It was nearing midnight when Cahalane pulled into the driveway, the boxes of guns safe in the back seat.

On a bright spring day in March 1973, three weeks after their clandestine pickup from the Palaces', Danny Cahalane pulled his work van off the West Chester Pike, the suburban highway that connected Philadelphia's suburbs. His oldest son, a teenager, was along for the workday so Cahalane left the van unlocked, the back doors wide open as he stepped away to make a phone call.

It was easy, then, for the lurking ATF agents to see. The back of the van was cluttered with all sorts of construction supplies — tarps, debris, plasterboard, a ladder. But tossed haphazardly among it all was something familiar: five long cardboard boxes, each with a bright red-and-white sticker.

CHAPTER 21

"THE IRISH PROBLEM"

THE STAKES OF what American agents had come to refer to as "the Irish problem" had seriously escalated across 1972. Rather than a prosecutorial coup, the case that had come from those Cobh suitcases — in which five New York NORAID men were subpoenaed to appear before a grand jury in Fort Worth — had dissolved in perhaps the worst possible outcome for Alvey, Merkle, and the Justice Department: the debacle was a publicity boon for NORAID and an abject failure in the courtroom. After three months of detention for their refusal to testify before a grand jury, the five NORAID men were released without charge. The gunrunning case associated with those suitcases on the Cork docks never materialized, and among NORAID's faithful, it had been energizing rather than a deterrent. First jailed in the spring of 1972 for refusing to testify, the men were denied bail, then released without charge, and then jailed again. The debacle would be easily packaged by NORAID as an extension of the legal injustices that were happening in Northern Ireland.

In the meantime, other, smaller NORAID criminal cases began surfacing. There was one in San Francisco, and another in Baltimore, where five men were charged in an IRA gunrunning case that involved 175 rifles. They were trotted out as significant prosecutorial successes, and proof that American legal officials were taking the issue seriously. But investigators knew they were dealing with small fish — the numbers in those cases paled in comparison to what was moving through New York and Philadelphia.

Despite its efforts to thread the shrinking eye of a political needle, the United States instead found itself on every wrong side of a war of which it would have preferred to remain ignorant. Now constant dispatches were flying between London, Northern Ireland, and the States, tallying up more and more American rifles found in the hands of the IRA. If there was ever room for doubt that Northern Ireland's ArmaLite problem came from the United States, it had long since disappeared. The evidence was all over the streets of Belfast, in every raid and every arms seizure. British Army and RUC investigators were regularly sending serial numbers back and forth to America, and the web that they drew was chilling: the same American guns were being passed around IRA brigades and used in ambushes across Northern Ireland, their bloody trail laid out over months and sometimes years.

That was what defined West Belfast and Andersonstown now. The ArmaLites arrived, and for the Provos, the drought of the early days was over. "The Provos seem to have an endless supply of arms," one member of the Official IRA remarked gloomily to a sympathetic reporter in 1973. And everyone knew where the weapons were coming from: "We find it harder to get arms than the Provisionals," the Official IRA man said, nodding toward NORAID and its support for the Provos. "The Irish-American groups no longer support us."

In Lurgan, a sectarian town in County Armagh about twenty miles southwest of Belfast, British authorities recovered an ArmaLite just before Christmas. The gun, they would find, had recently killed a twenty-nine-year-old officer with the Royal Ulster Constabulary; Robert Megaw was shot by a sniper while on patrol. Ballistics would show that months before it had killed Megaw, the same ArmaLite was used in a separate, fatal attack on two other RUC constables. Raymond Wylie, twenty-five, and Ronald Macauley, forty-four, were ambushed by IRA gunmen while investigating a stopped car on a country road near Lisburn, outside Belfast. Wylie, a new father, was shot twice and died that evening; Macauley would succumb to his wounds a month later. Later, another ArmaLite turned up in Lurgan, where the gun had been used to kill Phillip Drake, a twenty-year-old private in the British Army.

Meanwhile, in Newry, a sectarian town in Northern Ireland that straddled the border between County Down and County Armagh, an ArmaLite was found on the town's hospital grounds and traced to three different attacks on RUC policemen. It was also traced to a gun attack on a patrol of British soldiers.

And in a pile of rifles found in Derry, police found a clue that tied the weapons to a string of violent ambushes that had befallen British soldiers and RUC officers. Among the guns, most had the serial number scrubbed off. On one, though, the number was still readable. Once it was sent off to the ATF, the gun was traced easily. "One of the weapons," a British investigator would soon type on a growing list, "purchased by the Philadelphia 5."

The bloody reality was that the Irish-American problem was no longer a simple matter of a few men breaking the law. Instead, it was a multistate conspiracy, involving several cities, dozens of coconspirators, and multiple organizations. The failure of American law enforcement to stop it had become a thorn in the side of the US-Britain relationship, one of the Western world's most significant alliances. "The Irish Problem has become a serious problem and a source of embarrassment to the United States," one FBI memo scathed, noting that the State Department was in a diplomatic spiral over the gunrunning rumors. In notes to law enforcement, diplomatic officials pleaded with agents to prosecute NORAID members, going so far as to refer to the group as a "terrorist organization."

It would be months before the Justice Department would formally coordinate its various probes, but in September of 1973, Brandon Alvey and Robert "Mad Dog" Merkle's bosses at the Justice Department convened a meeting in Washington, DC, with several other high-ranking US government officials from across the American law-enforcement apparatus. There were officers from the FBI, the State Department, the ATF, and the Justice Department. For nearly two years, they had all respectively probed NORAID, mostly uncoordinated, and the efforts needed to be organized. Pressure from British authorities had mounted so that the Justice Department was eager to bring a larger case, one that might successfully link NORAID to the violence in Northern Ireland.

The meeting that September clarified two separate investigations that targeted NORAID. The first, handled by the FBI, sought to legally force NORAID to register under the Foreign Agents Registration Act as an agent for the IRA. The second was already well underway, managed by Brandon Alvey and Bob Merkle, and handled by the ATF, investigating instances of gun smuggling committed by NORAID members.

NORAID had, of course, filed its paperwork under the Foreign Agents Registration Act since its inception, but Mike Flannery and the NORAID front office had played a coy but dangerous game when listing the organization's foreign principal: that group, to whom they sent money in Belfast, was a benevolent organization headed by Joe Cahill. Cahill, of course, also happened to be a high-ranking commander for the IRA. The maneuver allowed NORAID to establish a theoretical distance from the Provos, making itself more palatable to a wider Irish-American audience. But by 1973, FBI investigators and the State Department had enough of the trick. NORAID, they decided, needed to change its registration statements and formally declare itself as a front for the IRA.

Such a change would be a victory for British and Northern Irish officials, who for years had pressured their American counterparts to more clearly link NORAID to the Provos. It would also land a serious — potentially fatal — blow to NORAID, whose more moderate members were already fleeing the group thanks to various investigations and gunrunning rumors.

The FARA case was fully launched after that September meeting. Among other things, it gave American law enforcement officers the opportunity to placate their worrisome British colleagues, who feared the propagandistic power of personalities like Dave O'Connell, Gerry Adams, and other Provo figureheads. Under the guise of the FARA suit, FBI agents could now keep watchful eyes on NORAID's pamphlets, tracking when certain personalities were expected to visit America as part of a NORAID tour and speak to its chapters. Agents would then pass the information along to the State Department, who made sure those people were denied visas.

The other investigation was the one managed by Alvey, Merkle, and the ATF, the one that was already targeting the gunrunning activities of NORAID-affiliated men. The two cases, of course, worked in concert. To prove that NORAID was a front for the IRA, investigators needed to prove that people connected to NORAID were funneling guns to the Provos. Despite the long list of ArmaLite recoveries by British and Northern Irish authorities, federal investigators still struggled to disband the larger network that was sending bulk orders of rifles into Northern Ireland. That needed to change, and it needed to change fast. In a chiding note to the FBI, a senior Justice Department official underscored just how critical it was that NORAID's gunrunning investigation be equal in priority to its FARA probe.

"As members of your staff are well aware, the Department of State together with the British Government have requested the Government of the United States to make all efforts to halt the shipment of weapons and explosives to Northern Ireland," one official wrote. "I cannot express too strongly the seriousness of this situation."

The official needn't have stressed the stakes, at least not to Brandon Alvey and Bob Merkle. By September 1973, the men and their team were well on their way to prosecuting the government's most significant NORAID case yet.

CHAPTER 22

"SAY NOTHIN' "

THE UNION HALL on Torresdale Avenue was packed with people who had paid $100 a piece to get inside. Most were union men and businessowners, almost all of them connected in some way to John McCullough, the gruff former marine who led the city's roofers' union. McCullough threw the bash under the guise of a fundraiser — a ham-and-cabbage dinner, in the spring of 1973 — but the men who went knew they were giving money to the IRA and the Philly men who supported them.

A brawler from Philadelphia's Fairmount neighborhood, McCullough had ensured the city's reputation as a safe haven for the Irish. His union had become a harbor for fugitive Irishmen — many from Tyrone, Armagh, and Donegal, who had run from trouble in Northern Ireland and surfaced in Philadelphia later, under new names, working for the roofers.

McCullough cultivated his own lore as a brass-tacks union boss, unafraid to get his hands dirty in a city where politics increasingly required it. With close-cropped hair and tightly tailored suits, McCullough seemed always just out of place among Philadelphia's aristocracy, one wrong look away from bursting through his polished façade and reverting back to a brawling infantryman. (It's perhaps no surprise that during McCullough's tenure, nonunion roofers in the city tended to have their job sites mysteriously bludgeoned, their vehicles destroyed, and sometimes, their family homes set on fire.) McCullough's dichotomy had made him a close, valuable ally of Hugh Breen in the Northeast, from which much of the roofers' union hailed.

THE NEXT ONE IS FOR YOU

Breen had presided over a difficult winter. But as the new year dawned, things were improving. Through their arrangement with Marjorie Palace, Cahalane and Byrne had clawed back Philly's reputation for gunrunning. Despite the whispers surrounding NORAID, its inner circle remained intact.

Still, trouble was obviously ahead, and that knowledge had brought a dark and inevitable paranoia to Irish America. Culturally, it had always been a tight-lipped community, but now there were whispers about turncoats and informants. On this, Breen and his group of confidants were unequivocal: there was perhaps no greater sin. Loose talk was unforgivable — even speaking with a journalist was its own needless risk.

It was just such a posture that made the union hall prickly that night, especially when an unfamiliar man managed to slip inside. The stranger watched as the roofers unfurled a tricolor flag across the ceiling, and he was still there around eight thirty that evening, when Hugh Breen arrived, escorting an escaped IRA prisoner from Northern Ireland. After all, the evening wasn't just a fundraiser; the night would also host a meeting of Philadelphia's so-called IRA war board, a collection of the city's various NORAID heads and ex-IRA men.

The stranger in the union hall looked on quietly as the board convened. Each respective NORAID chapter reported their latest plans to Breen. It was a strange ritual, heavy on rhetoric, and among the Irish union men it seemed less about execution and more about talk. "We could've blown up Belfast nine times, with all the plotting and planning going on," one union man chided. (Far outside the inner circle, the observer likely didn't know he was looking at some of the IRA's preeminent American gunrunners.)

The war board meeting ended and Breen lingered at the bar. It was then that the stranger approached him, shepherded by a friend. The man was a journalist who was writing about Irish Philadelphia, his interlocutor said. It was a good opportunity for NORAID, especially given the rumors swirling about gunrunning, and the IRA's vicious assaults through Northern Ireland. Here was a sympathetic reporter, right as NORAID could use some good publicity.

Breen was quietly furious at the intrusion.

"No press," was all he said, and unceremoniously dismissed the pair.

The Irish culture is not a particularly forward or direct one. It prizes discretion and restraint, owing to centuries of being ruled under the strange combined thumbs of the Catholic Church and the British Empire. These standards are doubly true when it comes to Irish Republicanism, which expects — perhaps above all else — that its adherents will hold and keep secrets. "Say nothin'" — the phrase immortalized by Derry poet Seamus Heaney — remains a colloquialism across Ireland and Northern Ireland alike. It's used to quell chatter on just about anything, from something as innocent as a fledgling juvenile romance, or as serious as a murder. "Say nothin'." Keep your mouth shut and your head down. Don't make it your problem. If you know, don't say.

This tradition has borne out across centuries of Irish rebellion, with certain characters elevated to canonical status for their ability to stay mum under pressure. It is the ultimate test of fortitude, an absolute exercise of principle, and a standard that among Republican families, was instilled as early as childhood. Brendan Hughes, the Provo volunteer who first attempted an inroad with NORAID for ArmaLites, recalled playing cards on the streets of West Belfast as a boy. When the police showed up, the group of them scattered but Hughes, a child, was arrested and interrogated by British police about the game — and he dutifully turned over the names of the other boys he had been playing with. When his father later asked what had happened, Hughes was smacked. "Not for playing cards," Hughes would later say, "but for giving the names of the other people who were involved with me."

In 1970, though, those standards would be put to the test in Irish America. Most devoted Irish Republicans adhered to them vigorously, but NORAID was a different beast. It wasn't just filled with hardcore supporters; it was a more widely palatable organization, eager for anyone's money and membership. That strategy had helped NORAID's bank account but also diluted its core. As NORAID stared down federal authorities, it had become a serious liability. Unlike the more selective Clan-na-Gael, NORAID was susceptible to hobbyists and casual adherents to the Republican code — people who, when faced with the choice, would far rather cooperate with police than go to prison. And as the noose began to tighten around Irish America, the unsettling truth became clear: in its eager expansion, NORAID had started leaking like a sieve.

CHAPTER 23

"I RESPECTFULLY DECLINE"

THE GRAND JURY subpoenas arrived to Philadelphia that May, a few weeks after investigators first tracked those boxes with the red and white labels to Danny Cahalane's van. The summonses blanketed the Delaware Valley and Northeast Philadelphia. Everyone, it seemed, was going to be pressured to talk. Marjorie Palace was called. William Corry, too. So was Charles Shulberg and his nosy secretary, from the Montgomery Loan Company. Jeffery Reh, Dan Duffy's colleague, and John Nigro, his underworld city hustler. And, of course, the summonses arrived at the homes of Neil Byrne, Dan Duffy, and Danny Cahalane.

The universe of evidence against the Philadelphia cell was circumstantial, but overwhelming: Investigators had records of phone calls between Cahalane, Byrne, and Bill Corry, and undercover agents had heard from Marty Lyons about the NORAID scheme with Clancy & Cullen, the shipping warehouse in the Bronx. The communiqués between the men, agents had noticed, conveniently lined up with dates that Dan Cahalane was buying guns. There were those strange nights and overheard conversations from undercover ATF agents, who had tracked the men through secret meetings up and down the New Jersey Turnpike and back and forth to Breen's pub. And, perhaps most damning, investigators had a whole list of rifles that were getting recovered from IRA hands in Northern Ireland, weapons with serial numbers that traced directly back to the men in Philadelphia.

The establishment of a grand jury panel for Philadelphia's gunrunning marked a significant advancement for Brandon Alvey and Bob Merkle. No longer was the ATF on an investigative fishing expedition; the bureau had collected enough evidence that the prosecutors believed they could finally do what British authorities had been pressuring them to for years: connect Philadelphia and NORAID definitively to the IRA.

Still, it marked just one step in a long process. In America, it's not federal prosecutors who decide to bring a felony criminal case; it's a grand jury, a fiercely secretive affair whose traditions date back to colonialist England. If prosecutors believe someone has committed a crime, they will impanel a group of uninvolved, impartial Americans to whom they will outline their evidence for the case — the grand jury. As part of the process, suspects and witnesses will be compelled to testify. But unlike public court cases, the grand jury process is guarded by intense secrecy rules; it's forbidden for jurors, lawyers, or courtroom staff to speak about what goes on behind its doors. It's the grand jurors who will eventually vote on whether there's sufficient evidence for prosecutors to indict suspects in a criminal case.

But given the context, the target of the grand jury probe was obvious to Philadelphia's Irish, who responded to the summonses with predictable outrage. It was proof, it seemed, that the American government was colluding with British authorities. BRITISH TERRORIST REGIME ENLISTS SUPPORT OF US JUSTICE DEPARTMENT TO STOP AID TO THE OPPRESSED PEOPLE OF NORTHERN IRELAND, read one picket sign outside the city's federal courthouse. Dozens of protesters — many in traditional Irish wool sweaters — marched in front of the building, playing Irish music and waving the tricolor flag. The case would eventually be dubbed "the Philadelphia Five," in reference to the five defendants who found themselves most seriously in the government's crosshairs.

For the city's Irish, the federal grand jury summonses fell politically flat from Richard Nixon's Justice Department, which was embroiled in its own web of alleged corruption and illegalities. In the minds of Philly's Irish, the White House's targeting *them* was yet another example of the stacked deck that existed whenever one dared challenge British oppression. The case tapped into a well of fury and contempt, much of it channeled directly at the White House.

Beneath the outrage, though, a more insidious fear took root. A grand jury is perhaps the highest-stakes phase of a federal criminal proceeding. The panels are critical prosecutorial tools — they are where investigators have intense leverage to turn suspects into informants, or turn witnesses against one another. And as NORAID had already begun to realize in other cities, its members might not be as principled or discreet as the group's leaders might have hoped.

It's easy, of course, to maintain an oath of silence before a figurative, abstract legal threat; quite different when you're under oath, in a witness chair, staring down accusations of mayhem and murder. Who is to blame, after all, for the pulling of a trigger that's an ocean away? The person holding the gun, or the person who sent it there in the first place?

On the morning of June 1973, Daniel Cahalane first walked into the grand jury room, buried inside the federal courthouse at Ninth and Market Streets. The building sat like a fortress not far from Independence Park, the leafy plaza that housed Independence Hall, where the city had orchestrated its own rebellion against British rule two centuries before.

The grand jury process was succeeding in some of the very ways prosecutors had hoped — it was placing Philadelphia's Irish under serious strain. There emerged a consuming paranoia over who might cooperate with the federal prosecutors, and who would stay silent. Many of the subpoenaed individuals had enlisted their own lawyers, fueling suspicion that someone, in the interest of self-preservation, might cut a deal.

Cahalane's initial appearance in front of the grand jury had both said plenty and said nothing at all. The facts of the case, as Alvey described them to the panel, were stark: Cahalane, aided by a group of men from Philadelphia to New York, had conspired to send hundreds of rifles into the hands of the Irish Republican Army, fueling the conflict. The man before them, a lawyer told the jurors, had spent three years pouring gasoline on a sectarian war that had already taken hundreds of lives and was well on its way to taking hundreds more — and investigators would show proof of his bloody impact: many of the guns Cahalane purchased were eventually seized by British investigators in West Belfast. Cahalane alone had bought nearly two hundred rifles himself, collecting them from a variety of brokers all across Pennsylvania.

"Mr. Cahalane," Alvey asked, "do you still have those weapons?"

Danny Cahalane sat stone-faced. He pulled out a small notecard and read from it, so softly a judge had to ask him to speak up.

"I respectfully decline to answer that question on the advice of my counsel because the answer might tend to incriminate me."

"Mr. Cahalane, did you purchase these weapons for any illegal purpose?"

"I respectfully refuse to answer those questions on the grounds previously asserted."

It went on for hours. Just like the men in Fort Worth, Cahalane refused to talk, reading out the same line in monotone, over and over. Frustrated and running out of time, prosecutors finally let him go.

Circumstances, though, changed after that first day of Cahalane's non-testimony. Despite their wide-reaching net of subpoenas, Alvey, Merkle, and the federal prosecutors knew they weren't looking for just anyone. Dan Cahalane and Neil Byrne were two of the IRA's most serious gunrunners. And more than that, if one of them turned, he could likely crack open the entire NORAID operation, from Philadelphia to New York to Belfast.

Byrne, a bachelor with few ties to the community, would be a difficult man to pressure. Cahalane, though — he had something to lose. A family, children, a nice house, a business. Certain principles are no match against self-preservation, when faced with such high stakes. It was why prosecutors decided to dangle an intriguing deal, to try to get Danny Cahalane to talk.

With nearly four hundred rifles being traced to the Philadelphia men, the defendants were looking at the prospect of serious jail time if the case went to trial. And so, federal prosecutors made a calculated gamble. Cahalane was important, sure, but he was only one part of NORAID's operation. It was why, in the spring of 1973, federal prosecutors offered Danny Cahalane immunity. All he had to do was tell them everything.

How to face the enormity of those last three years? Danny Cahalane's path to the grand jury room was perhaps inevitable, ever since that spring day more than a year before, wedged between Vince Conlon and Neil Byrne at the counter of the Montgomery Loan Company. It was Vince's last day shepherding them in their quiet mission, the day he passed the baton. It was a poetic sort of beginning, the three of them there together, fulfilling the Philadelphia legacy that Joseph McGarrity had left, all those years before. Together, they bought twenty-five rifles that day, all of them ArmaLites. Danny and Neil went on to buy hundreds of rifles and tens of thousands of rounds of ammunition.

It was easier, perhaps, to see the gunrunning forest instead of its trees. The Provos went from fledgling guerrillas to a well-heeled army overnight. There were brigades across Northern Ireland now — in Derry, in West Belfast, along the border in Armagh — that were armed with Philadelphia guns. The NORAID men had almost certainly changed the state of the war.

To change a life, though, doesn't take hundreds of guns. It doesn't even take twenty-five. It only takes one.

PART IV

GUN
GIRL

CHAPTER 24

SHOOTER

THE PANTS GERALDINE Crawford pulled on that night were a dusty pink. It was the kind of outfit better suited to a dance, or a night out with girlfriends. It would have been, anyway, in a different place.

But this was a Saturday in West Belfast in September 1973, the edge of a chaotic summer that seemed primed for an even more deadly fall. Nowhere was that more true than Lenadoon, an estate in Greater Andersonstown. In the years since the Falls Curfew, the ghetto had become the fortified center of the Provisional IRA. Most of its young recruits came from these streets, which doubled as a hidden network of armories, makeshift hospitals, and safe houses. The neighborhood was intense and claustrophobic, its residents sandwiched between the Belfast city border to the west, the inhospitable Black Mountain to the north, and a scattering of Unionist neighborhoods to its south.

A middle child in a large family, Geraldine was bright with long brown hair and sad eyes. She was eighteen years old as the seasons turned in 1973, on the cusp of the rest of her life. She had found work as a typist, transcribing shorthand. She was creative and likable, good at crafts, and a talented guitar player.

What was eighteen, though, in a place where you grew up fast, anyway? It was impossible to separate adolescence from violence, especially in Lenadoon, especially in that dangerous autumn. Trips to and from school were interrupted by British soldiers. Midnight knocks at the door, signaling imminent raids, were everyday occurrences. Mothers escorted their teenagers home from discos, for fear they would be targeted in sectarian killings. In Rosapenna Square, the small circular street where the Crawfords lived, a neighbor had only just died after locals said they had seen her be shoved by a British soldier and collapse; the mother of eight had been trying to reach her young teenage son, whom she believed was in the custody of British troops.

What else, then, was there to do? The notion of choice was a funny thing in West Belfast, and Geraldine had made hers. The pink pants were not for a disco. September 22 would be far more significant. It would be the night of her first operation in active service for the Provisional IRA.

The labyrinthine streets of Andersonstown and Lenadoon are their own tactical chip, of great use to those who live in them and of great challenge to those who don't. Roads that continue unhindered in one direction cut abruptly to another, or double back on themselves. The neighborhood's crowded houses are stacked neatly like dominoes up the hillside, and even today, long after the Troubles formally ended, the buildings themselves still seem nearly alive with suspicion. There is little rhythm or pattern to the streets, their paths constantly intersected by shortcuts and narrow alleyways that connect a network of housing estates. Gravel paths hug brick walls and cut between backyards, rarely passing completely into the open air or an unobscured line of sight. It is a neighborhood of shadows, and even in the daylight it's an easy place to get lost. To enter as a stranger is to feel watched. The name alone comes with a weighted significance: Andersonstown is its neutral reference; to call it Andytown, its colloquial name in nationalist circles, telegraphs one's politics.

Northern Ireland is often referred to by Republicans as an occupied territory, and in 1973 Andersonstown felt like one. The nationalist neighborhood, home to more than thirty thousand, was a no-go area in the early days of the Troubles, seen as too dangerous and hostile for British troops or policemen to even enter without reinforcements. The streets weren't fully barricaded but Andersonstown's reputation said enough: "The police never went near it, and when the army dared to enter, they did so in fast-moving vehicles with the doors closed and the gunslots up. Children of town had a reputation for being excellent shots with stones, and the IRA with guns." That line was written in the *Andersonstown News,* a local paper that began in 1972 primarily as a way for the insular neighborhood to communicate news about internment, so disproportionately affected was the community by the policy. More than half of Andersonstown's men were arrested at some point between 1971 and 1973, and the first Republican woman interned during the Troubles, Liz

McKee, hailed from its streets. In mainstream coverage at the time, Andersonstown and Lenadoon were spoken of with a fearful reverence, understood to be the spiritual and operational home of the Provisional IRA, a place that housed "nests of bombmakers," where accused murderers and gunmen walked freely.

South of Lenadoon was Finaghy, a Loyalist neighborhood. Many of Lenadoon's Protestants had fled there as refugee Catholic families moved west during the early 1970s. If the Troubles had front lines in 1973, the Lenadoon interface was one of them. The dangerous neighborhood border marked where the IRA's Andersonstown territory ran into that of Loyalist paramilitary groups, and the neighborhood lived in the shadow of guerrilla war. It was a flash point for sectarian violence, the kind of place that could spiral abruptly into chaos. The British troops took to calling the residents of the place "rabble rousers."

It was a young neighborhood, too — Andersonstown was said to have Belfast's highest proportion of children as residents. Many would grow up to be the new generation of the IRA, as the young volunteers of the Provos. Many would be the first in their families to join the cause, which was a significant shift in Republican tradition — most families associated with the Official IRA came from long ancestral lines of IRA volunteers. That would change in Andersonstown.

The ghetto was defined by survival, inside the home and out. The nights were pockmarked by the sharp *pop* of gunfire. Trips to the grocery store included searches by British soldiers, housewives argued with uniformed policemen in the streets, and trips to church could be interrupted abruptly by a bomb. Living rooms became hospitals amid street gun battles, and a quiet evening could be stopped short by a bloody body at the door — for an illegal organization like the Provisional IRA, private houses and makeshift surgeries were far safer than medical centers, which were often guarded by British soldiers. In the early days of the Troubles, the IRA created its own autonomous zone in Lenadoon and Andersonstown, arranging quasi–law enforcement and court systems, doling out rough justice, and patrolling the streets as a deterrent to Loyalist gangs from Finaghy and elsewhere. The IRA became as ubiquitous in Andersonstown as a town council in suburban America, albeit with far more violent tactics. Andersonstown, after all, was effectively a war zone, under assault from all sides. Beyond the British Army, Loyalist gangs routinely kidnapped and sometimes killed Andersonstown residents in sectarian killings, and the IRA, too, sometimes turned on its own, menacing families who declined assistance and, sometimes, killing those it believed had turned against them.

Not until internment in 1971 did British soldiers formally enter Andersonstown, and when they did, they did so decisively. The ghetto was blanketed with seventeen military installations, which took over everything from schoolhouses to bus depots to sports grounds. Billed as a peacekeeping mission, the troops' arrival — like elsewhere in Northern Ireland — was originally welcomed by Catholic residents, who hoped they would bring some sense of order. But that sentiment soured quickly, aided by the thuggish behavior of British troops and the continued incursions of Loyalist paramilitary groups into Andersonstown. That such organizations could operate in West Belfast only underscored nationalist suspicions that the RUC and the British Army — four thousand strong, in the ghetto alone — were quietly enabling extrajudicial Loyalist paramilitaries who were targeting Catholics.

British soldiers did little to assuage such concerns. The legions of troops stationed in Andersonstown — from two elite infantry units, the King's Own Scottish Borderers and the Green Howards — arrived with a mission, one that seemed less to do with peacekeeping than surveillance. They sought to create a sweeping civilian dossier of households, a job they approached with cold and ruthless efficiency. Men, women, and teenagers were frequently detained and brought in for hostile interrogations, pressured to spill details on Republican activity in their neighborhood. Social gatherings were interrupted, their attendees hustled on to buses and forced to give their names, addresses, and religions; in Lenadoon, one man was detained for questioning eight times in two nights.

The effort, perhaps more than anything else, created a deep-rooted hostility between British troops and the residents of Andersonstown, who lived in fear of a midnight knock on their door. Often, the raids were haphazard and retaliatory; in one instance, a mother was kicked as her young son was taken by British troops for an interrogation. In another, a young Andersonstown girl refused to wish British soldiers good morning on her way to school; those soldiers arrived at her family's door at 1:20 a.m. that night and, after the girl's mother refused to let them in, poured milk through her letterbox. Seventeen-year-old Daniel Rouse was kidnapped and murdered by Loyalist paramilitaries after British soldiers callously ignored pleas for help, saying they couldn't follow up on every "whimsical report" they got. Despite public assurances that bad behavior would be addressed, the numbers spoke clearly;

in 1971 alone, residents of Andersonstown filed 635 civilian complaints against the RUC. Only forty were substantiated, with little expectation that any of the offenders would be punished.

Even British officers often acknowledged the Army was its own worst enemy in places like Andersonstown, its aggressive tactics and heavy-handed patrolling doing little but driving residents toward the IRA. The blunt hammer of internment fell heavily in Andersonstown, radicalizing an entire generation of young men and women who saw brothers, fathers, husbands, and sons "lifted," or detained without cause, and imprisoned for extended periods of time without charge. Even childhood didn't protect you from such fates; by 1973, British soldiers were routinely arresting and jailing children as young as their early teens, pulling them into rough interrogations and demanding information on local paramilitaries.

The slights manifested in ways large and small, but their top-line implication was clear: Andersonstown was under siege by hostile outside forces, uniformed and otherwise. For the young volunteers who flocked to the Provisional ranks, the symbols of this conflict were ubiquitous parts of daily life: heavily armed soldiers on street corners and checkpoints; RUC officers, who occasionally entered to serve court summonses; the British Army outposts that dotted the neighborhood.

Perhaps the most visible of all was the Woodbourne barracks, an industrial-looking wart on Suffolk Road. It was an old estate, eventually fortified with corrugated iron and cages over the windows and doors. If British troops had once claimed to be in Northern Ireland on a peacekeeping mission, the Woodbourne post now belied that assertion. The fortress, its ominous watchtowers backing right up to the quiet backyards of Andersontown's housing estates, left little ambiguity as to its purpose. There was nothing about Woodbourne House that spoke to peace. Woodbourne House was a facility of war.

That September week was a busy one in Andersonstown. At the Suffolk Inn, a pub off Andersonstown's western border, police busted four men with a car full of explosives. Flurries of gunshots were traded between British soldiers and pockets of IRA volunteers, and that Monday, a volley of shots went off at a British patrol as they walked through Lenadoon. After sundown, Andersonstown was dark as night — British troops had shot out the streetlights, preferring to work in the dark, their faces tarred with black. Once the night fell, Andersonstown came alive, the silence shattered by the rapid tap of ArmaLites.

The Provos were careful with the guns. No one ever knew when the feast would turn back to famine, so operations and patrols often only had one or two weapons dispersed between them. That was the case that Saturday, as Geraldine and a small group of volunteers prepared for their operation.

Hers was to be a simple enough mission, another tit-for-tat skirmish that had become commonplace in Andersonstown's theater of war. There would be four other volunteers alongside her: three men and another woman, Aine McCotter. At seventeen, Aine hailed from a staunchly Republican family and had grown up steeped in the tradition; she lived in Andersonstown and had joined Cumann na mBan, the IRA's women's auxiliary, as a teenager.

The group shared a single ArmaLite between them, and the plan was clear and low-risk. They would prowl the streets of Lenadoon on a reconnaissance mission, then, if all was clear, one of them would take a snipe at the Woodbourne barracks. When it came time to decide who would hold the ArmaLite, it went to the newest hands. For her first mission, it would be Geraldine Crawford who took the shot.

The two girls stayed close as they approached the dark street corner where the Woodbourne barracks sat. Conditions seemed nearly perfect; all was quiet on Suffolk Road, and a brief sweep of the premises revealed nothing and no one. Satisfied that the coast was clear, the girls took their shooting post, closer to the barracks. Clutching the rifle, Geraldine inched to the street corner.

She had hardly aimed the ArmaLite when a shout came from the hedge across the road.

Halt or we'll fire!

It was over in a millisecond and a blur of sound: two *pop*s of gunfire and a metallic *thud* as the ArmaLite clattered to the ground.

CHAPTER 25

PROVO

SHE HAD GROWN up just down the road from that pavement, on the Lower Falls. There were twelve of them: her parents, Ned and Brigid, and ten children. She was the third youngest among eight sisters and two brothers. Like so many other youth in Belfast, she had been left in confusing limbo as the Troubles began. Spontaneous violence was always present, but never in Geraldine's short lifetime had it struck so swiftly and decisively: The burning of Clonard. The riots that followed. The raids on the Falls. Internment, Bloody Sunday — the list went on and on.

They had grown up in the shadow of Belfast's linen mills, down the road from the docks and the shipyard at Harland and Wolff, the British shipbuilding company that had become a symbol for the city and all its troubles. Its cranes, spindly and yellow, would loom so large in Belfast's psyche that they got their own names: Samson and Goliath, two unholy giants towering over a city of Davids. Like most things in Northern Ireland, the cranes were divisive and politically loaded. They were the heartbeat of the city's industrial center, emblematic of the prosperous port that Belfast had become, visible from nearly all corners of the urban center but just out of reach for Catholic residents like the Crawfords. In Samson and Goliath was everything the Protestants of Belfast had, and everything the Catholics of Belfast didn't.

Like most families on the Falls, the Crawfords felt this disparity acutely. Ned Crawford, Geraldine's father, had once been steadily employed, working as a fishmonger, then taking a job across the Irish Sea, working the docks in Heysham, a small port village on Britain's west coast. But luck in Belfast didn't last long, and as unrest percolated in 1969, Ned Crawford had already spent much of the decade back in Belfast, at home and unemployed. He was a blue-collar man and grew deeply involved in the Transport and General Workers' Union, but as the Troubles neared, his children watched him bounce from job to job, a trend that was reflected across Belfast, where Catholics were unemployed at a rate 2.5 times that of their Protestant neighbors. His wife, Bridget, had regular work as a janitor for buildings and businesses in the city's center, but it wasn't the kind of life kids ought to have; they spent their summer holidays not at the sea but rather at work with their mother, hanging around as she cleaned.

Ironically, it was the move to Lenadoon that was meant to bring the Crawfords some sense of security and to keep their children farther away from the fault lines of the Lower Falls and Clonard. They moved, along with thousands of other families, not long after the 1969 riots, part of the mass migration of Belfast's Catholics that had seen Andersonstown and Lenadoon balloon in population — and become a fertile recruiting ground for the Provisional IRA.

If the Crawfords had any hope that the move westward would shield them from Belfast's violence, that illusion was shattered quickly. Lenadoon had, by 1973, become one of Andersonstown's busiest fronts, the scene of some of the city's most heavy fighting and the battlefield for most of Northern Ireland's variously opposed sides: the British Army, the RUC, the Provisional IRA, the Official IRA, and the Loyalist paramilitary groups that operated in neighboring, non-Catholic ghettos. The estate would cement itself in Troubles history in the summer of 1972, when it was the scene of one of Belfast's most sustained, bloodiest encounters: the Battle of Lenadoon, fought over a week in July, marked the end of a two-week ceasefire struck between the Provos and the British Army, and it sent the city into a deadly spasm of violence. Dozens were killed across Belfast over those six days; five were sixteen years old or younger.

Such were the grim contours of the Crawfords' new home and the forces that defined the adolescence of their children. Surrounded by death, faced with their own mortality, they found their own means to cope. Geraldine's older sister, Laura, was a fiery, athletic young woman who quickly established herself as a political organizer. Laura and Geraldine were close, and Geraldine watched as Laura threw herself into activism. She signed on with Provisional

Sinn Fein, the IRA's political wing, and led the Jordan and Finucane Accordion Band, a nationalist musical group that took part in local marches and demonstrations against internment. And Laura started reporting for *An Phoblacht,* the Republican newspaper that was the IRA's main publicity channel.

Why, then, had Geraldine Crawford joined the IRA instead of other, less risky pursuits? She would never quite be able to point to a specific incident, or night, or happening that had pushed her to such a brink, or explain why she opted for armed resistance instead of politics, as Laura had appeared to do. Up against Belfast's proverbial walls, Geraldine had finally decided, during that hazy summer of 1973 as she watched British troops tear through her neighborhood, pummeling her family and friends into submission. It was a secret she would keep from everyone, including her family. She wouldn't even tell Laura, even though she had started off on her own respective Republican journey. No; the decision that Geraldine made was one she would make alone, and in the Republican tradition, she would say nothing. She would take up arms against the British Army. She would join the Provisional IRA.

Women extremists are complicated figures, in fictional and nonfictional retellings. Among the IRA, they drew — and still draw — on inevitably gendered stereotypes, equally fetishized and villainized. "In taking up arms, they commit a double atrocity, using violence, and in the process destroying our safe, traditional view of women," wrote Eileen MacDonald, in one of the few studies of the phenomenon.

History has borne this out across any number of conflicts: the women of Germany's Red Army Faction, female revolutionaries in Cuba, women founders of Italy's Prima Linea. The same was true of the IRA's women. Newspapers called them "inhuman," the work of war "unwomanly," monikers that stuck with them into the 1980s and 1990s, and still linger today.

Women were always a part of the Irish Republican movement, from its contemporary beginnings in 1900. The Daughters of Erin, the first iteration of a Republican women's army, advocated for women enlistees to be treated the same as men as early as the turn of the twentieth century. That group would eventually merge with Cumann na mBan, which was first established in 1914. Even in early days, many female volunteers fought to learn how to shoot and handle a gun, eager to leave the restrictive domestic mold that was inherent in the Irish tradition in the early 1900s. But despite small bursts of change, it was a widely held belief among male volunteers that their women comrades ought to stay in subservient roles, outside of direct combat.

That changed quickly in 1971, as the nascent Provisional movement faced an increasing challenge of retention due to imprisonments, injuries, and deaths. Women, the Provos found, not only bolstered the ranks, but they also brought a unique skill set to a guerrilla war, which was increasingly fought in crowded towns and cities. Women avoided the more obvious suspicion under which male volunteers often fell, and could convincingly use gendered props like baby carriages to hide sinister cargo like bombs, or lure amorous British soldiers out of bars and into the line of fire. Some women volunteers cultivated their own cults of personality, hypersexualized as cunning, ruthless operatives capable of seducing and killing. That brand was embodied by the likes of volunteers like Dolours and Marian Price, two sisters from Andersonstown who were jailed for orchestrating a notorious campaign of car bombings in London. They were romanticized as glamorous villains in the mainstream discourse, criticism which they did little to counter. Media darlings, they became known in newspapers as the "sisters of death."

By the summer of 1973, teenage girls and women had become central to the movement, enlisting in the IRA by the dozens. Some had male family members tied to the IRA — brothers, fathers, boyfriends, and husbands — but many joined of their own volition, pushed toward the cause for the same reasons as their male counterparts: the brutality of Belfast was impossible to ignore, and there were few other options.

But that September night made Geraldine an anomaly: she was one of the first IRA women to be shot in combat. Norms were shifting, but the IRA was still reticent to place women volunteers in combat-facing roles. Even today, the IRA still brings to mind an inherently masculine brand. If Provo women are remembered, it's mostly via personalities like the Price sisters, their polished brands providing a canvas through which to tell the complicated story of the Troubles. Through them, the entire ordeal feels almost romanticized. But perhaps just as — if not more — critical to the Provisional IRA's success were the throngs of less remembered, ordinary women and girls who joined the army's ranks in its early moments. In 1973, men were still the overwhelming majority in the Provos, but courtroom reports from local Belfast papers stand as testament to what was, at the time, a significant change:

by the early 1970s, Belfast's blotters were not just full of young men from Andersonstown. Almost daily, there were women being charged with IRA membership, too.

She had heard plenty about being shot, but no one had ever described it like this. Most of the people she talked to said they hardly realized it when it happened, as if their body was detached from their mind. This, though — this slammed into her like a brick wall, as if a huge blast had buckled the soft tissue behind her knee. The scream coming out of her mouth was bloodcurdling, and the pain made it impossible for her to move anything in her lower extremities. She went bone-chillingly cold, pressed against the pavement. Nothing moved the way it should.

Walk toward us.

The soldiers shouted to them from the hedge.

I can't walk.

She was shocked she wasn't dead; they were close enough, with a clear enough shot, that she ought to be. Aine McCotter lay next to her uninjured, a hole in her pants where the bullet had just barely missed.

Crawl toward us.

The rest of the brigade was nowhere to be found. Were they safe, or injured, too? Those days it was hard to even track how many of them had been shot — such statistics weren't recorded in the IRA's network of secret, makeshift hospitals. Surely, that's the sort of place the rest of that night's brigade was headed; as she would later learn, the three boys with them had also come under fire as the girls had inched closer to their shooting post. One was struck but managed to scramble away.

Geraldine, though, wasn't so lucky. She knew then, lying on the pavement: it was her legs. Both kneecaps, blown out. She had never felt such pain, so sharp and heavy that even crawling was impossible. Bright-red stains spread across the pink fabric of her pants. The blood looked nearly alive, pumping out of her.

She scraped across the pavement, using her arms to drag herself toward a nearby hedge. It was useless. She was stopped short by the hard, metallic press of a gun barrel jammed into her chest.

If you have any other weapons, the soldier said, looming over her, *throw them out.*

It was just the rifle; only the rifle. The ArmaLite, ferried into the back streets of Belfast from America. It was her first night, the first thing she was set to do, and she was the only one with a gun.

Do you have a field bandage? she asked, knowing the soldiers often carried first aid materials in their kits. But the man above her made no move to provide it. The British soldiers, indeed, seemed wholly unconcerned with the dangerous amount of blood leaving her body. It was only later, sure that the situation was under control, that the soldier who'd been pressing the gun to her chest tossed her a bandage to dress her own wound.

There was something familiar then, in the soldier's detachment. Plenty of British troops had hurled abuse at her and her family, hassled her neighbors, targeted the people she loved. But there was nothing personal, then, as the man faced Geraldine Crawford's possible death. He remained coldly professional, and in later years, Geraldine would have little bad to say about him. They were just two people at war, in the dark.

CHAPTER 26

PRISONER

THE RIFLE THAT dropped from Geraldine's hands onto the pavement that night became one point in a legal constellation, part of the mechanism that was scrambling, daily, to tally the growing list of seized ArmaLites and connect their serial numbers back to America.

The work had been manageable at first, but by the time the Provos were getting their hands on large numbers of Philadelphia guns, British authorities became overwhelmed by the sheer number of recovered weapons. Their system hadn't been built to handle such an influx; in 1972, at the height of the Troubles, there were only two people in Northern Ireland working to catalog the guns that were being seized from the Provisional IRA. The Royal Ulster Constabulary, the domestic police force, picked them up in raids and house searches. The British Army and its Royal Military Police picked up others, sometimes in searches, other times during shoot-outs and clashes with IRA fighters. It became such a pressing matter that the Royal Military Police soon set up its own so-called finding teams, tasked specifically with seizing weapons. The result was an overwhelming flood of court cases in Belfast and Derry — the seized guns were used in nearly seven hundred procedures a year.

It was a complicated legal situation in Northern Ireland. Being a member of the IRA was illegal, but that was often a less serious conviction than the violent acts associated with the secret army. In cases like Geraldine's, authorities would often opt to prioritize more serious charges like gun crimes and drop the charge of IRA membership, even if the violent acts were undertaken as a member of the IRA. It would eventually lead to a whole population of volunteers who were convicted of shootings and murders yet who were never convicted of being a member of the illegal army.

To prosecute these cases, though, required the guns, which was why British security forces so aggressively worked to find them. After they were used in a Belfast court, most of the weapons disappeared, turned over for disposal to the British Army. Some guns were melted or destroyed, others were used for training purposes, to teach newly deployed soldiers about the weaponry they'd soon face.

But by that autumn, some of the guns began taking a different journey. For the first time since the Troubles began — and the first time since British investigators started recovering piles of American guns — an arrangement was reached for British and Northern Irish investigators to assist their American counterparts in prosecuting the IRA's American arms network. What had begun as a casual dialogue in 1970 had, by 1973, become something else entirely. Investigators from the Royal Ulster Constabulary were in regular, intensive dialogue with the two American prosecutors — Brandon Alvey and Bob Merkle — about a potential criminal case in Philadelphia. They had even invited ATF agents to Belfast, to probe their own investigative leads.

Although US prosecutors had already brought charges in a handful of NORAID-related cases, Northern Irish and British investigators saw the potential for a very different kind of case in Philadelphia. Never before had they been able to so definitively show that American guns were directly tied to specific violent acts in Northern Ireland, and that the pipeline of NORAID-funded weapons ran directly to the IRA. In fact, British investigators could show, some of the people who were arrested with Philadelphia guns were prosecuted for membership in Provos and a whole host of related, violent offenses. One of the guns was even used to kill a police officer.

The ArmaLite that Geraldine had dropped on the dark corner in Belfast would become one of these evidentiary guns. She didn't know it at the time, but from the moment she dropped that rifle, two outward paths diverged. The first would lead to a court in Northern Ireland, where she would soon face her own criminal charges. The second would twist and turn through the American court system, dabbling back and forth across an ocean in a legal saga that would last decades. After all, every rifle that investigators found in Belfast could be used in two potential cases — one in Northern Ireland, against the person who used the gun, and the other in America, against the person who had sent it.

The first was a straightforward enough investigation. The second, though, required an extra clue, which investigators found on Geraldine's rifle: serial no. S11981.

The washing at the hospital mortified her, the utter lack of dignity in the exercise. The trainee nurse sent in to bathe her was her own age, so similar and yet so categorically different; Geraldine was girlishly embarrassed despite the heaviness of the circumstance. The nurse, in kindness, tried to quietly allow Geraldine some privacy, to bathe herself. But the gesture was fruitless. She hadn't been alone a moment when a large British soldier kicked the door in. The teenage patient, they claimed, was too dangerous to leave alone.

Even after ten days in the hospital, in and out of surgeries, the memory of that night remained clear. Geraldine had dressed her own wound as people gathered outside the army barracks, the soldiers milling about, trying to keep the nationalist crowds contained. They gathered almost immediately. Neighbors formed a crowd around her, and one particularly drunk woman from the nearby pub even managed to press through to them; go, Geraldine directed the woman, and tell her sister that she had been hit. The woman scurried off. The soldiers called for an ambulance, loading her onto a stretcher to wait in the bay of an Army transport until a civilian one arrived. She was rushed up the Falls Road to Royal Victoria Hospital.

It was a turn-of-the-century facility, its proximity to the Falls and Shankill Road making it a triage zone for the Troubles. The crowded wing in which Geraldine was placed felt less like a hospital and more like an interrogation room, so dense was the suspicion between patients and attending nurses and doctors. The wariness was not unfounded — the site was such a dangerous interface that British soldiers took up regular post at the hospital.

Geraldine was taken directly into the operating room, where doctors removed her right kneecap. A heavily armed officer was at her bedside when she woke. He peppered her with questions but she refused to answer. She hardly had a moment alone.

Among them, under close watch, Geraldine was a dark anomaly. Hostile glares from fellow patients followed her. Things grew so tense that nurses moved the teenager to her own room, which proved a small consolation. Heavily armed guards watched her constantly. There would be no respite, and she briefly went on a hunger strike, refusing to eat. On the third day of her stay in the hospital, she was charged with possession of an ArmaLite rifle, with intent to endanger life.

She spent ten days recovering from surgery at Royal Victoria, and then she was moved to Musgrave Park Hospital, a sweeping complex closer to Andersonstown. It was the only facility in Belfast that had its own security wing, and she spent her days there under close watch, as both patient and prisoner. It was the start of her life in confinement. The ward at Musgrave was less a city hospital than a battlefield triage center, its beds dotted with gruesome injuries of war and young, fellow IRA volunteers. Over her three months in the hospital, she fell into its strange camaraderie, making friends and growing close to one volunteer, Jim Lynagh, a boyish redhead who had been injured in a bomb explosion. She was taught by other Republican patients how to make handicrafts, like the woven and carved knickknacks that were often sent back to the States to be auctioned off at NORAID fundraisers.

How much could change, just from one night, one choice, one gun. It had all moved so fast on that corner in Andersonstown, but Geraldine remembered her sister, who eventually turned up with the rest of the crowd as Geraldine lay bleeding on the pavement. She had hoped for some flash of recognition, a show of solidarity, anything — but her sister's face stayed locked in a strange daze. She came to understand it with time, but Geraldine had noticed it that night and was perplexed; it was as if her sister was looking at a stranger, as if she was someone else, somewhere other than that dark street in Belfast's hell, somewhere far away.

By the time her trial arrived, it had been more than six months since that night in Andersonstown. She was still not well, her recovery befallen with setbacks. As she was transferred between hospitals and jails, she had to be stretched out across the back of police cars, her legs still too injured to sit properly. At her first court appearance, she leaned heavily on a cane.

Possession of an ArmaLite, with intent to endanger life. She was hardly the only one facing such stakes; the Provisional IRA's first generation of women volunteers were being yanked into court those days nearly as often as its men — the proceedings in Geraldine's case were often bookended by other teenage women from Andersonstown, caught with guns, arrested while carrying explosives, or accused of belonging to a paramilitary organization.

If convicted, she could be sent behind bars for years, and there seemed little hope that she would avoid such a fate — it's not like she was trying to defend herself, anyway. Yes, she had the gun, and yes, she shot it. But she didn't believe that what she'd done had broken the law; after all, that was a fundamental component of Irish Republicanism in the 1970s. Members of the IRA refused to recognize the legitimacy of any component of the Northern Irish government, including its legal system.

It was why, at her first court appearance, Geraldine turned her back to the judge, a symbolic gesture undertaken by many Provo defendants in Northern Ireland to underscore their rejection of the Northern Irish state.

Twelve British soldiers were flown in from West Germany for the trial, the same unit that had been stationed at Woodbourne House the night she was shot. Among them was the man who had pulled the trigger. Publicly unnamed, he testified that he was on patrol that night near the post when the two teenagers were seen, acting strangely. One girl, he said, had a rifle raised and was aiming it at the barracks. He shouted a warning, he said, but Geraldine refused to lower the gun. So he fired twice, hitting her in the soft tissue behind her knees. He had watched as she fell.

She was convicted, unsurprisingly, with little fanfare, and sentenced to eight years in HM Prison Armagh, known as Armagh Gaol. Eight years behind bars, for carrying a loaded rifle under suspicious circumstances, with intent to endanger life. A newspaper article at the time called Geraldine and Aine McCotter the "Belfast Gun Girls," and noted their refusal to recognize the court, even as the magistrate sent them both to prison. Indeed, as the judge read her sentence into the court record, Geraldine's voice cracked defiantly through the stale air of the courtroom:

"Up the Provos!"

In a different moment, with different purpose, the light-drenched halls of Armagh Gaol might've looked like the eaves of a cathedral. But there was nothing holy about the place. The aged facility was the only women's prison in Northern Ireland, thrust into a role for which it was unprepared and unequipped. Prior to the dawn of the Troubles, it had never housed more than a dozen women at any given time, and most of them were in for relatively minor, nonviolent crimes — at times, it even served as a sort of de facto shelter for the poor, who sought out minor infractions to find a bed and a safe place to sleep. The guards functioned more as caretakers than wardens, and the space was more comfortable than foreboding. The only other inmates were troubled juvenile boys, who usually spent some time in Armagh before being sent back to other facilities.

A sparse, Victorian-style structure, the prison was a simple design: a circular center, from which two cell wings went outward, an A Wing and a B Wing. They could be entered from the center by double secure openings — a gate and a door. It was manned around the clock by a guard, ensuring the sleepy prison stayed secure, and stayed locked.

That all changed at the start of the Troubles. In 1971, there were only two female political prisoners in Armagh Gaol. From 1972 to 1976, that number ballooned to more than a hundred. In the early years of the conflict, it was a miserable place, bursting with disrespect and suspicion between guards, wardens, and prisoners, Republicans and Loyalists alike. By the time Geraldine arrived, though, that had changed. A significant policy shift had occurred in 1972, when Republican prisoners were afforded "special category," or political status. It was an important change both in theory and in practice. IRA prisoners were no longer treated as petty criminals. Instead, they were allowed to wear their own clothes, have access to educational facilities, and socialize freely. It was an important political distinction, too, one which British authorities would quickly regret having clarified. By designating IRA captives as so-called political prisoners, it legitimized the organization as a political body and validated the IRA's movement as something more than criminal, a matter of semantics that carried — perhaps unintentionally, on behalf of Northern Irish authorities — serious weight.

As she arrived for the first time to Armagh, Geraldine hoped for a quiet entrance, welcomed, perhaps, by an older volunteer, someone to show her around and introduce her to her new life. She stripped and washed herself, shuffling through the main hall to the double-gated entrance into A Wing, where most women Republican prisoners were held.

There, Geraldine's hopes for a discreet arrival disappeared. As she stepped through the gates, a roar came from the top of the steps, where a throng of her new cellmates had gathered. Their faces swam above her, many of them teenagers. They were from all over: Derry, Strabane, some from Lurgan. Bubbly and curious, they were full of excitement, and peppered Geraldine with questions.

She was mortified at the raucous welcome, but it was its own show of solidarity, too. She was among the initiated now, the women prisoners of the Republican movement. She may not have known it then, but the sisterhood she entered that day in the cold cells of Armagh Gaol would last for decades, well beyond the 1970s, well beyond her own time on the front line, and well beyond the war that had put them there.

CHAPTER 27

SISTER

THERE WAS NO denying that the stark cells of Armagh Gaol made it a hard, dark place. But in the era of political status, it was an exciting place, too, full of laughter and sisterhood. Most of the prisoners were more girls than women — like Geraldine, they were mostly in their late teens and early twenties. It was a motley mix of comrades, many of whom were from the same streets on which Geraldine and her siblings had grown up. They were led by Eileen Hickey, a veteran Republican volunteer who was widely recognized as the leader of A Wing. The women there had constructed their own hierarchy, a disciplined command structure that mirrored the one they had left outside the walls — even the guards acknowledged Hickey as the primary arbiter between the prisoners and wardens. There was Ellen McGuigan, Geraldine's cellmate; Madge McConville, a legendary, elder Republican woman in her fifties. And, in a highly publicized debacle, Dolours and Marian Price arrived to Armagh's A Wing the spring after Geraldine's conviction. They were transferred there from a prison in London, where they were convicted of setting off a string of car bombs in 1973. (Their arrival to Armagh followed a hunger strike by the sisters that had gone on for more than a hundred days, as they demanded to be moved from Great Britain to an Irish prison — an example of how the IRA used hunger strikes as a political negotiating tool.)

The camaraderie made life easier, but it didn't compensate for the jail's dismal conditions, or the tension that simmered between its prisoners and certain members of its staff. Chief among them was Armagh's attending physician, Dr. Cole, so careless that Geraldine and her co-inmates referred to him

Geraldine Crawford, seated at left, with the Price sisters and another prisoner in Armagh Gaol, sometime in the 1970s

as Dr. Frankencole, after the monster — one inmate drew a caricature of him, with bolts in his neck, and pasted it to his door. Cole was assisted by a nurse whom the inmates called Ratchet, after the character Nurse Ratched from *One Flew Over the Cuckoo's Nest*. It was dark humor, but the reality was anything but funny — many of the prisoners in Armagh, like Geraldine, had suffered traumatic injuries, and the doctor's lack of expertise did little to help. He soon became known as Dr. Death for his liberal use of tranquilizers and painkillers to quiet inmates down.

Geraldine was unimpressed with the medical care — she often referred to the prison doctors as "quacks" — but otherwise she was among friends. "It was like a holiday camp," she said, years later. Cells were unlocked for the day around 7:30 a.m., and wardens would start inspections around ten, but otherwise the women were left mostly to themselves. They drilled in the yard, then spent most of their days socializing, cooking communal dinners, and making crafts.

It was a strange time to be a prisoner, made stranger by the girls' adolescence. The days were filled with a mischievous innocence, in bizarre contrast to the circumstances that had brought them all together inside Armagh's locked doors. Geraldine regularly broke out her guitar and sang, usually landing on her favorite tune, "Me and Bobby Magee." She and a friend acquired a taste for fried mushrooms, and a group of them would gather in the kitchen and cook them in butter, music floating in the background. Films were shown on Wednesdays, in the prison chapel above the jail's central circle, partitioned so Loyalist and Republican prisoners stayed separate. The girls lugged pillows, juice, and sweets, spreading out on the floor to watch the film. Sometimes they even dragged up mattresses, huddling together for comfort if it was a horror film.

They traded the job of making home-brewed liquor in bottles under their cell beds, a tradition that kicked up around Christmastime. It was during one such mission that Geraldine and her cellmate, Ellen McGuigan, were woken up in the middle of the night by squeaking from under their beds. Girlishly spooked, they flagged the guard — a "big country woman," Geraldine recalled — and begged her to search for mice. But the woman found none. Instead, the two girls spent the night in the cell of a friend. It was only the following evening, when they heard the squeaks again under their bed, that they realized the noise was from the containers of fermenting homemade alcohol; they didn't know that they had to periodically release the built-up gases.

Fearing trouble, the girls snuck down to the garbage cans and dumped the fizzing bottles, covering them in blankets. "It was like the bomb disposal unit," Crawford would joke, years later. The debacle enraged Eileen Hickey, the wing's commander, but entertained the girls for weeks. It was an ironic story, in hindsight: Ellen McGuigan, Geraldine's cellmate, was serving time for planting an IRA bomb.

The lore surrounding the imprisoned looms large in the Irish Republican consciousness. In the 1970s, entire infrastructures sprang up in Catholic ghettos to support prisoners and their families. Newspapers and newsletters were established solely to pass news about who was arrested and when, and to serve as a message service from outside the walls to within. It was the prisons, really, that became a unifying touchstone for the communities of West Belfast, and nationalist ghettos everywhere.

NORAID, too, became an auxiliary part of that apparatus. Members organized ceaseless letter-writing campaigns, and *The Irish People* regularly published the names and addresses of IRA prisoners, encouraging readers to send notes of support. In later years, NORAID would organize tours to Northern

Ireland, where members would often stay and live for a time with prisoners' families. Much of the group's purpose, as publicly stated, was to collect money and goods to support the families of imprisoned IRA men in Ireland. Far from being an invented cover, following internment in 1971, that need became quite real: more than half of Andersonstown men were interned at some stage, leaving entire families with unreliable streams of income and unpredictable futures. In the claustrophobia of Northern Ireland's violence, many families inevitably dealt with at least one member in prison. The debacle became communal experience: making the long treks to jail for visits, collecting donations, passing news back and forth between prisoners and respective jails, to keep the IRA's network of communications running. The *Andersonstown News* became its own de facto notice board, smuggled into prison with messages of solidarity from the outside.

The plight of the Republican prisoner became a cause célèbre, tangible evidence of the discrimination and bias the British ruling class had wrought on Irish residents almost entirely in the North. Statistics did little to counter those concerns; despite the equally brutal violence committed by Loyalist paramilitary groups, it was Irish Republicans who made up the vast majority of wartime prisoners in the early 1970s, their cages becoming like dog whistles for nationalist politicians and IRA supporters — Long Kesh, Portlaoise, and Mountjoy prisons became their own shorthand for the Republican cause. Andersonstown and neighborhoods like it responded in kind, organizing marches against the internment and imprisonment of Republican volunteers.

For the girls in Armagh Gaol, no amount of camaraderie could dull the horror of what was happening outside. Rumors of an assassination campaign ricocheted around Andersonstown, with fears that Loyalist paramilitaries from Lisburn would enter the Catholic ghetto to conduct sectarian killings. Parking restrictions went into place along the Lower Falls, to deter the placement of car bombs near pubs. Two members of the security forces were accused of shooting a young man in the back as he ran through Andersonstown. Other British regiments like the Scots Guards and the Queen's Own Highlanders were deployed to the neighborhood and embarked on a brutal turn. Among other things, they were accused of beating and interrogating children and teenagers.

Most of the women in Armagh had been drawn to the IRA's cause of their own volition, but by virtue of Ireland's conflict and its intimate connections, nearly all had boyfriends, fathers, husbands, or brothers who carried the same banner. The group of them watched in terror as a fire tore through the cells of Long Kesh, a men's prison where many had loved ones behind bars. Not long after, the women of Armagh staged their own riot, taking the prison's staff hostage and retreating to a top floor with food and water. They unfurled a banner outside the jail's walls, advertising its dismal conditions. A priest would later serve as mediator, and the riot ended without incident; the only change was that doors were once again put back on the girls' cells.

Despite the dynamics outside the prison, the respective groups got on well enough inside. Geraldine and her fellow Republican inmates were fascinated when Loyalist prisoners eventually arrived to Armagh Gaol. Accused of a particularly brutal murder, they were covered in tattoos — the Republican girls had never before seen such women. For the most part, the groups left each other alone.

Certain mornings, though, haunted the wing, and they were those mornings that Father Raymond Murray, the jail's chaplain, arrived and called one of them out for a talk. Such a summons was never good, and his arrival alone was enough to telegraph that something tragic had happened to a loved one on the outside. The otherwise rowdy wing would fall silent, the girls speaking in hushed tones. Most days, the churn of A Wing could keep the looming sense of helplessness at bay. Not so, on the days Father Murray arrived. The girls retreated into themselves, murmuring prayers. Those were the sort of mornings that left them all in fear, and as the decade wore on, Father Murray seemed to arrive on such macabre errands more and more often. For most of them inside, the bad news seemed to just be a matter of time.

Geraldine, of course, wasn't the only Crawford to be drawn to the Republican cause. Laura, her older sister, also threw herself into work for Sinn Fein. It was the start of a new generation of Republicanism, which, up to the Troubles, had largely been a family affair. The vast majority of the Official IRA had come from the same generational stock — families who for years had volunteered to fight, fathers who passed the mission to sons, who passed it on to theirs. But in the 1970s, that changed. Neighborhoods like Andersonstown were full of sisters like the Crawfords, a new era of volunteers who became the first in their families to pick up the Republican cause. There was a whole spectrum from which to do so. Geraldine gravitated toward the IRA, but Laura leaned toward the softer power of politics and journalism, writing for *An Phoblacht,* the preeminent Republican newspaper, and volunteering for Sinn Fein.

That's what Geraldine thought, at least — it was she who had enlisted with the cause's more militant ends, an endeavor about which the sisters spoke little. In West Belfast, though, some realities speak for themselves. Around the same time Geraldine went to prison, her mother, Brigid Crawford, was vacuuming the house when she made a disconcerting discovery: there, in Laura's room, was a blond wig.

PART V

THE
SECRET
ARMY

CHAPTER 28

"WE ARE ALL LOYAL AMERICANS"

THE BANNER AT the Presidential, a large hotel on Philadelphia's City Line Avenue, said it all: WELCOME HOME, DAN CAHALANE!

The year 1973 had been a long one for Cahalane, first in Holmesburg Prison, then farther from the city, in Berks County Prison, and he had felt every minute. The prosecutors, Alvey and Merkle, had been right, that Cahalane had much to lose. But they had been wrong in thinking the stakes would convince him to talk. Instead, Cahalane declined their offer of immunity, refused to cooperate and was jailed for contempt of court. For six months, he was kept from his work, his wife, and his children. Berks County, where he had spent most of that time, was more than an hour from Philly and difficult to reach on public transit. It made their regular visits seem even farther away.

Jail had also kept Cahalane from his other great priority: NORAID. The fact seemed to frustrate him nearly as much as other, more tender estrangements. He spread out his limited ration of prison visits between family and NORAID colleagues, who despite the obvious legal danger, had carried on in Cahalane's absence. Frustrated at jail's monotony, Cahalane read the same books over and over, and tore through local newspapers like Philadelphia's *Evening Bulletin*. He looked forward to daily walks between meals and furiously wrote letters back and forth to friends and family. They kept Cahalane updated as best they could, sneaking him copies of NORAID newsletters and other Republican literature.

"I got a copy of *The Irish People*," he wrote to his daughter, not long after he was transferred from Holmesburg to Berks County. The issue shipped to him clandestinely by "the Sister" — the nun who ran the NORAID-affiliated newspaper in New York — made it through the jail censors and was good. The issue had moved him — inside was a list of interned Irishmen and women, and Cahalane recognized many of the names.

"Imagine all the poor guys and girls in jail over there," he wrote. "My heart bleeds for them."

This, as Cahalane was facing his own legal troubles. Despite Alvey's and Merkle's hopes, he had never given their immunity offer even the briefest of considerations. Across two full days of testimony, Cahalane said nothing more than his scripted, stubborn citation: *I respectfully decline to answer that question on the advice of my counsel because the answer might tend to incriminate me.* And, just like the men in Fort Worth, Cahalane had landed in the same place: behind bars, held in contempt, and a national rallying point for NORAID.

"We would be well off in this country in using the forces of law and order to snuff out abuses of the courts, and not using them to persecute those fighting for freedom and justice like Dan Cahalane," said Paul O'Dwyer, one of NORAID's lawyers who spoke on behalf of Cahalane. "If this man is guilty of a crime, then charge him before a jury of his peers. It is not right to send him to prison without a fair trial."

It was a strange space for Cahalane, who eschewed the spotlight. By the summer of 1974, his face was splashed across national Irish-American newspapers as a reluctant martyr. "A sense of outrage pervades the Irish community here," a front-page story in *The Irish People* said, next to Cahalane's US Army portrait from the 1950s. As far as NORAID and Irish America was concerned, Dan Cahalane's imprisonment wasn't so different from the imprisonment and internment of so many in West Belfast and Derry. Cahalane's supporters quickly established a legal defense fund, which was used to offset his expenses and keep Jane and his children afloat while he was away.

Much of that hardship, though, was a distant memory that night at the Presidential, on City Line Avenue. The mood was buoyant. Just like the men in Fort Worth, Cahalane had finally been released without charge, and he returned to Philadelphia a hero. In an event billed as the Philadelphia Freedom Dinner, NORAID celebrated his return. If the threat of legal jeopardy concerned anyone, one wouldn't know it from the packed hall. The group that gathered was full of familiar faces. Frank Durkan, the NORAID lawyer hired by Michael Flannery, made the trip down from New York. Father Sean McManus was there too, the divisive, exiled preacher who had spoken at the Irish Center that night so many months ago.

Cahalane, looser and more emotive than usual, eventually took to the podium. He had always considered himself a dedicated patriot, both to his ancestral home and his adopted one. For the rest of his life, he would find it hard to disentangle his view of America — a land of freedom, which had conquered the same British imperialists two centuries before — from his loyalty to Ireland. Philadelphia had trademarked the exact sort of self-determined rebellion in which the Irish had long taken part. The dissonance would trouble Cahalane for the rest of his life. By the US government's standards, his Americanness and his Irishness seemed criminally at odds.

"The American nation has nothing to fear from Irish Northern Aid," Cahalane told the crowd that night. "We are all loyal Americans."

Of that contingent, Cahalane took special care to note two: Neil Byrne and Dan Duffy. The pair of them had kept Philadelphia's NORAID apparatus operating in Cahalane's absence, he said, even as they faced the same legal pressures and constant threat of jail. Led by Cahalane, the room applauded them.

It was a triumphant return. They danced and celebrated, Cahalane's children zipping in and out of photographs, music floating through the hall. The city's Irish, it seemed, had stared down the American justice system and won. Asked by a reporter to pose for a photograph, Cahalane gave a sly grin. "The FBI probably could give you one quicker," he said.

The morning, though, would bring more sinister questions. Danny Cahalane had returned a hero. But who else might Alvey and Merkle pressure? And how sure could they all be, that everyone would carry the torch like Danny?

After all, he made clear that night at the Presidential that the preceding months had changed little. When the aforementioned journalist questioned whether the time in prison had made him more determined, Cahalane cut the man off. "Absolutely," he said. "With more fervor than before."

Despite the celebratory theme of Dan Cahalane's return, Irish America was still very much in the woods. And it wasn't just legal issues that were dividing them. Questions of policy, long-term solutions, and the IRA's strategy were beginning to create fissures within NORAID.

The Provos arrived to 1975 low on men and in deep need of a reset, political and operationally. Over Christmastime 1974, they declared a ceasefire, establishing what would become a pattern over the long arc of the Troubles. Secretly, Unionists arranged official contacts with IRA leadership, to discuss the prospects for peace. The pause in hostilities lasted through much of 1975 before dissolving into sectarian violence and distrust.

In practice, the 1975 ceasefire was a disaster for Provo leadership. Their discussions with Unionists hurt their credibility with the rank and file and left them with little to show for the trouble — hard truths that they would later acknowledge nearly snuffed out the IRA. In theory, though, the debacle would serve as a cautionary starting point, as the IRA dabbled in and out of ceasefires and peace talks for decades.

Such political experiments, though, cleaved the movement, both in Ireland and in Irish America. Amid the confusion over the ceasefire and a spate of IRA bombings, NORAID and the IRA's American auxiliary found it more difficult to recruit believers; among two of the most lethal blows were an IRA bomb in London that severely injured an Irish-American lawyer from Philadelphia, and a botched IRA bomb that nearly killed — but missed — Caroline Kennedy, the daughter of Irish America's patron and presidential saint, John F. Kennedy. Those incidents were promptly added to the growing list that US authorities trotted out to dissuade Irish Americans from supporting NORAID.

It was a shift that even the most dedicated NORAID ideologues couldn't ignore. In the months following their brawl with the grand jury, Philadelphia's Irish helped start the Irish National Caucus, a lobbying front headquartered in Washington to promote Irish reunification. In theory, it was a new organization built to create a more legitimate political movement in America and create inroads with US lawmakers, since NORAID had become too controversial for most mainstream American politicians to touch. In practice, though, the Irish National Caucus included most of the same NORAID and Clan-na-Gael voices that had gotten the organization into trouble in the first place. Among the Caucus's executive board were Father Sean McManus, the expat Baltimore priest; Brendan McCusker, an old friend of Neil Byrne and Vince Conlon's in Clan-na-Gael; and Danny Cahalane. The group's mission, decided at a meeting in New York, was to "establish Irish Freedom as an American moral issue."

Was it naivety, principle, or a bit of both that kept them all working, even as the threat of prison loomed? Just because Dan Cahalane had been released didn't mean that the danger was gone; the threat from a grand jury doesn't go away just because the panel is dismissed. Prosecutors have time afterward to decide what they might do, in order to bring a case. The release of Danny Cahalane and the Fort Worth Five hadn't placated Brandon Alvey and Bob Merkle, and it certainly hadn't placated the British investigators who were pressuring them. Contrary to what the celebrations may have suggested in Philadelphia, the case against NORAID was still very much alive. And more than that, what Danny Cahalane might not have known, even as he had toasted freedom in the Presidential Hotel, was that the tight-knit circle around him was actually full of holes.

CHAPTER 29

THE TOUT

AFTER CAHALANE'S RELEASE, 1974 had been relatively quiet, lulling them all into a false sense of security. But a looming betrayal would soon change all of that. John Casey, the officer with the Yonkers NORAID chapter and reluctant member of Marty Lyons's inner circle, never really wanted to be a gunrunner; his interest in NORAID was limited to family history and a sense of injustice. It was Frank Grady, Casey's colleague in the plumbers' union, who first pushed Casey into NORAID's darker missions.

The stakes of this had been easy to ignore, until federal agents came knocking. Casey had refused to cooperate at first, but facing serious prison time and a federal investigation, he committed the exact sort of betrayal NORAID had long feared. Just as the legal heat seemed to be quieting, John Casey — riddled with fear of retaliation from Marty Lyons — became a federal informant.

Despite his junior status among Marty Lyons's inner circle, Casey became the NORAID Rosetta Stone that Brandon Alvey and Bob Merkle had been looking for — a "tout," in the Irish slang, who betrayed his coconspirators by cooperating with law enforcement. In pages and pages of testimony, Casey walked them through NORAID's inner workings in New York, and the group's various smuggling operations through the warehouse and the docks. There were the M-1 carbines, purchased at the bait shop. The late-night trips, dropping crates of weapons. The transfers, using the names and identities of dead Irishmen. The boxes of pistols and the statements from Marty Lyons and Frank Grady, constantly on the hunt for more firepower.

Casey's cooperation was a coup for Alvey and Merkle, but they wasted little time enjoying the spoils. His cooperation came as the prosecutors unveiled a case against Frank Grady, who was charged in the spring of 1975 relating to the weapons he and Casey had purchased from the J&J bait shop, all those years ago. It was concerning timing for plenty of reasons, but it was especially worrying for Philadelphia.

Since the grand jury debacles of 1973, the criminal cases against the Philly men seemed to have sat on ice, fading slowly into obscurity as the statute of limitations approached. The case against Grady, unveiled just days before the grand jury would have expired, left little doubt: if Grady could still be charged, it meant the Philadelphia case could be, too.

There was even more reason to be worried, though the Philadelphia cell may not have realized it at the time. The Grady case was a victory for American and British investigators, but it fell short in a significant way: Grady was only charged with illegal exportation, and falsely filling out firearms forms at the bait shop in Yonkers — the instance in which John Casey helped file false transfer forms with the names of dead Irishmen. The case did little to directly tie those weapons to violent incidents in Northern Ireland, and it failed to prove the British line: that American guns, funded by NORAID, were the Provos' main source of firepower.

That proof actually lay in the Philadelphia case, which British investigators had been increasingly pressuring their American counterparts to charge alongside Grady's. It was a watershed investigation, one that built on years of collaboration between British and American law enforcement, and one that British authorities viewed as the most important to date in their fight against NORAID. Investigators from the Royal Ulster Constabulary even began sharing sensitive court documents from Belfast with Brandon Alvey and Bob Merkle, and were offering something that had never before been attempted: sending the recovered IRA guns *back* to America, to use as evidence in the courtroom.

"It is one of the first cases where some of the guns which the men are alleged to have exported have been linked directly to terrorist activities in Northern Ireland," one British officer wrote in an internal letter about the Philadelphia case. "The case of the Philadelphia Five is by far the most important of the gunrunning cases so far."

For British and Northern Irish investigators, such sobering evidence would settle, once and for all, the role of Irish America in the Troubles. Reminders of

Irish America's lethal impact played out every day on the streets of Belfast and Derry, but there was something more intimate, and horrifying, about seeing those tallies laid out one by one, every bullet wound and body that was felled by an American trigger.

Among them was a curious toddler named Andrew Fennel who had walked outside his family home in Belfast, wandering near the cars that were parked on the street. There, underneath one of them, the boy had found a Magnum handgun—bought in the States, investigators would later determine—and pressed the trigger. It was a passing bread man who found him, collecting his small bloodied body and rushing him to Royal Victoria Hospital. Whether the gun had been dropped there or stashed, no one could know. But at three years old, a little boy shot himself in the head with an American gun on a Belfast street.

CHAPTER 30

"THE POLITICAL HORNET'S NEST"

IT WOULD HAVE been delicate, under any circumstances, for American investigators to join forces with a foreign government to build and prosecute a domestic case. But in the fragile diplomatic balance between America, Ireland, and Great Britain, such a collaboration threatened political disaster. American investigators, wary of public perception and the Irish-American voting bloc, would resent appearing as if they were doing Great Britain's bidding. British investigators, meanwhile, needed to be sure that ham-handed American investigators didn't upset their own delicate investigations in Northern Ireland. And, perhaps most importantly, the Brits needed American investigators to believe that the fight against NORAID had been *their* idea, not simply a favor to the Crown.

"Although we should not wish to embarrass the US authorities by dwelling on this in public, there was extensive cooperation between the UK and US authorities on the preparation of evidence for the 'Philadelphia Five' trial," one internal British memo wrote about the case.

In a world of such subtleties, there was perhaps no less subtle man than Bob Merkle, and no more careless than Brandon Alvey, who was known to kick his feet on his desk, explode in anger when couriers dropped messages to his door, and, occasionally, drunkenly flip off of his chair. Among colleagues, it was common knowledge that any important conversation with Alvey had to happen before lunchtime, when he traditionally began drinking. Merkle, meanwhile, would be remembered for a large safe he kept in his office, into which he would shove paperwork with which he didn't want to be bothered.

By the mid-1970s, the political and legal challenges of pursuing NORAID had become clear, and the Justice Department was split mostly into two camps.

The first, more conservative group was wary of a full frontal assault on NORAID as an organization, and had often blocked attempts to more forcefully pursue criminal charges against the group. Instead, that contingent advocated for end-around solutions like charging NORAID members with gunrunning, or prioritizing the FBI's probe of the Foreign Agents Registration Act.

The second camp wanted to bring the full weight of the US Justice Department against NORAID. This group included young, ambitious prosecutors like Merkle, who cared little for the political hazards of the moment. NORAID, in Bob Merkle's mind, simply needed to be shut down by the Justice Department.

In theory, Merkle was the dream ally for British and Northern Irish investigators, a young, aggressive lawyer whose ambitions aligned with theirs. In political practice, though — and in a pattern that would come to define Merkle's life and career — he was a bull in a very expensive diplomatic china shop. There were few subtleties of the NORAID problem that couldn't be fixed with some rough justice in a courtroom, Merkle felt, and he set about constructing his legal assaults with little regard for any sensitivities he might be violating on the other side of the ocean. One British diplomat in Washington, tasked with coordinating communications between the two legal systems, put it bluntly: Merkle, he wrote back to Belfast, should be watched — because his ambitious plans to shut down NORAID might be more of a problem than a solution.

"He seems, incidentally, oblivious," the man wrote, "of the political hornet's nest that this would undoubtedly stir up."

In December 1975, there was a sudden flurry of significant, pre-holiday developments. Internment, the detention policy that had brought grief and havoc to Northern Ireland's nationalist ghettos since 1971, was formally ended, and the last of the prisoners detained under the policy were freed from jail. The numbers would stand for themselves: of nearly two thousand people who were interned, 1,874 were Catholic. The end of internment was celebrated in Irish-American communities, but it also sparked great fear. In the end of internment, the

British lost one of their most unchecked strategies for combatting the IRA. Perhaps, Irish America feared, losing it would spur British and American investigators to pursue NORAID more aggressively as a means of cracking down on the Provos. Indeed, this was underscored when British officials directly targeted NORAID in public statements. "Those who subscribe to the Irish Northern Aid Committee…are not financing the welfare of the Irish people, as they might delude themselves," Harold Wilson, the British prime minister, told a room full of American correspondents at a dinner in London that December. "They're financing murder."

The second development — perhaps connected to the first, or simply an accident of timing — was a visit to Washington, DC, by two investigators from the Royal Ulster Constabulary. They went to meet with Brandon Alvey and Bob Merkle with a very specific goal in mind: to outline what an American prosecution of the Philadelphia network might look like, and to determine how evidence from Northern Ireland could be used against the Philadelphia men in American courts.

It was critical timing, for both the British and the Americans. Alvey and Merkle had finally drafted a formal indictment in the Philadelphia case, in which they would accuse and charge the Philadelphia men with gunrunning to the IRA. The pair were awaiting word from the Justice Department higher-ups as to whether they would approve the case.

But as promising as this development was for British interests, the ensuing conversation with Alvey and Merkle that winter was challenging and worrying. The pair seemed confused, one British investigator wrote, about how many different agencies existed in Northern Ireland, and how to sort through the available evidence from both the British Army and the Royal Ulster Constabulary. More than that, Merkle and Alvey hoped to use confidential evidence from British courts to prove their case against the Philadelphia men and show their connections to the IRA — a tactic that would reveal some of the most sensitive intelligence collected by police officers in Northern Ireland. The suggestion rattled investigators within the RUC, who impressed upon Alvey and Merkle just how delicate such information was — and just how dangerous such revelations could be for British soldiers and police in Belfast. There was so much concern among the RUC, indeed, that the visitors told Alvey and Merkle that they would not permit their officers to testify in open court with their real names, and, further, would require security details and disguises, even in Philadelphia, far from the dangers of Northern Ireland.

Among the most significant and concerning proposals was that the seized Philadelphia guns be returned to America, something that Alvey and Merkle hoped would serve as both useful propaganda in the US media and convincing evidence for a jury. But the British investigators feared the outcome if the Philly men were acquitted. Could the guns be returned to Danny Cahalane and his men — and sent on again to the Provos?

After a long dialogue, however, the American and Northern Irish officials ended their visit optimistic. Alvey and Merkle, satisfied with the security requirements, believed they had all the evidence they needed to reincarnate the Philadelphia case. And no, they promised the RUC men, there was no way the weapons could possibly be returned to the Philly cell, even if the men were acquitted — more than that, Alvey and Merkle would personally ensure the guns were looked after.

Their visitors, too, had reason to feel upbeat. On the last day of the trip, just before Christmas 1975, the Belfast investigators heard important news. "We were informed," one of them wrote, in an after-report of their American journey, "that the Attorney General had consented to the indictment."

The case had more potential than the British authorities may have even realized at the time. Alvey and Merkle had unearthed a significant piece of information. One of the Philadelphia men — a member of the same group that was subpoenaed to appear before the panel two years before — had once been an informant for the FBI.

CHAPTER 31

PH T-1

THE RADIO SEGMENT might've gone unnoticed on any other day, white noise in the background of a busy holiday season. It was three days before Christmas, and Dan Duffy — an AM radio junkie who nearly four years prior had caught the news about Bloody Sunday live in the car with his family — might well have been listening now alongside his teenage daughter, had he not been in and out of shops, running holiday errands with his wife.

It was a disorienting December, marked by a mix of good and bad news. In Philadelphia, the Irish neighborhoods held dances and parties, and the union halls buzzed with fundraisers and events. Lights dotted the city's parkway, a skating rink bustled outside City Hall, and Wanamaker's, the iconic department store in the city's heart, put on its annual light show. An unexpected snowfall would blanket the city on Christmas Day. But in Belfast and Derry, the disastrous end of the IRA's ceasefire had ushered in a new round of sectarian attacks. Among them, a young mother was shot and killed while putting up Christmas decorations.

These harsh realities were never far from the minds of Philadelphia's Irish, who were still on edge following Grady's indictment in New York. It had been nearly two years since the grand jury flipped the community on its head, and each day without an indictment seemed to bring just the slightest sigh of relief.

But now, just before Christmas Eve, a news announcer sent a breaking bulletin across the airwaves: Five Irish Americans, the program announcer said, were indicted in Philadelphia after a yearslong investigation. The crime, he said, was straightforward: sending hundreds of guns to the IRA.

Duffy's daughter was out with friends when she heard the news broadcast on the radio, so surreal it made her heart stop. Still, she knew it was no mistake. One of the accused, she was certain, was her father.

It was an inevitable ending in many ways, telegraphed for years by the shadow of federal inquiry that had hung over the city and its suburbs. The case in New York against Frank Grady was an ominous sign of things to come. Of course Brandon Alvey and Bob Merkle would come for Philadelphia; of course it would be soon; and of course it would be sweeping.

Five of them, charged with trafficking hundreds of rifles to the IRA: Danny Cahalane, Dan Duffy, Neil Byrne, Vincent Conlon, and a fifth man, Thomas Regan, who, like Conlon, had long ago returned to Ireland. These principal defendants would come to be known as the Philadelphia Five. An even larger group were named as unindicted coconspirators, including Eugene Marley, Marty Lyons, Marjorie Palace, and Cahalane's friend Bill Corry. Beginning in August 1970, prosecutors asserted, the men had acted as agents of the IRA, conspiring with gun dealers to send rifles and bullets to Northern Ireland. They had been a key supplier of a sinister weapon of choice with which the Troubles were now associated: the ArmaLite.

The timing of the charges was confounding: it was December 22, and the banks were preparing to close for the holiday. The possibility of obtaining cash bail was slim, and government prosecutors argued the men ought to be detained; they were affiliated with an organization that had a history of transatlantic crime and fugitive smuggling. For Philly's Irish, the maneuver was designed to be punitive: Byrne may have been a bachelor, but Daniel Duffy and Danny Cahalane both had young children and families at home, all prepared to celebrate Christmas. Now they would spend it scrambling for collateral in the hopes of staying together. It was an aggressive legal move from Alvey and Merkle that baffled even the case judge, who had ordered Duffy and Cahalane to spend Christmas at home. Byrne was released too, his bail money fronted by NORAID. All of the men were ordered to turn in their passports, and were due back in court on New Year's Eve, to be arraigned.

It was a case, prosecutors said, that was connected to a larger investigation probing the IRA in America, including criminal cases in Baltimore and Frank Grady's in New York. But there were two serious distinctions that set the Philadelphia case apart. The charges were not just related to guns; instead, there was an additional accusation, one that British investigators had hoped for years to have declared in an American court. The Philadelphia men were charged with acting as agents of the IRA, an allegation that if proved, would directly link NORAID with the Provos.

The second: the charges were not solely based on American evidence. Instead, the indictment listed out pages of specific serial numbers and linked them to the guns recovered in Northern Ireland. In a chilling degree of detail, the prosecutors laid out the NORAID-linked American trail quite clearly. Prosecutors could connect each of their names with a serial number, and provide a date on which the weapon had turned up in Belfast or Derry. In many cases, they could describe the specific circumstances under which the gun had been seized — and the lives changed, in the process.

In the court of public opinion, the men struck a bizarre image. Here, prosecutors alleged, were some of the Provisional IRA's key arms dealers, whose guns had left a bloody trail through Northern Ireland. It was an odd accusation to drape over these bookish suburban men. They could have been anyone sitting at that defendant's table, staring emotionless as the charges against them were read in court. As one writer said of the men's arraignment, they looked ordinary and harmless; in fact, Danny Cahalane, accused as one of the most successful IRA gunrunners in America, almost looked boring.

The fiercely secretive Republican movement did not take kindly to informers. Indeed, the Provisional IRA created its own internal group, known as the "Unknowns," who killed people they believed were guilty of this very crime. It would become one of the most notorious chapters of the Troubles, one that still, more than five decades later, tears open wounds in Northern Ireland.

It wasn't just the streets of West Belfast, though, where that paranoia festered. Irish America carried it, too. The worries would bear out with John Casey's betrayal in New York. But the truth was, NORAID and Clan-na-Gael were riddled with informants as early as the 1960s. The information those individuals provided to authorities was usually innocuous — reports on demonstrations or protest marches, information that could have been gleaned from any public observer. But the reports — filed in FBI papers beginning in the 1960s — are more significant for their implications than their contents: Irish Philadelphia, it turns out, was deeply divided over the direction of the IRA, so much so that many felt comfortable enough to talk to US authorities about it.

At the time, the Official IRA was firmly in control of the group's direction, and whispers of more radical cliques were the exception rather than the norm. Irish America had, to that point, operated in alignment with the Officials, without much interference from US authorities; it's natural to think that as Vince Conlon oriented Irish America in a more radical direction, Irish-American supporters preferred the status quo, and perhaps saw such changes as a step too far.

But it's hard to ever know, really, what makes someone turn. Sometimes it's money, which the government can — and often does — offer. Sometimes it's self-protection and fear, of the type that drove John Casey to the ATF; faced with one's own stiff sentence, a person might rather spill what they know and cut a deal. Perhaps rarer are the true believers, those who have become so disillusioned with the people around them that they feel as if informing, somehow, is the more righteous choice. Others still may not even know that the government ever considered them an informant — what one man views as a casual conversation could, in fact, be considered much more serious by the FBI. In such gray areas, it's impossible — especially decades after the fact — to know certain truths.

But buried in an internal Justice Department document is one. At some point in the 1960s, until 1971, Daniel Duffy — one of the accused Philly Five — was listed by the FBI as one of its confidential informants.

There had always been a schism between Irish America and the more radical factions of Irish nationalists, and it has mostly come down to political leanings. It was the same ideological gap that dogged Bernadette Devlin during her visits to the States, and caused early friction over Irish support for causes like Black liberation and Palestinian autonomy. Irish Americans radicalized in America simply weren't as extreme as many born-and-bred Irish Republicans, and many viewed the movement's tilt toward social justice and Marxism with unease, at best, and vitriol, at worst.

Dan Duffy was one of them and made little secret of it. The ideological division had pushed him to early clashes with Vince Conlon, whom Duffy at one time believed represented a faction of IRA supporters who were communists. The thinking picked up a common thread used to criticize some Irish-American activists, lumping them in with militant, far-left groups. It was a division that was established as early as 1960, when Duffy appears to have first come into contact with FBI agents. The information the Justice Department says Duffy provided was of relatively low value, and publicly available — agents claimed Duffy told them about a high-profile visit from Cathal Goulding, then chief of staff of the Official IRA. It was a far different, relatively benign time for the army; Goulding was years away from his falling-out with Conlon and the Provos, and the Troubles were not even yet a concept. But it *was* a kinetic time for Philadelphia's Irish, right as Conlon and Byrne reincarnated Clan-na-Gael and headquartered the fledgling group out of the city's various Irish clubs. Agitators with a singular mission, to reinvigorate the IRA's arms supply, the pair were divisive figures who played various factions of the city's diaspora against one another, and frequently ran afoul of Philadelphia's benevolent Irish societies, where Dan Duffy was a member at the time. A man mostly matching his description, known as PH T-1 in the FBI's documents, shows a clear distaste for Conlon and Neil Byrne, describing them as self-aggrandizing hard-liners.

"He described these individuals as hard-core diehards who were pushing the CNG for their own personal glorification," an FBI report from the 1960s says. "PH T-1 advised that the majority of Irish in the Philadelphia area did not hold them in high regard and were not supporting their aims and purposes."

Indeed, Duffy was hardly the only person with whom the bureau claimed to be talking. In its own documents, the FBI traced its interactions with a web of confidential informants within Philadelphia's Irish community, though it's nearly impossible to know how confidential or informative those sources were, or if the people listed ever considered themselves informants; Duffy, after all, would talk about Irish issues with just about anyone who would listen. Most of the FBI's listed informants in Philadelphia were identified in varying degrees of detail, referred to by code names, and most dipped in and out of usefulness until their relationships with the feds eventually fizzled.

According to the Justice Department, its relationship with Dan Duffy ended in 1971, the last time he had any contact with FBI agents — significantly also just before Bloody Sunday, the tragedy that pushed him to become more involved with NORAID's inner circle. There is no evidence that a relationship continued after that time, that Duffy ever provided anything of criminal value to the Justice Department, or that Duffy turned on his friends during the trial.

People change; ideologies change. And interestingly, even in 1965, PH T-1 held the line when asked if he would say anything about guns or money in Irish America. Whether or not he even knew about any gun trafficking at the time isn't clear, but it was clear to the FBI: PH T-1, an agent wrote, "has no information concerning money or any other aid being furnished to the IRA."

Now Dan Duffy faced a stark choice.

The federal indictment spelled out in painstaking detail every name attached to every serial number in Philadelphia — and Danny Cahalane, Vincent Conlon, and Neil Byrne were all over the document. One name, though, was missing. Duffy, long irritated by what he saw as the men's naive insistence in signing their own names, had never used his real identity when he signed for a weapon; he used only fake names, usually from dead Irishmen. Duffy was tied to the conspiracy, but as far as investigators could say, he had never sent an ArmaLite to the Provos.

"It's a relief to me," Duffy growled to the press, after the charges were filed. "There have been men following me around, taping conversations and I don't know what else."

But what now? For years, NORAID had pledged to represent any of their members who were ever pulled into court over the group's activities, and that offer extended to Philadelphia. Duffy, though, was in a strange position. He could likely get out of the charges against him, but it would mean having to distance himself from the other men on trial, and NORAID in general — and it would also require lying, claiming he had never bought a gun for the Provos and that his affiliation with the group was a mistake. It was a poisonous proposal, one that Duffy knew would risk isolating him from the Irish community, tarring him as undedicated or worse. But he had children and a wife.

Facing the threat of prison, Duffy got his own lawyer and agreed to the man's defense strategy: Duffy needed to distance himself from Cahalane and Byrne. It would be an uphill battle, the man warned him, but Duffy ought to fight for a severed case, or at least claim that he had never purchased a gun for the IRA.

"He's a pacifist," a friend said of Duffy at the time to the newspapers. "He's been raising money for a Catholic glass factory in Derry. Based on a lot of knowledge, Dan Duffy has never been involved in anything illicit."

Not everyone had such harmless views of Duffy, though. Someone, clearly, was watching and didn't like what they saw.

Around the time of the indictment, Duffy's teenage daughter found a blank envelope stuffed in their mailbox. Inside was a note, with no return address. "You are brave enough to send the guns to kill others but not brave enough to stand up and do battle yourself," the note said. Tucked inside the fold of the envelope was a bullet, with a chilling message: ***The next one is for you.***

Dan Duffy perhaps never was a productive informant. But in one last ironic turn, he *had* actually given Brandon Alvey and Bob Merkle everything they needed to close the case against the Philadelphia Five. He just wasn't the one who told them.

Instead, in Duffy's ham-handed eagerness to buy weapons, he had pursued that strange, doomed arrangement with John Nigro, the city hustler from whom he had tried to buy rocket launchers back in the fall of 1972. The arrangement had, like so many others, fallen apart, something Duffy and the NORAID men attributed to the sorts of seedy characters one tends to find in gunrunning.

Nigro's disappearance, though, was far from innocuous. What Duffy didn't know was that in addition to moonlighting as a gun dealer, John Nigro had another hustle on the side. And unbeknownst to Duffy, Cahalane, or Byrne, as soon as they called asking about guns, John Nigro turned straight around and made his own call: to his handler. Because for years, as it turns out, John Nigro was an informant for the ATF.

CHAPTER 32

"THE BITTERNESS OF CENTURIES"

AT THE NORAID event, inside the gymnasium of Philadelphia's Incarnation Parochial School, there was no hint that the city's Irish were facing their darkest moment. Just days before, the group inside was accused of one of the biggest gun-trafficking heists to one of the most notoriously violent guerrilla organizations in contemporary history, but on this evening, lively Irish jigs and reels lilted through the packed hall. NORAID members of all ages pulled themselves off chairs to dance. Some wore traditional Irish costumes, others pumped accordions and banjos. It certainly didn't look like a room under siege.

If the indictment was meant to spook Philly's NORAID faithful, it had failed. Just days after the indictment was revealed, they all arrived to the school gymnasium — two hundred people at $2 a piece for entry — and bought up souvenir bookmarks, bumper stickers, posters, and records of Irish rebel songs. Much of the money was earmarked for Cahalane's and Byrne's upcoming legal battle.

If Cahalane himself was on edge, he didn't show it. He arrived in good spirits, NORAID's embattled, bookish marshal. Affable and pleased with the turnout, he bounced from table to table, shaking hands and greeting friends and neighbors. It was a lopsided celebration against the backdrop of the ominous battle ahead. The event itself gave mixed signals: amid the dancing and singing, posters were taped along the walls, celebrating the IRA's violent victories.

It may have been lost on diehards like Danny Cahalane, but a visiting reporter couldn't miss the strange juxtaposition. "Through history there has always been a dark side," he remarked, "to the fun-loving Irish spirit."

NORAID's Northeast and Delaware County chapters stayed firmly behind Cahalane and the other indicted men, but the case had exposed just how far those more extreme pockets had grown from more moderate, mainstream Irish-American circles, which scrambled to publicly distance themselves. A messy, public debate over NORAID and the IRA took place. In local newspapers, letters raged to the editor about the Philadelphia men. Some accused Danny Cahalane and his supporters of fueling a conflict about which they knew little. "The greatest need for Ireland is for Irishmen of goodwill, not expatriate fanatics who would try to keep alive the bitterness of centuries," wrote one angry letter. Others defended them. "Britain is not the policeman but the thug," wrote John McGee, a NORAID member who was rumored to have helped ship some of the Philly guns to his native Donegal in boxes of books.

Others dismissed the entire situation, ridiculing the arbitrary, secret codes under which Cahalane and his gang seemed to operate. "They'll trust you 100 times, but the 101st they clam up," said one passing observer. "When they start talking about this secret stuff I just leave the room."

Freed by the indictment, though, many of the city's Irish finally began to talk. In anonymous dispatches to newspapers, they spilled about the hushed meetings at Breen's, and the strange smuggling networks on the docks. Many had visited Northern Ireland and had a general inkling of what exactly the Philly men had been up to, even if they were mum on the details.

"Damned if I know how they get in there," one Philadelphia Irishman said. "I've seen ArmaLites there, but I don't know how."

Two weeks after the indictment was filed in Philadelphia, Brandon Alvey — stressed and frustrated — was headed to a meeting at the British embassy. The news wasn't good. Hardly a month had gone by since they charged the Philadelphia men, and already there were significant challenges. Now one appeared that was completely out of Alvey's and Bob Merkle's control.

By the prosecutors' standards, the trial judge to whom the case had been assigned was an unlucky draw. Judge Raymond Broderick, an affable former politician, had been appointed to a federal judgeship by President Richard Nixon five years before, and had kept a mostly low profile. But he was also an Irish Catholic, a product of Irish Philadelphia, having grown up in the city's west and attended its parochial high schools. Broderick, Alvey feared, nursed his own political sympathies for the Irish — and he crassly told the British embassy that the jurist "retains his brogue." He and Merkle were optimistic they could convict the Philadelphia men, he told his Northern Irish and British colleagues, but with Broderick at the bench, they would need all the help they could get.

"They say their money goes to widows and orphans," Alvey said at the time, underscoring just how difficult it was to track NORAID's finances. "That's what they say, and I can't prove otherwise."

Unsettled by Alvey's reports, British investigators scrambled to protect the case.

"We are very anxious that this prosecution should succeed, and that the five defendants should be convicted of all these offenses, especially that of acting as agents of the IRA," a rattled British officer wrote, after their conversation. "A conviction on the 'foreign agents' charge should clearly damage NORAID, since one of the defendants is known to be head of the Delaware [County] chapter."

Further complicating the case, Alvey realized, was the fact that its ringleader, Vince Conlon, wasn't in America at all; he was back in Ireland, having pivoted from his role as an IRA volunteer and into politics, as a representative for Sinn Fein.

The country house, set on a leafy, quiet hill in Rakeeragh — just outside Monaghan town's borders — was never still. Vince Conlon made sure of that. He was a different man now, a different soldier than he had been when he first left for Philadelphia all those years ago. And it was a different time, far different than the haphazard offensives of the border campaign in the 1950s, his last turn as a full-time IRA soldier. By 1975, Northern Ireland was irreversibly at war: nearly a thousand people had been killed in the violence of the Troubles, and there was no sign that the conflict was slowing. Conlon had brought his family back to Northern Ireland's dangerous border for plenty of reasons, and rejoining his colleagues in the Provos was one. No amount of risk would change that.

Rakeeragh was far from the fronts of Belfast and Derry, but for Conlon the location was strategic. Their home, away from the bustle of town and just a few miles from the Northern Irish border, had become a busy IRA safe house, where traveling Provos could stay for a few days on their way to operations — or hide out, in the safety of the Republic. In Rakeeragh, Provisional commanders could safely meet to plan border attacks, or store packages that needed to be moved into and out of Northern Ireland.

Marina, Vince's wife, had found a new life on the border. There were certain cold realities of being married to a rebel: the shadow of danger, the restrictions on movement, the pressure, always, to do more. She embraced the life regardless — maybe for love, maybe for her children, or because she had found her own revolutionary spirit. She stayed far from the front lines, but that didn't mean she stayed away. With Vince's fugitive status making it difficult for him to operate in Northern Ireland, it was Marina who often dealt with their cross-border responsibilities — errands as mundane as visits to the market, or as clandestine as smuggling people and things into the North. It was Marina who helped make their home a reliable, safe place for the young IRA volunteers who passed in and out, their presence as fleeting as a whiff of smoke. They used the children's bedrooms for secret meetings and war planning.

It was a ceaseless rhythm. Rare was the moment when there wasn't an extra man or more in the house. And danger made its presence known in ways large and small. The fact that Conlon was back in Ireland — and back in the fight — didn't go unnoticed; his reputation was so well known that even the IRA's gentleman's agreement with the Garda Síochána couldn't protect him from scrutiny. In police raids, officers tossed the Conlon home and seized anything that looked dangerous. (After one encounter, Conlon was so troubled that he rushed to his son's school and pulled the child out of class. The Garda had seized something important, he told the boy, and if the child was asked about it, he was to claim the contraband for himself and say he had received it from a boyhood friend.)

Such choreography was a part of daily life in Rakeeragh. One afternoon, when Conlon's son made to answer a knock at the door, he was stopped. A senior IRA man appeared next to him, leaning against the doorframe; the man was peering out the window, clutching a pistol. The children's bedrooms were regularly used for IRA meetings, full of gruff, older men and lingering cigarette smoke. At night, the boys were woken by nightmares, sure that they were under attack. "There's a bomb in the room!" Conlon's son shouted one night, half asleep, as he hammered at the bedroom door to escape. (The boy's brother, used to such fears, hardly rolled over — "Try the handle," he mused, and went back to sleep.)

Not all horrors, though, were imagined. The young men who passed into and out of the Conlons' home were drifting across a front line. Most were hardly adults, barely older than Conlon's own children. The boys arrived home from school one day to find Marina sobbing at the kitchen sink; a young IRA man who had stayed with them the night before was hunted down and killed by British soldiers.

In a war remembered for such collective, dramatic moments — Bloody Sunday, the Falls Curfew, the Battle of the Bogside — the smaller, more intimate traumas are perhaps the more enduring burden. Half a century later, Vince Conlon's son still remembers the funeral of the man who was shot and killed while staying in their home, but his most lucid memory isn't the casket, or the grief, or the heaviness of an IRA military funeral. The boy, dispatched on an errand, accidentally wandered into the morgue. Decades later, he can still see the cold slab, its hard surface covered in blood and tissue, the trappings of war that you can't take with you, when you go.

If Conlon had been more engaged on the IRA's front line, perhaps the British, Irish, or American authorities might have been able to prosecute him. But by the time the Philadelphia case was revealed, Conlon had successfully won a seat on the Monaghan County council, part of a prescient strategy by Gerry Adams and the Provos to bring political legitimacy into the Provisional movement. Given the awkward politics, there was little diplomatic energy or means to extradite Conlon, the ringleader of the entire Philadelphia operation. It was an unfortunate conclusion with which the British reluctantly agreed.

Alvey and Merkle were preparing for a long slog. The lawyers whom the Philadelphia men employed were already maneuvering to delay or dismiss the case, and they seemed uniquely well versed in the political optics associated with Irish America. It was conspiratorial, Alvey believed, but he expected the attorneys might try to delay the trial until the summer, when Queen Elizabeth was expected to visit the city. If the trial were to coincide, it would create a nightmare of publicity, protests, and security issues.

It may have sounded alarmist, but Alvey's concerns weren't so far-fetched. The visit was certainly on the minds of Irish Philadelphia, particularly the hard-liners who remained firmly behind the Philly Five as they faced trial.

"I know Dan Duffy and Cahalane and Vincent Conlon. Their activities are nothing unusual," said one of Cahalane's friends in a local newspaper, around the time the case became public. "If I were the Queen or Prince Philip, I wouldn't feel secure sitting in the middle of the Delaware — it would be damn easy to float a rowboat filled with dynamite.

"I wouldn't recommend it," the man added, as a helpful aside, "but it has possibilities."

CHAPTER 33

TROPHIES

THE ORDER CAME into Belfast in late February, trickling up to an officer in the Royal Military Police, one of the many agencies tasked with handling the rifles that authorities were seizing on the streets of Belfast. The officer, a veteran of the British Armed Forces, had been selected for an urgent mission, an assignment that was the culmination of the effort that the British and Northern Irish authorities had begun years before, when they first nudged American investigators to seriously consider charging the Philadelphia case. As a trial date neared, the group of them were preparing the dozens of Philadelphia ArmaLites and rifles to be sent back to the States as evidence.

It would be the first time such a maneuver was used in an American court, and it would require that the British officer travel to Kinnegar, an ordnance base on the far reaches of Belfast's city limits. Most of the weapons seized by British forces were stored there after being scrubbed, filed, and cataloged for criminal cases in Northern Ireland. The logistics of removing the guns from storage and preparing them for transport back to America were daunting, however — and when the officer arrived at Kinnegar that day, it was clear why he had come.

The sheer number of guns that the NORAID men had sent to Ireland was startling. Taken together, the weapons — dozens of them — stretched across the span of the war, the earliest having been seized as far back as 1971. There were Lee-Enfield long guns, M-1 carbines, sleek ArmaLites. It was a transatlantic arsenal, perhaps as chilling for what was there as what wasn't: the men, investigators now knew, had sent over hundreds of guns. Less than half had been seized. In a war of elusive truths, the pile showed one thing clearly: the Philadelphia men had made a significant impact on the Troubles, fueling a conflict from three thousand miles away.

Most of the guns at Kinnegar had already been used as evidence to prosecute dozens of IRA men and women in Belfast. Some of those defendants were convicted of simply possessing the guns. Others faced more sinister accusations, like shooting soldiers or murdering police officers. The rest of the guns were found abandoned in parking lots and backyards, their roots — and histories — a mystery.

Spoils of war, they were trophies now. The officer watched as a staffer placed small, white trigger guards on the guns. Each weapon was tagged with a small blue label, bearing a unique string of digits, the numerical fingerprint that would irrefutably connect the gun to the Philadelphia men. Packed away in large crates, there were nearly 140 guns — less than a third of what the men had purchased in the US.

It was a nerve-wracking exercise for the Northern Irish security officers, to now be sending the weapons themselves back to America. There was something more comforting about having them locked away in Belfast, never again to be in proximity to the Provos or those who supported them.

But Merkle and Alvey were adamant: the Americans needed as much and as powerful evidence as possible in order to successfully convict the Philadelphia men and prove NORAID had been supporting the IRA. The numbers and paperwork surely spoke to the scope of operations, but there was something visceral about actually seeing the piles of guns in the courtroom. It could be the difference between a conviction and an acquittal. What's more, the Americans had promised that the weapons would never be allowed to hurt anyone ever again, even if Cahalane walked free, even if the whole lot of them beat the charges. Satisfied, British authorities approved their transfer back to America.

Not long after the trip to Kinnegar, the officer boarded a plane, escorting the precious cargo across the ocean. He would chaperone the weapons to America, into the hands of Alvey, Merkle, and the ATF agents who would ensure their safekeeping. It was a strange sort of full circle, in the end — a Philly gun shop, to a freighter, to West Belfast, and then, finally, back again toward home.

CHAPTER 34

BEYOND A REASONABLE DOUBT

THAT DANNY CAHALANE, Neil Byrne, and Dan Duffy had bought the guns was clear. But what Alvey, Merkle, and the British investigators really needed was proof that people who were found with those Philadelphia guns in Belfast were convicted members of the IRA, and had used the weapons for violent assaults on the police, British soldiers, and civilians.

Officials in Belfast and London had been making the case, nearly since the Troubles had started, that the majority of the IRA's arsenal came from American hands; it seemed natural to believe that there was plenty of evidence proving the link — after all, simply being a member of the IRA was illegal in Northern Ireland, and the region's court registers were full of cases. For Merkle and Alvey, the ask was simple: just show that some of those people convicted of IRA membership in Northern Ireland had been in possession of a Philadelphia gun. It would be clear evidence for what had become the most politically important part of the Philadelphia trial: proving the NORAID men were directly sending guns to the IRA, a poisonous accusation that both British and American investigators had long leveled against the suspects, but which the officials couldn't yet prove. Given how adamant British officials had been on the matter, both in public and private conversations, Merkle and Alvey just wrote up the indictment without first collecting all of the documentary evidence from Northern Ireland, or confirming that such paperwork would meet the standards of an American court.

By springtime, the Americans found themselves with a mess.

Rather than a silver bullet, the court documents from Northern Irish and British investigators arrived very late, in a disorganized state, and below the standard of evidence of an American court. And even more troubling, the Northern Irish authorities seemed to have prosecuted few actual cases in which people with Philadelphia guns were formally convicted of membership in the IRA. Sent on an errand by Bob Merkle to find such evidence, a Northern Irish officer had arrived back troublingly empty-handed.

"In cases where the weapons were found in someone's possession, ... the person often faced more serious charges, and the IRA charges were often dropped in favor of the more serious ones, like murder, or attempted murder," a Northern Irish official wrote, not long after the Philadelphia men were indicted.

The lack of clear connections had thrown the case's most critical tenet into jeopardy. Proving the Philadelphia men had acted as agents of the IRA was nearly as important as — if not more than — proving they had sent the guns. In doing so, British and Northern Irish investigators had hungrily seen an opportunity to neutralize NORAID writ large.

Alvey and Merkle were banking — perhaps naively — on the premise that the British would provide everything they needed to prove the case's central accusation. But when pressed to back up their claims, British and Northern Irish officials balked, sometimes for lack of underlying evidence, other times because they feared the political repercussions of showing their hand. When Alvey and Merkle requested proof for a seemingly innocuous issue of verbiage showing that the IRA was a "body of insurgents," their allies in the Crown declined, fearing that any courtroom judgment on such language could help the Provos; and privately they considered pulling their support for the Philadelphia case altogether. Because of the Americans, it seemed, they were being forced to risk public statements on a group they preferred to pretend was just a collection of violent amateurs.

"The British authorities," one British officer wrote internally, "are not responsible for the way in which the United States authorities draw up indictments in the US courts."

British, Northern Irish, and American authorities were running up against the central principle of the US Department of Justice: convictions require proof beyond a reasonable doubt. Much of the Philadelphia men's gunrunning had, by 1975, become self-evident. There was ample evidence that the men had purchased the guns, ample evidence that the guns were eventually recovered in Northern Ireland, and ample evidence that the men all had ties to NORAID. But while some of these facts might have been convictable offenses in Great Britain, none of them — taken together or separately — were necessarily illegal in America, nor could they necessarily convict the men of a crime in an American federal court.

But the Philadelphia case still provided a critical forum: through it, American prosecutors could present those legal documents from Belfast courts, showing clearly how the guns purchased by the Philadelphia men had wrought death and destruction in Northern Ireland. Even if such paperwork might not lead to long sentences for Danny Cahalane and his friends, it would likely be enough to clarify for Irish America that NORAID was not, in fact, the humanitarian front that it claimed to be. This is why it became so important for those court documents from Northern Ireland to be publicly presented in American court.

It's hard to say what might have happened had those bloody details ever seen the light of day. They were meant to, of course. But like most searches for truth in the Troubles, Alvey and Merkle's seemingly straightforward errand was doomed from the start — in fact, not only would those Northern Irish court documents be tossed from the Philadelphia case, the details of American guns in Northern Ireland stayed buried for more than fifty years, outliving NORAID, all of the Philadelphia men, and even the Troubles themselves.

As the trial date of the Philadelphia Five neared, Brandon Alvey and Bob Merkle faced a serious complication. The final set of legal documents from Northern Irish and British investigators — the records showing that the Philadelphia guns had landed in the hands of the IRA — had not satisfied the prosecutor's standards. They were haphazardly arranged and difficult to follow, totaling more than a thousand pages.

The documents came from a web of institutions, from the military to the police, detailing dozens of gun seizures in the IRA strongholds of West Belfast, Derry, and along the border. They were carefully curated by Merkle and Alvey, who spent months in a back-and-forth with officials in Belfast, choreographing what documents went where. The packet of papers was meant to be the crown jewel of the Philadelphia prosecution, a testament to transatlantic cooperation and a damning, concise indictment of NORAID.

Instead, the packet was a mess. Many of the documents were incomplete or not properly labeled; some contained entire narratives, details about shootings, dark nights in West Belfast, raids in Derry backyards, and car stops, while others were half-told stories, with tantalizing details but no endings or in-betweens, glances of guns seized and forgotten, the full stories lost to bureaucracy and oversights. And the documents weren't turned over to Cahalane and Byrne's legal team until days before the trial, jeopardizing the process of discovery, a cornerstone of American jurisprudence that affords a defendant the right to examine in advance any evidence presented against him or her.

The paperwork might have been a mess, but even so, it contained details that perhaps even the Philadelphia men themselves hadn't known: the intimate mechanics on the receiving end of their operation, the conclusion of a story that started in Philadelphia and then disappeared off the New York City docks. When it was all cataloged, the scale of the operation was staggering.

There were nearly two hundred clear instances of violence connected to the Philly guns, names and dates and shootings, guns seized under various circumstances and tied to dozens of convictions, injuries, deaths and criminal indictments in West Belfast and Derry. The majority seemed to have come from police seizures, no doubt turned over during the curfews and raids of British Army and police patrols across Andersonstown and the Bogside in Derry. Eleven weapons came from the British military, picked up during active shooting engagements. The soldiers' reports were far more comprehensive, involving summary sheets and witness statements detailing the clashes and violent skirmishes that had eventually led British authorities to the guns.

It was proof, it seemed, of what the British and American authorities had been claiming for years, and what NORAID had fastidiously avoided saying publicly: the bloodshed in Northern Ireland was a direct product of American bullets and American guns, bought and paid for with American dollars, by men who were connected to NORAID.

That disorganized pile of paperwork from Belfast was actually one of the most significant legal documents of an era, one that in hindsight, might have clarified decades of rumors around American gun trafficking to the IRA. They made clear what it's taken more than half a century to say, plainly: the

Philadelphia ArmaLites were critical to the formation of the Provisional IRA, and it's hard to say what the fledgling army might've become without them.

They might not have been as polished as Merkle and Alvey preferred, but those papers proved what no court case had — and what few investigators, journalists, reconciliation panels, and prosecutors have been able to since. It showed the direct impact of American guns in Northern Ireland, the lives and people and families that the Philadelphia bullets had hit.

For prosecutors, it was clear evidence that NORAID members had been directly aiding the IRA in its campaign of violence.

But for Danny Cahalane and the other members of the Philadelphia Five — whose attorneys would eventually see the documents as part of the discovery process — those papers offered stunning evidence of their success. The papers were proof that NORAID's inner circle had been able to concretely help the IRA from three thousand miles away, proof that some in the diaspora had never forgotten the plight of their ancestral home. Far from being limited to the nationalist ghettos of Belfast and Derry, the Provisional IRA had an impressively robust American army. And for years, it turned out, they had been fighting the British without ever firing a shot themselves.

"I SHOULD BE HAPPY"

"THE IRISH REPUBLICAN Army is not on trial," Merkle said in his opening statement at the proceedings that started just before Memorial Day 1976. "Neither are the policies of Great Britain.

"This is a trial of three individuals," he continued, "who are charged by a grand jury of ladies and gentlemen from your community with violating the laws of the community. The evidence in its entirety will be overwhelming and there will be no reasonable doubt whatsoever."

Contrary to Merkle's statements, the proceedings quickly devolved into a legal circus, with Judge Raymond Broderick as a reluctant referee trying to impose order in juvenile gripes between prosecutors and defense lawyers. With its twists and turns, the trial — which would last for twenty-one days — at times felt more like a sitcom than a serious court proceeding. Lawyers threw barbs at one another, sniped about guns and morality, and endlessly interrupted each other over petty slights. The group was constantly pulled into chambers or to a sidebar, lectured by Broderick for a lack of professionalism.

Alvey and Merkle had a litany of witnesses. John Nigro, Duffy's failed gun dealer, revealed his status as an informant and spoke of his encounters with Duffy, who had said unequivocally that he was working via NORAID for the IRA — Nigro had even recorded some of their phone conversations. Also on the witness list were defected NORAID members and gun shop owners. Marjorie Palace, listed as an unindicted coconspirator, walked jurors through her dealings with Vince Conlon and the late-night gun pickups by Danny Cahalane and Neil Byrne — though conveniently, she told investigators, a flood had damaged many of her firearms records through March 1973, coincidentally covering the period of her dealings with the Philadelphia men. At one point, a NORAID lawyer from New York, Frank Durkan, interrupted from the courtroom's audience; later, the entire trial was put on hold because a years-old, pro-IRA news article had been slipped into the jury room. (The culprit was never found.) Federal agents mapped out their surveillance of the Philadelphia cell. One had hidden in the bushes outside Danny Cahalane's house; another had tailed Neil Byrne around Philly's outskirts. There was the agent who followed the men into the Irish Center that December night, another who saw them at Breen's bar, and another who had once watched them slip into Marty Lyons's apartment in New York.

There were political witnesses too, tasked with setting the stage for the IRA's bloody campaign. There was a State Department analyst who detailed the dynamics of Belfast's conflict, and a journalist who covered the war. Three security officials from Northern Ireland, having flown in from Belfast, testified about the guns and their stories. Fearing retaliatory violence, the group was placed under strict security protocols, required to wear sunglasses and civilian clothes, and stay locked in their hotels unless otherwise chaperoned to and from the courthouse.

It was those security officers who were flown in to handle the matter of the guns, detailing the Northern Irish court documents to an American jury. They were meant to clearly testify about those court documents, detailing the nearly two hundred incidents that involved the Philadelphia rifles. But the admission of third-party law enforcement evidence in American court was a tricky legal maneuver, fraught with legal challenges. Put simply, it was difficult for American prosecutors to independently verify the information contained in the British investigators' documents, when the standards were obviously very different in the midst of a war. Further complicating the matter was that the source for the documentation — the British government — was an obvious stakeholder in the proceedings. How could American prosecutors be so sure that the testimony of British police and soldiers in the Northern Irish documents was accurate? In relying on them, the American justice system perhaps unwittingly backed the British in their attacks against Irish nationalists. It was a confusing position for the Americans to take — after all, Washington had for years publicly taken pains to avoid inserting itself into the Northern Irish conflict. But if it ratified the legitimacy of those RUC and British Army documents in the Philadelphia case, was it not siding with the British? After all, if *those* documents were good enough for American courts, what separated those raids and seizures from any other instance in which the British government had justified its behavior in Northern Ireland, from the injustice of internment to the tragedy of Bloody Sunday?

Such implications were not lost on Judge Broderick, the Irish-American jurist whom Alvey — rightfully — feared would deal the case its most significant blow. As prosecutors prepared to describe the Belfast court papers, and tell the stories of the guns' recoveries in Northern Ireland, the judge stopped them.

"What I'm worried about, frankly, as the judge in this trial, is that we are getting to the point perhaps of bringing in testimony that may in some way inflame the jury," Broderick said. "I don't think those inflammations should be permitted unless they are necessary to the case."

Sufficiently agitated at the petty back-and-forth between Merkle and defense lawyers, Broderick issued a ruling that would cloud forever the role of Irish America in the Troubles: the details contained in the documents from Northern Ireland, Broderick ruled, were not admissible in an American court; they were simply too fraught and too far removed from the acts the American men were accused of committing. The months of work, mapping out IRA incidents and arrests involving the Philadelphia guns, were moot. That the guns existed and were recovered in Northern Ireland was a fact inherent to the case, but the details around how those guns were found — and *whom* they had been found with — would never see the light of day in an American courtroom.

It's hard to say how memory might be different in Irish America if the consequences of the gunrunning had been revealed. Perhaps it wouldn't have changed much; after all, almost everyone around the Philadelphia men assumed the guns were going to the Provos anyway, and probably assumed they were being used for its violent campaign. But perhaps it's easier to assume such things from an ocean away, graciously buffered from Northern Ireland's true carnage. At any rate, such lost details wound up obscuring for decades the impact of NORAID and its more sinister elements.

Broderick did make an exception, though. To underscore the sheer amount of firepower alleged to have come from Philadelphia, he allowed the seized guns shepherded to the city from Kinnegar to be paraded into the courtroom. There were more than a hundred of them, piled into carts, walked in front of the jury box. There were so many they filled up the courtroom, making the space feel cluttered and dangerous. Each day, the guns were lined up against the wall, their serial numbers noted on those small blue tags attached to the scope. As the trial neared its end, Bob Merkle picked one up and waved it around the courtroom.

"This is a type of weapon," he said, "that creates widows and orphans."

It was a funny kind of irony, to have every element of the story but to be forbidden from telling it to the jury. Each gun, after all, had two lives attached to it; the person who sent it and the person who pulled its trigger. Like, for example, the ArmaLite bearing evidence tag A-44, recovered one September evening in West Belfast, on a dark street corner in Andersonstown, dropped by a teenage girl after she had both her knees shot out by a British soldier. The ArmaLite she was holding had been purchased by Vince Conlon, Danny Cahalane, and Neil Byrne in March 1972, that last outing before Conlon returned to Ireland. Such details, though, such intricate facts would take decades to piece together.

Did the Philadelphia men ever know just how much bloodshed they helped cause, on the far side of the ocean? Such details were casualties of a long, complicated war. Leaving the courtroom one day, Dan Duffy found himself near the piles of recovered guns. Irreverent as ever, he sidled up to the attending officer. "We bought them," Duffy quipped toward the rifles. "Can we have them back?"

One of the last witnesses to take the stand was a familiar face. John Casey soberly walked the jury through the mechanics of the Philadelphia operation: how the group had secured an ArmaLite supply, how Marty Lyons had snuck on and off the New York docks, how they had used Connie Buckley's warehouse as an arms dump to package the goods and send them to Ireland as plumbing and household supplies. And, in perhaps his most damning recollection, Casey detailed the afternoon he had found Marty Lyons in his office, near giddy at the group's recent successes.

"The boys in Philly," Casey said to the jury, reciting Lyons's words, "really came through for us."

The trial lasted three weeks. On the afternoon of June 21, 1976, the jury reached a verdict. They filed back into the courtroom.

"Mr. Foreman, on Count 1, does the jury find the defendant guilty or not guilty?" Judge Broderick asked, instructing the courtroom not to react.

"Guilty."

And so it proceeded, through nearly every charge. It was a damning outcome. Danny Cahalane and Neil Byrne were convicted of exporting hundreds of Philadelphia rifles illegally. Now it was official. But the government failed in its bigger goal, of proving that the NORAID men had acted on behalf of the IRA. They were found guilty of an obscure weapons-exportation violation, and released until their sentencing.

If Judge Raymond Broderick had political leanings, they weren't evident across the three weeks of the trial. But after the verdict, he did allow himself a statement, one that perhaps discreetly telegraphed his own view on the island's future. As he sentenced Neil Byrne and Danny Cahalane to prison, Judge Broderick issued a missive to their supporters in the courtroom. Do not, he said, turn your backs on Northern Ireland. "Double or triple your energies," he said, "to bring about peace."

Despite the verdict, British officials were frustrated at the case's conclusion, and particularly bitter that prosecutors had failed to prove that Cahalane and Byrne had acted as agents of the Provos. "This is disappointing in view of the amount of work we and the RUC put into helping the FBI in this case," one internal British memo said privately of the verdict. In scathing cables, they lay blame mostly at the feet of Broderick, whom they described as "unhelpful," an opinion no doubt colored by Alvey's earlier political concerns.

Still, they would eventually come around to the case's conclusion. "The outcome," they later noted, "is much better than we and the Department of Justice had feared."

Only one of them walked out of court a free man that day. The strategy of Dan Duffy's defense lawyer had worked. He was acquitted on the only charge he faced, and Duffy would never again face the wrath of the American court system.

"I should be happy, but I'm not," he said after the verdict, nodding toward Cahalane and Byrne. "It's a way of life, for the Irish, prosecution and persecution."

Rumors swirled in the months after the trial over why Duffy had escaped jail time, and old friends grew suddenly cold. But, as the decades wore on and memory faded, Duffy was remembered along with the rest of the Philadelphia Five, the verdict's reality forgotten amid the grander accusations of gunrunning. Today, Duffy is widely considered part of the Philadelphia gun trafficking ring.

Not for everyone, though. Verdicts aren't limited to juries, and Irish memories are famously long. Fifty years after Danny Cahalane went to prison, an old Philadelphia hand leaned forward during an interview and asked in a hushed tone: *Did the FBI documents say anything about informants?* Because there was a man named Danny Duffy, the person said, and they had always suspected something was off.

CHAPTER 36

LAST SHOT

NEIL BYRNE WAS hunched at a bar, hours after the verdict that would change his life. What a strange turn it had all been, with all its absurd twists. Even the smaller machinations of the trial seemed at times laughable — just that afternoon, Byrne had been shepherded out of the courtroom by their lawyer, Jack Levine. Fearing the press would be swarming outside, Levine graciously passed Byrne a newspaper to hold up to the side of his face, shielding his likeness from throngs of photographers and cameramen as he departed the federal building. Byrne, though, mistakenly had held the paper up to the wrong side of his face.

Alone at the bar, Byrne was sipping a beer as a breaking news bulletin crackled across a nearby television. Two Philadelphia men, the announcer said, had been convicted of gun trafficking to the IRA.

Byrne watched quietly as his likeness flashed across the screen. A nearby patron broke the tension.

"Isn't that you?" the man prodded, pointing at the television. They all huddled there together, watching as the segment played on TV.

"I did it," Byrne would later say, "to protect Irish people from murdering British troops."

Did he even need to confirm it? They all had known, of course. The news went on, reading out the headlines of the day, and they all went back to their drinks. Besides the whole felony debacle, it was like any other night. A few months later, Danny Cahalane would be named NORAID's "Man of the Year" for his trouble.

For in that City of Brotherly Love, the home of America's own rebellious spirit, Neil Byrne, Danny Cahalane, and the IRA's Philadelphia gunrunners — after a trial, after guilty verdicts, and even after prison — were still among friends.

Verdicts, of course, are rarely the end of things. Danny Cahalane and Neil Byrne were in and out of federal court for two years after the June 1976 ruling, trying — and failing — to appeal their convictions. Their primary argument was that John Nigro, the petty criminal turned government informer, was an unreliable, botched witness, and that his recording of Duffy was akin to an illegal wiretap (an argument with some merit; Pennsylvania was and remains a two-party consent state, meaning that recordings by private individuals must be consented to by both parties. Nigro, then, had recorded Duffy illegally when he switched on his homemade wiretap during their first phone call, recording the conversation that would help put Cahalane and Byrne in prison).

But appeals take time and money, two things NORAID didn't particularly have to spare, especially in 1976. That year, the FBI's parallel legal maneuverings were finally coming home to roost. In 1976, NORAID and its affiliated newspaper, *The Irish People,* were charged with violating the then-obscure Foreign Agents Registration Act (FARA). No longer could the organization coyly register as an agent of the Northern Aid Committee in Belfast; under the statute, prosecutors alleged, NORAID was legally bound to register as an agent of the IRA.

Such declarations would cut to the heart of everything Dave O'Connell and Mike Flannery had first tried to build all those years ago. For NORAID to formally declare itself as an agent of the IRA would signal a clear end to the group's formative chapter, solidifying the exact sort of public associations NORAID's founders hoped to avoid.

The FARA victory against NORAID thrilled the British authorities, who had watched the Philadelphia case so closely and were so disappointed in its shortcomings. Over drinks with British embassy officials in 1977, Bob Merkle said the NORAID case had been a hard-won compromise between the Justice Department's two camps — the first being his, determined to close down NORAID entirely, and the second being the more conservative element, who preferred less direct maneuvers.

For NORAID, the development of the FARA case was expensive, and not just reputationally — the group was forced to redirect funds to a whole variety of legal defenses, of both itself as an organization and of individual members like Cahalane. Though they made initial efforts to appeal their verdicts, Cahalane and Byrne were soon irked by the amount of money getting diverted to American courts and backed off. NORAID's funds were already running low, thanks to years of reputational damage inflicted by the US government. The last thing the organization needed was a bloodletting to defense lawyers. Resigned, Cahalane and Byrne abandoned their appeals in 1978. They were sentenced to a year in prison each.

Among Merkle and Alvey's counterparts in Northern Ireland, the conclusion was a relief after such a protracted case. Despite whatever disappointments had existed over the inadmissible Northern Irish evidence, the outward facts of the Philadelphia Five remained. Two men from NORAID were definitively connected to guns that eventually landed in the hands of the IRA. More immediately, the Provos' channel of American ArmaLites was successfully staunched.

On a cold night in Philadelphia in April 1978, a grizzled barman named Mickey Haggerty was pulled away from the counter by a phone call. It was a summoning that he and his business partner, Mike Doyle — a publican who, together with Haggerty, had helped manage a network of pubs that propped up Cahalane and Philadelphia NORAID — knew would come eventually. Solemnly, Haggerty traipsed out of the bar and drove through the streets of Northwest Philadelphia, finally arriving to pick up his friend and take him to the airport.

Again Danny Cahalane was headed to prison, and again it was a long way from home. He was due to check in to the federal prison at Alabama's Maxwell Air Force Base, to serve a sentence that was more daunting for its distance than its length. He would hardly see family, and his contacts were limited to letters from home and the rare visit from his daughter Mary Jane, who made just one trip to Alabama, alone. It was a tolerable enough way to live, he later wrote to her; compared to places like Holmesburg Prison, where he had spent those dark months after the grand jury summons, Alabama was "pretty good." The food was decent, the guards were nice, there were no walls or fences, and it was more like a "work camp" than a jail. Cahalane would eventually take over

Danny Cahalane and his daughter, Mary Jane, in the prison yard in Alabama

as the manager of the prison dormitory, and his only task for the year was to make sure the quarters were clean and well kept — after morning inspections at ten, the day was his. He trimmed hedges at the warden's house, and cut grass. Usually he spent his time reading *The Irish People* and *An Phoblacht,* the IRA's newspaper. He also cultivated a talent for making leather handicrafts — the same kind made by IRA prisoners overseas. He sent them back to Philadelphia, including to the MacSwiney Club.

"You try to make the best of it," said his wife, Jane, in a rare conversation with a reporter after Cahalane was denied an early release to a halfway house. "I thought they would send him home."

Byrne, sentenced to the same fate, was sent separately to Florida. With few ties and no one to miss, he was in decent enough spirits. His prison job, he would later joke with friends, was to feed the alligators.

The year went fast, and Cahalane was out and back in Philadelphia the following summer. The time in Alabama had changed so much and nothing at all; Cahalane himself, perhaps, was more changed than anything. But if Brandon Alvey and Bob Merkle had hoped to make an example of him, it had fallen on deaf ears. Cahalane had never quite stopped plugging into NORAID, even from Alabama, even in prison. Tommy Flynn, a friend from West Philadelphia who helped run NORAID in Cahalane's absence, had called regularly, bringing news of picnics, fundraisers, and Gaelic sporting events.

The fight kept on in Northern Ireland, and despite Irish-American fatigue, Philadelphia kept fostering it. NORAID, though, was never quite the same after its legal brawls of the 1970s. It would eventually settle with the government and agree to do what it had fought, since its founding: NORAID would register under FARA as an agent of the IRA, though it only did so with an accompanying stipulation, that such admissions came purely because of a contested court order. The organization sputtered along for years, hemorrhaging members, but the Philadelphia contingent stayed vigilant, if relatively neutered. British authorities, seemingly realizing the fight against NORAID was mostly won, noted the futility of chasing after these remaining, extreme pockets. "We really are down to the hard-core of supporters whose views are never going to change," an officer wrote in an internal cable.

The details of what Cahalane got up to after his release remain murky, but his family and friends know one thing: until the day he died, he helped get guns to the IRA. Times changed, after all, but Philadelphia didn't. The city remained a safe haven for Irish rebels, a place where wanted men could land with the unions, pick up a guild card and a fake name, find a warm bed, and meet a friendly face like Danny Cahalane or Bill Corry.

That's where an IRA volunteer named Michael O'Rourke headed in the late 1970s. An explosives expert, O'Rourke had blown himself out of a Dublin prison in 1976 and headed to Philadelphia as a fugitive. He was so deep underground that neither British nor Irish authorities had a clue of his whereabouts — and his reputation was so formidable that authorities believed, briefly, that O'Rourke helped plan the assassination of Lord Mountbatten, a member of the British royal family who was targeted and killed by the IRA in a 1979 bombing. He would eventually be cleared of any connection to that killing — after all, at the time, Michael O'Rourke wasn't even on the right side of the Atlantic. He was posing as a young roofer named Pat Mannion, who worked for John McCullough and lived with an old friend of the IRA in suburban Philadelphia, in Newtown Square.

It was a common enough occurrence at homes like the Cahalanes' — the kids, emerging from sleep and headed for the breakfast table, would find a stranger there with an innocuous name and a brogue. Raised in the Irish tradition, they knew not to ask questions but do as they were told. That's what the Cahalane kids did when Michael O'Rourke arrived at the house.

Cahalane opened his doors for scores of Irish fugitives, a tradition that he carried on even after prison. Still, though, for as strong as his principles remained, prison had changed Danny, made him less healthy, less magnetic. "He was never quite right after his sentence," a friend said.

O'Rourke's visit did little to help. Like so many IRA men before him, he had fled to Philadelphia to wait out the heat, and joined John McCullough's roofers' union under his fake identity, as Pat Mannion, from Dublin. (O'Rourke's IRA talents would prove transferrable, especially during McCullough's brass-knuckle tenure: once in Philly, O'Rourke occasionally put his skills to use, causing modest explosions at nonunion job sites.)

O'Rourke, though, never seemed to understand the dynamics of being a wanted fugitive. Bold and impulsive, he moved through Irish Philadelphia with little discretion, attending marches, protests, and anything else that would keep him on the front line of the Irish fight. It irked Cahalane, ever the pragmatist, who urged O'Rourke to keep a lower profile.

Cahalane had his own reasons for needing O'Rourke to calm down. The Troubles were still raging, the IRA still needed guns, and people in America could get them. Cahalane just needed to be more careful. And he needed the people around him, like O'Rourke, to be more careful, too.

It all came to a head in the fall of 1979, as O'Rourke toiled along in the Philadelphia scene. The *Queen Elizabeth II,* the ocean liner that had emerged as the key conduit connecting America with Ireland — and a key smuggling route for getting ArmaLites to the IRA — was docking in Philadelphia, an event that traditionally inspired waves of anti-British protests at its moorings. It was the exact sort of event that O'Rourke tended to frequent, and Cahalane passed along very specific instructions: stay the hell away from the *Queen Elizabeth II,* and whatever protests popped up around it. The Philly docks would be crawling with FBI agents and law enforcement, eager to catch glimpses of Irish-American malcontents and probably snag any photographs of potential fugitives. More than that, Cahalane himself needed the docks to stay quiet — the *Queen Elizabeth II* was headed back across the ocean, and he needed to get some clandestine cargo onto it.

O'Rourke didn't listen. Instead, as Cahalane predicted, the FBI spotted him clearly at the rally that day. The debacle would explode publicly, revealing O'Rourke's true identity and causing an international debate over whether he should be sent back to Ireland. He was eventually deported and rearrested in Dublin in 1984.

Cahalane, though, would never see the end of the O'Rourke story. He was dead of a heart attack in 1980, an ending that seemed sudden, but inevitable after his stint in prison. *It primed Danny for death,* the Philly Irish often say now, with mischievous glints. *But the debacle with O'Rourke — that was what finally killed him.*

A group of them gathered the night before the funeral, collected friends and colleagues that Danny had known all his life. One was the young laborer who, years before, had followed Cahalane out of Breen's Café on that ambiguous errand up the New Jersey Turnpike, dropping the green work van at a rest stop.

Danny needed a send-off, they all decided, something fit for the dean of Philadelphia's Irish, one of its most avowed disciples. He may have never volunteered with the IRA in Ireland, but he had more than proven his worth to the army in the States. The IRA's Army Council in Dublin had even approved a rare Republican honor guard for his funeral.

That, though, was the group's conundrum that evening. After all, a traditional Republican funeral should include a volley of gunshots over the casket. The idea sounded fitting and right, in theory, but for the realists in the room it was a nonstarter. It was too much, too risky, too on the nose, given Danny's own spotty history. After all, this wasn't West Belfast — this was Holy Cross Cemetery in Delaware County. A round of gunshots could get the whole lot of them cited, and they already had enough trouble. Some of them weren't even supposed to be in America in the first place. Grudgingly, they agreed to give Danny a more muted send-off, his coffin draped with the tricolor and accompanied by a uniformed Republican honor guard.

The funeral was one of the biggest Irish Philadelphia had ever seen, thronged with mourners who had traveled from all over to pay their respects. Hundreds gathered around the plot, in solemn testament. "Danny Cahalane shed his blood for this country," a friend said, noting Cahalane's American military service. "But he died for Ireland."

All proceeded according to plan, until a crack in the air sent the throngs of mourners into a mass panic.

Rules, of course, were never really how Philly — or Danny — operated. As the crowd collected itself, a shadow slinked off from behind a headstone, clutching a rifle. The rogue operator had popped up in one final, obstinate tribute, firing a single, booming shot into the air.

CHAPTER 37

"DANCING A LITTLE TOO MUCH TO OUR TUNE"

A SCATTERING OF NORAID-related gunrunning cases followed the trial in Philadelphia, though none seemed to pack the same heft. American prosecutors briefly weighed charging Marty Lyons — whom all sides knew was the key to the NORAID scheme — but ultimately decided against it, a decision that disappointed their British counterparts. Still, the Philadelphia case would eventually be viewed as a success, especially by the British. Alvey and Merkle held onto the seized guns throughout the appeals process — they eventually became dust collectors for the Philadelphia police, who stored them in a holding cell at a local jail. Finally, after Cahalane and Byrne abandoned their case, the weapons made their way back across the ocean to Belfast, where they were disposed of by British authorities.

In internal communications, as the guns were returned, Northern Irish investigators debated ways to thank Alvey, Merkle, and the ATF. They considered planning a trip to Belfast for the agents who had worked on the case, and other shows of appreciation. But a more astute diplomat shut down that effort, well attuned to the delicate optics around such displays of gratitude. It all felt too choreographed, too effusive. Any gratuitous show of thanks, the man wrote, "might inspire the Americans to ask themselves whether they were not dancing a little too much to our tune in pursuing these prosecutions."

Matters between the American and British governments would remain fraught over the Northern Irish conflict for years. Not long after the Philadelphia trial closed, British authorities formally requested their own channel of lethal American support — to combat the Provos' American ArmaLite stores, they wanted to export sixteen submachine guns of their own from the States.

It was a politically brazen ask, one that American officials immediately sought to bury. "The supply of arms for use by the British Army in [Northern Ireland] was very difficult politically and would be likely to give rise to awkward questions in Congress and from Irish-American political circles," one internal British cable said of their discussions with the Americans. It sent the Brits off in a huff, warning that any American questions about the British Army's behavior in Northern Ireland were "inappropriate." Such fragile egos and delicate dialogue would come to define the America-UK relationship when it came to the Troubles.

By the time Cahalane and Byrne were preparing for prison, their influence in Northern Ireland had waned. The Provos were increasingly looking to other international channels — namely, Muammar Gaddafi in Libya, whose support would be central to the Provos' next chapter — for bulk weapons shipments. Based on their own figures, British authorities said they were fairly confident the days of large-scale American gunrunning from the United States to the Provos were over.

"There seems little doubt that the procurement of weapons in the US for terrorist use in Ireland has been made materially more difficult," read a 1977 cable from the Northern Ireland Office. "We have no evidence of recent bulk purchases there, though weapons from earlier bulk purchases continue to be recovered."

PART VI

A NORMAL LIFE

CHAPTER 38

THE VETERAN

THE ARMY JEEP that snuck up behind her might've startled another driver, but the woman was used to all this trouble by now; she had hardly known anything else. This was just daily life in West Belfast, where surface tension seemed to be the only thing holding the city together, like a glass on the cusp of overflow.

It had been twenty long years, and still the fortified tanks and jeeps of the British Army remained on the streets, sentries in a war that perpetually simmered. This was what they did, this was how they operated. If they weren't shooting with bullets, they were harassing with badges. Resigned to a confrontation, the woman steered off to the side of the road.

She was driving that afternoon, sometime around the early 1990s, on a brief errand from the Falls Taxi Association, a car service that had become synonymous with West Belfast and nationalist neighborhoods. Established in 1974, the association was formed by Catholic taxi drivers when riots and violence interrupted the public transport services that served nationalist Belfast. In the years since its formation, its signature black taxis had become a symbol for Republican Belfast, and a reliable employer for ex- and current paramilitaries — known as a friendly place for IRA volunteers looking for a job, or as a resource for volunteers on the run.

In her thirties, with a slim face and sharp, glinting eyes, the woman worked for the company, selling taxi parts. That day's errand was innocuous and unrelated: she was driving her boss to fetch bread and milk. Nothing was normal, though — still, after all these years — in West Belfast. They were tailed by the

British Army jeep even on this short journey, and now, with the car at a stop, she prepared for the questions. These interactions hardly stressed her anymore. Years had passed, and it was just more of the same.

These tit-for-tat encounters had come to define West Belfast, skittish interactions that always carried the threat of escalation. But the woman was smart. She had been around long enough to know: one single slipup could turn an annoying hassle into a headline. It was what most of the soldiers seemed to want, anyway, to prod until they were given a reason to do more. Sometimes they taunted, lobbing insults. *Whore. Slut.* Once, they had even taken her car apart under the guise of a search, looking for guns or bombs. Usually they asked for her ID, and an intelligence officer would quiz her. No matter the bait, she answered each time simply, with her name, address, and canned statement that she was over twenty-one years of age. Technically, they were owed nothing more.

Hope in West Belfast often seemed naive, but the new decade was bringing flickers of promise. The Republican movement, via Sinn Fein and its figurehead, Gerry Adams, seemed to be securing inroads to political legitimacy. More and more often, there were ceasefires, rumors of talks and negotiations that could see Northern Ireland at peace. Maybe someday. But that afternoon, as the soldiers approached her car, such futures couldn't have seemed further away.

It was a blessedly brief interaction, and the soldiers let the woman off after some needless hassling. She continued on, tacking the incident onto the endless list, these incursions into her peace, these invasions into her home. There was a strange sort of familiarity in it, though. They knew her, she knew them, and the hatred had hardened into a strange sort of mutual pity over the years. Most of these uniformed men, she knew, never wanted to be in Belfast. Some may not have even been old enough to remember those early, horrible days of the 1970s. Most had probably been sent to the tortured city against their will, ordered by the same military institution that had stolen her childhood. She didn't hate them. Most days, she felt sorry for them.

Every now and then, though, a particularly bullish or particularly mercurial soldier would jam his finger into the proverbial wound. It was always a reminder that for all that had happened and all that was to come, the playing field remained uneven. Whether at a traffic stop on the Lower Falls or on a dark corner in Andersonstown, one of the parties in these exchanges remained indisputably more powerful, more in control, and more protected than the other.

"How is your leg, Geraldine?" one had growled at her, not so long ago. "You have got some fucking history."

Whether the soldier meant such snipes for her, alone, was unclear. After all, Geraldine wasn't the only Crawford sister who had made headlines. She was the only one, though, who was still alive to hear about it.

Bespectacled and wide-eyed, Father Raymond Murray hurried through the doors of Armagh Gaol in December 1975, a cold winter day for an even colder errand.

The young priest had hardly been ordained five years when he was first sent to Armagh Gaol in 1967, tasked with serving as the curate at what was — then — a sleepy women's prison that was hardly used. It was a welcome return for Murray, an Armagh native who had joined the Church in the midst of a ministerial surplus, in 1962. Rather than stay in his home parish, he was loaned out by his home diocese along with ten others. In what would turn out to be a fortuitous posting, Murray was one of four who was sent to Belfast, where he worked for five years.

That time in Belfast would foreshadow the rest of Murray's life. Who could have known that, though, in the early 1960s? West Belfast and Northern Ireland were wrought with tension but it had not yet calcified into a war, and when he was sent to Armagh Gaol, the facility was mostly decayed, and still mostly empty.

That had changed, though. Oh, how it had changed. The entire debacle would prove darker than even Father Murray could have imagined. What was supposed to have been a brief pastoral assignment had turned into his life's mission. He remembered vividly the day in 1971 that he learned of the British government's internment policy, and the darkness that had fallen over the jail in the weeks that followed. It was no longer a sleepy low-security shelter for petty criminals. Its population ballooned, and its halls were soon filled with the same parishioners he had met as a young priest in West Belfast. Such patterns would play out across the course of his life, in dark symmetry — he ministered to some in jail, counseled their families outside it, and buried others. And even the cloth hadn't protected him entirely. His work in Armagh, ministering to Republican prisoners, had landed a target on his own back, and by 1975, anonymous, threatening letters arrived regularly. Police officers often warned he was being hunted; a bullet once arrived in the mail.

Still, the work in Armagh had become hugely important. The plight of the women prisoners had moved him deeply, and he had become a trusted confidante and mediator between them and the jail's staff — it was Father Murray who helped negotiate the end of the prison riot that had seen several staff taken hostage. Perhaps most serious and tenderly of all, Father Murray was tasked with guiding Armagh's prisoners through their darkest moments. It was he who brought bad news in from West Belfast, news of murdered mothers, dead fathers, and missing friends. And it was Father Murray who helped negotiate for compassionate releases so Armagh's women could help bury their dead.

It was clear, as 1975 had worn on: it was only getting worse, and these macabre journeys were becoming more and more frequent. Father Murray entered the prison that December morning knowing the next visit was only one bomb or bullet away.

In the priest's view, his job was purely spiritual; he never asked what had landed Armagh's women prisoners behind bars in the first place. He knew, of course; many were associated with the IRA and Cumann na mBan, the women's militia that had predated the IRA's acceptance of women fighters. And, many of the prisoners had connections to well-known IRA families or operatives. Father Murray, for one, abhorred sectarian violence — but having grown up Catholic in the North, and after years of work in West Belfast, he understood the sort of forces that drove people to it. Still, he confronted the fatal realities daily.

Slipping inside the austere stone structure that winter day, Father Murray set himself to the grim task at hand. He didn't know everything about the operation in Belfast the day before, but he knew the basics. The IRA had planned a host of bombings — tragedies in their own right — and one of them had failed. Two young volunteers were transporting a bomb when it went off prematurely in their parked Hillman Avenger on Belfast's King Street, turning the avenue into a fireball and killing both occupants. Another two strikes added to a grim and growing tally. Another two young people, vanished in the fog of war. The car's passenger, a man named Paul "Basil" Fox, was only twenty and had been a lieutenant in the Belfast brigade. The car's driver was more senior, a twenty-five-year-old woman who had enlisted in 1973. Ambitious and politically savvy, she was a Cumann na mBan staff officer from Lenadoon, and over her short service, she had become known as a ballsy, chillingly efficient operative.

©Victor Patterson

A British soldier examines the remains of the car in which Laura Crawford was traveling when a premature explosion killed her and Paul Fox in December 1975.

She was pulled from the car by passersby, still alive but barely breathing, her body on fire. For almost ten minutes, a man attempted CPR until the woman took a shuddering last breath and died in his arms. It had taken them nearly as long to notice Fox's body, which had been launched from the car in the blast, slamming against a nearby wall.

Years later, memories of Father Murray's bereavement visits still haunted the women of Armagh Gaol. These dark occasions were such formative experiences that many still vividly remembered the days and the victims' names, like when Tommy McElwee's fiancée heard he had died on hunger strike, or when Maire Drumm was summoned to hear news of her mother's passing. And, they remembered the morning Father Murray arrived and called for Geraldine Crawford to break the terrible news. Her sister, Laura — she who was supposed to be a writer, a politician, whose rebellious ends were supposed to have stopped at the ballot box — had disappeared like the rest of them, like smoke into Belfast's gunmetal sky.

If anyone had known how deep it went in the Crawford house, they hadn't said. It was a wall of secrets so strong that even sisterhood hadn't breached it — Geraldine had always believed Laura's involvement in the cause was limited to the ink-stained battlefield of newspapers and politics, her pledges stopping at the political limit of Sinn Fein, the IRA's burgeoning political wing. Instead, around the same time as Geraldine, Laura, too, had taken her own militant oaths, joining the women's wing of the IRA in Cumann na mBan. She rose quickly through the ranks. Older and more sophisticated than Geraldine, Laura embraced a flashier modus operandi: she drove her own car, dressed sharply, and rarely went out without makeup.

After enlisting in 1973, Laura had already proven herself as a volunteer by the time the IRA embraced the car bomb, a weapon that would become ubiquitous with the IRA's strategy and the Troubles. So looming was the threat of vehicular-bound explosives that parking limits went into effect around Belfast, restricting cars from stopping near pubs or storefronts (a dark legacy that continues to the present day in Belfast, whose city center is still pedestrianized).

Laura was partnered that December night with Fox, a young IRA man from Belfast with a terrier-like disposition. Fox was an ambitious soldier, constantly ducking down Belfast's labyrinthine streets and harassing British Army units. At seventeen, he had narrowly escaped a British raid on his home; not long after, soldiers had opened fire on a car in which he was riding. The driver, a comrade in the IRA, was killed.

The bombing operation was meant to be straightforward, the front end of what would become a decades-long campaign in Belfast's center. Laura and Paul were tasked with transporting one of the IRA's bombs into the city, where it would explode along with several others that were placed elsewhere by other volunteers. Paul and Laura were supposed to be long gone by the time the explosive was set to ignite.

But in what was to become a regular, fatal pattern, the bombs were faulty and the fuse blew prematurely, igniting the explosive charge while Laura and Paul were still in the car. The ensuing detonation — which happened in Belfast's downtown, though not where the bomb was meant to be placed — brightened the night sky in a massive flash that was visible from miles away.

The extent of Laura's involvement with the IRA had been suspected, but not known, even by those closest to her; there was that blond wig in Laura's room, of course, found by her mother. But that discovery went where most such incidents did, among families in cloistered West Belfast: away. On that December night in 1975, it was so far from mind that when news of the explosion reached Lenadoon, Brigid Crawford murmured a blessing, oblivious that the tragedy would be hers to bear. "Lord have mercy on their souls," she said, of the then unknown victims.

The loss devastated Geraldine, for whom the revelation was two-pronged: for as long as the sisters had been alive, neither told the other of their involvement with the IRA. But starting in those frenetic months of 1973, they were fellow soldiers, fighting in such dense shadows that they never even knew they were in it just as they had always been: together.

Milltown Cemetery sits at the western edge of the Falls Road, where the avenue splits to encircle Andersonstown. It's a large cemetery, its plots crowded together in an odd patchwork, clustered in some places and spaced apart in others. By 1975, its hard ground seemed eternally tilled, torn open more and more often for younger and younger bodies. The story of the Troubles, by then well into five violent years, was etched in its gravestones, the vast majority of them Catholic, many of them Republican, almost all residents of nationalist West Belfast.

A large crowd gathered on a clear winter day and walked through the cold from Andersonstown to accompany the wooden casket to its grave. It had been a battle to get Geraldine out on compassionate release for the funeral, but Father Murray somehow managed it. Such negotiations were getting more and more difficult the more unstable West Belfast became. But Father Murray's efforts had been buttressed by those of Eileen Hickey, the respected commanding officer of the A Wing. Thanks to them, Geraldine walked through the gates of Armagh Gaol on a ticking clock, expected back in two days' time.

Laura's coffin had been laid across Geraldine's bed that day, attended on either side by an IRA guard of honor. As marchers escorted the casket eastward, through the winding streets toward Milltown Cemetery, Geraldine walked alongside it, one of six stone-faced women dressed in the traditional uniform of sunglasses, a black sweater, and a black beret.

It was their first and final mission together, on Laura's long, last journey up the Falls Road. By the week's end, one Crawford girl was in a Republican grave and the other was back in a Republican prison.

On the day Geraldine Crawford was stopped by the soldier, more than a decade had passed since the awful happenings of 1975. It had been a long time, too,

Crowds of mourners gather in Milltown Cemetery for Laura Crawford's funeral, as her sister, Geraldine, marches with the coffin's honor guard.

since Armagh Gaol, and that strange clash of innocence and violence in its hallways. She had been released early, two years after Laura's funeral, but life for Geraldine Crawford hadn't been easy in the time since.

She first left prison in the fall of 1977, and found work for the Falls Taxi Association, the company that ran the Black Taxis. She worked for a time in the company's garage, which doubled as a service station and a repair shop. It even occasionally serviced Gerry Adams's armored car, which he relied on for protection during trips around Belfast. Such security measures were prescient; once, while Adams's car was being serviced, a passing British soldier asked mockingly if the mechanic was scrapping the car. When the man said no, the soldier replied, "We'll have to scrap the fucking bastard who owns it."

For years she bounced between the garage and the taxi office, which was located just off the Falls Road. It faced Milltown Cemetery, where Laura was buried, in the graveyard's Republican plot, which had grown over the years. The Troubles' various chapters were mapped across its field. Now Laura's headstone was buttressed by those like Bobby Sands, a hunger striker who died in 1981, famously protesting the suspension of political status for Republican prisoners.

That decade brought new and different challenges, and the end of political status for IRA volunteers was a big one. In the early years of the Troubles, that designation had differentiated IRA prisoners from standard criminals, allowing them more freedom while behind bars. Political status was what had allowed such camaraderie among Republican prisoners in Armagh, in the early 1970s. But political status was abandoned by the British in 1976, and Northern Ireland prisons now resembled more traditional — and bleak — jails. Conditions were poor and Republican inmates were not permitted to wear their own clothing or to socialize freely. And there were more existential implications too: the removal of political status removed the legitimacy of Republican politics. The slight led to historic protests, both outside and inside prison walls, many of which eventually became colloquialisms in the IRA's vocabulary. There was the no-wash protest at Armagh women's prison, when the jail's female detainees refused to shower or bathe, instead smearing their own feces on the walls. There was the blanket protest, when male prisoners at Long Kesh refused to wear their jail uniforms, insisting instead on staying naked. And finally — and perhaps most tragically — there were the hunger strikes of the 1980s, when Republican inmates like Bobby Sands refused to eat unless they were declared political prisoners. Ten men would die, their emaciated, disintegrating bodies beamed across the world in television broadcasts and photographs. Such imagery was galvanizing propaganda when stacked against British prime minister Margaret Thatcher, who stonily refused the men's demands.

The hunger strikes were an energizing moment for Irish nationalists. But as the 1990s dawned, a new split was developing in West Belfast, the same divisive routine that had played out time and time again within the Republican movement. Sinn Fein began to negotiate with the British government and outside mediators, and the prospect sent the IRA's fringe extremists into a spiral. The factions were clear enough: West Belfast's own Gerry Adams, clawing for legitimacy as a political voice, was elected to the British House of Commons in 1983 for Sinn Fein, and began publicly distancing himself from the IRA's more violent ends. It was a transparently hypocritical — though arguably necessary — maneuver to lay the groundwork for progress between Sinn Fein and Unionist politicians. It would begin to shove a wedge between Adams and the foot soldiers who once carried out his violent directives. Beneath him, hard-liners like his onetime friend, Brendan "the Dark" Hughes, and Andersonstown's Price sisters rebelled, hunkering down into increasingly violent, isolated corners.

Geraldine, though, went in the other direction. She aligned with Adams and Provisional Sinn Fein, the same political movement Laura had joined before her death. By the time the 1990s had carried on, Geraldine had established herself in the community of women Republican prisoners, whose numbers had grown larger and larger every year. Among them, she was a respected — and veteran — voice. After all, that night at the Woodbourne barracks with the Philadelphia rifle had only been the beginning.

Geraldine arrived back in Armagh in the summer of 1981, four years after her initial release from its hallways. Captivity, though, couldn't have been more different. Gone were the sanguine days of the early 1970s, and the summer-camp-style camaraderie. The removal of political status had entirely changed the dynamic between the prison's staff and its inmates, which went from grudgingly cordial to openly hostile. Gone were the movie nights, the girlish hijinks, the freedom of movement and drills in the exercise yard. By the 1980s, each side of the prison complex seemed determined to make the other as miserable as possible. Among the indignities: women prisoners were strip-searched anytime they left or entered the prison, whether for court, hospital appointments, or familial visits. Forced to stand completely naked in front of a panel of female guards, the women were inspected front and back, an experience that so disturbed Father Raymond Murray — still the prison's chaplain — that he reported the practice to his superiors and begged for help in stopping it. He cited Geraldine as an example: she had been strip-searched thirteen times over ten days.

Times were different, and so was she. When Geraldine had first arrived in Armagh in 1973, she was greeted by women like Eileen Hickey, older, veteran Republican volunteers who helped younger girls transition into their adult life as IRA soldiers. By 1981, Geraldine was no longer the teenager from a decade before. It was she who guided young girls and women through their first days in prison now, their first nights behind bars, their first initiations into that storied sisterhood.

Some things, though, were the same. The debacle that had sent her back to prison had, again, involved an ArmaLite, and had, again, involved Andersonstown. It had happened at the funeral of Joe McDonnell, a Belfast native who had grown up in Lenadoon, like the Crawfords. Like Bobby Sands, McDonnell died on hunger strike, protesting Thatcher's refusal to grant IRA prisoners political status.

Republican funerals in Belfast were always risky endeavors. They were a magnet for conflict with British security forces, who kept close watch on such proceedings, using the gatherings for intelligence and occasionally provoking mourners into violent confrontations. Things grew particularly tricky when the funeral included a volley of shots over the casket, which was a traditional mark of respect for IRA volunteers who had died. Such endeavors were illegal in West Belfast. IRA membership alone was enough to get one arrested in 1981, let alone possessing a rifle, let *alone* shooting it. So, such rituals were often arranged with the utmost secrecy, the guns snuck over for the volley and then quickly returned to a safe house, where the gunmen would change in and out of masked outfits that hid their identity. It required a carefully coordinated operation, to ensure both the guns and the men got away safely. Such were the arrangements for McDonnell's funeral, as it wound its way through West Belfast and toward Milltown Cemetery, followed by thousands of mourners.

Not far from its final destination, McDonnell's casket stopped outside a shopping center in Andersonstown. It was there that a group of three masked, uniformed IRA men stepped forward. They followed along obediently as a fourth issued commands, ordering the men to lift their arms and shoot. With a decisive crack, the volley ended, and the four men disappeared into the anonymous thrum of the crowd, winding their way back to a safe house in Lenadoon to stash the guns and their disguises.

It was then that the chaos started.

Pursuing the masked men, British soldiers began firing bullets and rubber projectiles into the crowd of McDonnell's mourners, sending them all scrambling for cover in churches and doorways. The scenes bore a terrifying resemblance to those of Bloody Sunday, with unarmed civilians huddled together in fear.

Geraldine was there that day, though not at the march — she was manning the safe house back in Lenadoon, where the gunmen were due to drop their weapons and masks. But not long after the IRA firing party slipped inside, the British soldiers who were following them burst into the home, spraying the walls with bullets. Shots exploded through the small space, and two of the men from the firing party jumped out of a window. Geraldine, though, became trapped in the house, barricading herself into a bedroom as the soldiers neared. They would later say she unlocked the door herself, but years later, Geraldine would remember the moment clearly: they burst into the room, firing indiscriminately, the bullets flying in an uncomfortably small, dangerous space.

Oh no, she had thought. *Not again.*

She was beaten and arrested along with several others of the firing party, including Gerry Adams's brother. Inside the house, the British soldiers seized three rifles and a pile of IRA military uniforms: four sets of khaki-green combat jackets, trousers, black berets, belts, sunglasses, gloves, boots, and six masks.

The incident would send Geraldine back to prison, and she never quite forgot the chaos of that bedroom as the bullets flew. In it was a scene they had all seen play out before, plenty of times: there were no witnesses, no cameras, no rules. The soldiers would be able to tell whatever story they wanted, about how she died and why they shot her. She wasn't holding a weapon.

The bullets mercifully missed her. But it was different facing a barrel the second time, she would realize later. She knew what it felt like, by then, to be shot, the blood pulsing out of her, unsure what was lost and what was hit. It was different that time in 1981, huddled in that bedroom, plaster raining down. That time, older and wiser, Geraldine Crawford was scared.

CHAPTER 39

"SHIFTING SAND"

THE TALL MAN landed back in New York in 1985, setting foot on American soil for the first time in nearly fifteen years. The time between had seen an almost incomprehensible torrent of grief and violence. Friends who had once welcomed him home were dead. Fellow soldiers, raised in that same disputed borderland, were in prison or gone. His son — grown now, and back in Philadelphia — was spared his father's own militant obsession, but the conflict had raged for long enough that the boy's childhood friends were now moving up to the front lines. Civilians, too — neighbors, their friends, people whose only transgression was poor timing in crossfire — had fallen, one by one. How long could one country, or one man, bear such a toll?

He had made this journey back to America the same way as he had made the first, all those years ago: alone. The cause had taken plenty from him, over the long journey — his friends, his youth, his freedom. Marina didn't follow him to America immediately, but stayed at home in Monaghan while their youngest son finished school.

The man's hair was grayer, his face slightly more sunken, but so much about Vince Conlon had stayed the same. There was still a gleam in his eye, a darkness in his brow, a restless, rebellious spirit. He had returned to a different America, at a rapidly changing time, but his mission was the same as the one that first brought him across the ocean, so many decades before. He was needed, again, to fix a crumbling IRA support network in America.

Many things had fallen apart since that stretch in the 1970s, when NORAID and Clan-na-Gael organized their transatlantic gun trafficking network. It was a rare moment when the whole of notoriously fickle Irish America seemed to move at the same time, in the same direction. They had run into their share of complications, of course — there were enough warrants, enough trial convictions, enough strife to prove that — but that chapter was proof that the historically fractured diaspora could, in fact, unite under one cause.

That had all changed, though, by the time Conlon landed back in the States. Drained of financial resources from its long register of court battles, NORAID had limped through the 1980s and into the 1990s as a fractured organization, its ranks torn apart by warring ideologies and petty interpersonal disputes. Clan-na-Gael, too, was in the midst of its own split, its diehards in New York and Philadelphia spinning off into their own separate pockets. It had left the IRA's American support network in shambles, relegated to separate cells that operated with varying degrees of success and little coordination.

The guns, of course, had still come, but they came from far outside NORAID's sphere of influence. After its American network was destroyed by the court cases of the 1970s, the IRA pivoted to gun trafficking networks in Libya and the Middle East to fuel its needs. In shambles following its protracted court battles — and with many of its leading figures either in prison or fighting charges that would send them there — NORAID had become an obsolete ghost.

Most fatal to the organization's legacy, perhaps, was a final court case in the 1980s — the number finally came up for NORAID's well-coiffed Michael Flannery, who was charged with gun trafficking, along with Conlon's old friend George Harrison. The pair beat the charge, thanks to evidence pointing to a bizarre CIA connection that the American federal government couldn't quite refute, but the signal was final: NORAID was toxic, and sympathetic Irish Americans ought to find other avenues, lest they, too, be caught in prosecutors' crosshairs. By the 1980s, NORAID was seen as so radioactive that when an IRA operative was sent over to Boston to arrange a shipment of guns, the man was given clear instructions: stay away from NORAID and anyone associated with it.

The situation, though, was changing as the 1990s neared. This time, as the Troubles entered their third decade, there was hope that the war could end. It was still too far to touch, but for the first time since 1969, there was a potential ending in sight, so much so that a new effort was underway to once again reinvigorate the fractured network of Irish-American support. No longer, though, did the IRA need guns. What it needed was just the opposite: for the diaspora to stop encouraging violence, and to start supporting peace.

Conlon, of course, had aligned early with Sinn Fein, which had elevated him to the county seat in Monaghan. He was the first, but not the last. Sinn Fein had gone on to prop up whole rosters of IRA men and women into positions of power, effectively legitimizing the IRA's politics and earning it—however grudgingly—a seat at the negotiating table. It was hard won, and the success was not without sacrifice, but the telltale signs were increasingly clear: political solutions, long a source of strife and division in the Republican movement, were once again part of the conversation.

The debate over Provisional Sinn Fein and its political ambitions had torn apart Irish America much the same as it had torn apart West Belfast and the North. Faced with the prospect of negotiating with Unionists and Loyalists, NORAID and Clan-na-Gael splintered, and among the casualties was Conlon's friendship with Flannery and Harrison, both of whom remained staunchly against Sinn Fein's peace negotiations. It was a division not so dissimilar to the sort of separation that first led the Provisional IRA to split off into its own entity during the tumultuous arguments of 1969.

In a letter to both Clan-na-Gael and NORAID in 1990, Adams asked each group to send delegates to a gathering where the leaders of Irish America could get on the same page. Early talks had shown promise, and Republican leadership was optimistic that the two groups could be reorganized and redirected to support Sinn Fein's political aims. Key to the effort would be a series of delegates from Irish America, most importantly Clan-na-Gael, which for three decades had proven to be the IRA's most lasting and reliable source of American weaponry. And when it came to Clan-na-Gael, there was hardly a debate over who should represent the group.

"Vince," a handwritten note said, scrawled on Adams's personal stationery, "I think you should be the man to go."

It was indicative of just how highly Vince Conlon was regarded—and how capable a diplomat he had become. The various scatterings of the diaspora needed to set aside their disputes and find common ground—by the time peace negotiations were beginning in the 1990s, Clan-na-Gael and NORAID had turned against each other, sometimes working to actively sabotage each other's efforts. It was a disconnect that Sinn Fein's leadership realized could cause serious problems if they pursued a lasting truce with the British government; after all, Irish America had proven its lethal capabilities before.

Such potential, of course, was never far from mind. Not long after his return to America, Conlon reached out to an old friend, a man who had long since retreated into the shadows, soured by Irish America's infighting. But perhaps, Conlon hoped, he could be coaxed back into the fold, this time to work toward a much different goal: peace.

It had been a long time, though, and so much — too much — had changed. The meeting was cordial but brief. The man unequivocally turned Vince Conlon down.

"We both saw the accomplishments achieved from a zero start in 1969 to 1973, after 1973 in my opinion it became a free for all.... Dealing with Ireland since is the feeling of dealing with shifting sand," Marty Lyons wrote to Vince, after their reunion. "As for my own static of the present time, I support all who are helping the cause of a united Ireland, and will continue in that role, but I will not participate in a leading role until the climate appears to be favorable to reestablish a more effective and united front."

Whether or not Conlon knew it at the time, his return to the States was risky. Even though American, British, and Irish authorities had decided not to extradite him in 1975, the case against him was still open, at least as far as the FBI knew. Conlon set foot on US soil in 1985 as a wanted man, still a fugitive from the case that had sent his old friends to prison. A bench warrant for Conlon's arrest was still active, and the case in Philadelphia was still, technically, open. If it concerned Conlon, though, he had hardly shown it. He landed in New York and almost immediately set to work, at loud volume.

Nearly as soon as Conlon arrived in New York, federal agents received two tips. The first was from a so-called friendly intelligence service — almost certainly Great Britain — warning the agents that Conlon had returned and was back at the same work, liaising with the country's Irish-American organizations. The second was from an informant within Clan-na-Gael circles in New York, who warned the FBI that Conlon had returned. The FBI followed along obediently, picking up surveillance on Conlon and tailing him around the city. They even kept an eye on the Adams-sanctioned meeting that Conlon was dispatched to attend that winter, as a representative of Clan-na-Gael.

"Fundraising activities have increased in the last year, especially under the leadership of Conlon," one FBI surveillance memo wrote.

FBI agents, thrilled at the chance to finally bring Conlon to court, eagerly dug up the ATF's Philadelphia file. They were disappointed with what they found: the Philadelphia division of the ATF had actually shelved its legal pursuit of Conlon years before. Even as he toiled under their noses, the agency had little interest in reopening the charges — the gunrunning of the 1970s was old news.

Still, the FBI had its own priorities. It quickly opened a new case on Conlon, this time filing its own surveillance requests and secret subpoenas to monitor his whereabouts. In New York, agents plumbed a host of confidential informants for intelligence about their resurfaced fugitive. Undercover agents tailed him on his daily errands around the city. Investigators pulled his bank records and telephone logs, keeping close watch on who he was meeting with, and where. Their goal, written in an investigative report, included two things: "to determine asset potential of subject" and "to determine if subject is involved in [Provisional IRA] weapons procurement in the United States."

It became a good investigative endeavor, though perhaps not in the way the FBI initially hoped.

There was indeed real value in maintaining a close eye on Conlon. The preceding years had seen the United States pressed into an increasingly difficult and consequential position in the grander scope of the Troubles. No longer could the American government relegate the conflict to the status of a strictly British problem; instead, by the 1990s it found itself a self-appointed mediator. In this, Gerry Adams became a critical chip, the political arbitrator who could bring the Provisional IRA's violence to heel. But he came with serious baggage — while he may have publicly denied having ever been part of the IRA, such declarations were laughably hollow, and the 1980s and early 1990s had done little to soften the group's violent image. A trail of brutal attacks by the IRA — including a botched bombing that killed nine Protestant civilians on Belfast's Shankill Road — underscored accusations that the group bought and sold in terrorism. Adams was widely understood to be the future of the Sinn Fein party, and an unavoidable stakeholder if the United States was to artfully guide Northern Ireland toward a peace deal. But how such relationships would play, both with Irish America and with Americans in general, was a risky unknown; taken one way, it would appear that the US was endorsing the Provos' violence, and negotiating with terrorists.

Conlon, as a trusted confidant of Provisional Sinn Fein and a respected — if agitating — voice in Irish America, was a useful barometer for the government agents who watched him. That became doubly true when Adams sought his own inroads with the United States. At the turn of the 1990s, Adams began to cultivate a tantalizing image, one that he hoped to elevate with the help of the Americans: the onetime Belfast brigade commander had become the best chance for an IRA ceasefire, and an end to Northern Ireland's war.

Just as such political maneuverings were creating a schism in Belfast and Andersonstown, they were doing the same in the States, where talk of peace negotiations dealt NORAID its fatal blow. Michael Flannery and a cortege of loyal followers balked at Adams's approach, accusing Sinn Fein of undermining the IRA and selling out its mission in the pivot toward politics and peace. It was a messy, acrimonious split from which NORAID would never recover. Flannery and dozens more of the organization's best-known members abandoned the group and began actively attempting to sabotage it, at one point placing a half-page advertisement in Irish-American newspapers accusing NORAID of abandoning its principles. The Flannery camp knew that their approach personally hurt Adams and his supporters, but had little sympathy. "If it hurt them that badly," Flannery said, "they must know they are in the wrong."

Along with Flannery was Conlon's old friend and colleague George Harrison, perhaps the IRA's most reliable, independent armorer across the scope of the Troubles. He would split from Conlon and remain a staunch opponent of the Sinn Fein peace process for the rest of his life.

The FBI was presented with a strange turn of events. They had reopened their probe of Conlon to keep track of the IRA's militant ambitions in America. But ironically, their target had landed on the more peaceful, promising side of the diaspora's divide. For the first time in his travels across the Atlantic, Conlon and the American government were working toward the same goal.

Finally, after years of cat and mouse, the FBI backed off Vincent Conlon in 1992. Its investigation had failed to turn up any particularly incriminating evidence, and the years since the 1970s had seen a whole swath of safeguards put in place to prevent the indiscriminate investigation of US citizens, part of a national tilt toward civil liberties that followed the overzealous years of Hoover's FBI. Conlon, it seemed, had moved to a different game, and the FBI no longer had any clear reason to surveil him. Ordered by Justice Department higher-ups to back off, the New York FBI division protested; Conlon was still in the mix, they believed, and the links between Clan-na-Gael and the Provisional IRA were strong enough that he ought to be tracked. Still, they acquiesced; whether he knew it or not, Vincent Conlon became a truly free man that autumn.

And perhaps more unbelievably, he became part of the American government's best gambles, if they hoped to see the IRA and its American auxiliary accept peace.

By 1994, the path to Sinn Fein's political legitimacy was clear. The American government had emerged as the clear interlocutor between Great Britain, the Republic of Ireland, and Northern Ireland, and its endorsement of Gerry Adams's political veracity would change the balance of peace negotiations, forcing Great Britain and Unionist politicians to acknowledge Adams — and through him, the IRA — as a stakeholder.

As part of this legitimizing effort, Gerry Adams needed to visit America. But he needed a visa to do it.

It was no small ask, politically or operationally. Since the 1970s, the United States had denied visas to Provisional IRA figures, including Adams, because of his ties to the Provos. It was a tradition that started as far back as the 1970s, when American investigators were monitoring NORAID flyers for news of visits from IRA volunteers, then quietly ensuring that their visas were denied. For Adams to be granted a US visit now would be seen as tacit approval of his role within the IRA, and a slap in the face to the British, who viewed Adams — mostly correctly — as the mastermind behind some of the Provisional IRA's most heinous acts of political violence.

But there are rarely clear villains in war. In a gamble that would prove to be one of history's most prescient, President Bill Clinton granted Gerry Adams a forty-eight-hour waiver of restriction, and a two-day visa to visit the United States. The decision was met with predictable anger from British allies, but it would have significant historical consequences. In January of 1994, Adams arrived in New York, where he was invited to speak on Northern Ireland at the National Committee on American Foreign Policy. To a packed auditorium, Adams was the gleaming politician, shaking hands, rousing audiences, and convincing many skeptical Irish Americans that Sinn Fein's early peace talks — and an IRA ceasefire — were worth supporting.

"It is our intention," Adams said, "to see the gun removed permanently from Irish politics."

Among the small, trusted group of Irish Americans alongside him was Vincent Conlon.

CHAPTER 40

IN GRAVES

THE STORMONT POLITICAL complex sits directly east of Belfast's city center, across the River Lagan in a grassy parkland. On Thursday, April 9, 1998, it was the scene of one of perhaps the most consequential, fraught peace negotiations in postwar European history.

The four years since Gerry Adams's contentious 1994 visit to the United States had seen a distinct change in tenor in Northern Ireland. The Provisional IRA had skeptically embraced a series of ceasefires, part of a yearslong pivot that was, largely, the brainchild of Adams and facilitated by John Hume, a Social Democratic and Labour politician from Derry. Wary, but convinced by Hume's reputation, key Unionist delegations, British and Irish leaders, were coaxed into negotiations that could see the end of the Troubles. The peace talks began in earnest in the autumn of 1997.

It was a long, laborious process, full of false starts and near misses. The various ceasefires had paved the way for more serious talks, but also inflamed dissident splinter groups of the IRA, who had periodically violated the ceasefire agreements and engaged in violence, mostly in Belfast. Such incidents threatened the credibility of Adams as a potential peacemaker, especially among the Americans who gambled on him in 1994. It was an unenviable position, both for Adams and for those who backed him. They were left to both outwardly promote Adams's ability to negotiate with the British and, separately, convince the IRA's rank and file that such endeavors were not a complete betrayal of Republican principles.

Political legitimacy, too, had brought its own challenges for Adams and Sinn Fein. The party was widely understood to be the political arm of the IRA, even while its leadership maintained a performative separation from the group. But the logistics of that relationship were tougher to figure. Wresting a militant organization into politics was a daunting goal, and the transition was filled with bumps, both existential and practical. Common political processes like financial paperwork and election filings were new territory for Sinn Fein, a grassroots movement with militant roots that now faced the sudden, urgent need to become a polished political outfit, set for the international stage.

That effort, too, was rooted partly in America. In 1994, the same year that Adams first visited the states, the National Democratic Institute in Washington provided fundraising and election workshops to Sinn Fein. In 1995, as Sinn Fein cleaned itself up, it ordered NORAID and Clan-na-Gael to slow their respective fundraising efforts. No longer could Irish America's support networks be so ad hoc and under the table. Instead, in the mid-1990s, Sinn Fein began a momentous effort to wrest its disparate Irish-American support networks into the sunlight. Fundraising streams would be halted, party leadership wrote, until the political group could figure out how to collect them legally.

This process of reinvention led, finally, to formal peace talks, which began in 1997. Getting all of the stakeholders in the room, though, was only half the battle, and the lesser half, at that. The various sides of Northern Ireland's kaleidoscopic war were represented: there were Unionist representatives, members of the British government, members of the Irish government, more moderate Labour party representatives, and Sinn Fein, in the person of Gerry Adams. Many of them were wary of compromise; most were in direct opposition to each other. Tasked with refereeing them was Senator George Mitchell, a veteran American lawmaker who had been appointed by President Bill Clinton as an envoy to Northern Ireland in 1994, the same year as Adams's first consequential visit to the United States.

Even the added weight of American expectation, though, failed to bring consensus. 1997 came and went with Northern Ireland seemingly no closer to peace. To the contrary, dissident spinoffs from both the IRA and Loyalist paramilitaries — ignoring the ceasefire that was a prerequisite for talks — engaged in tit-for-tat killings across Belfast. Tragedies defined the New Year.

At his wit's end and fed up with the petty bickering and politicking, Mitchell declared a deadline for the talks: midnight on Thursday, April 9, 1998, the beginning of the Easter holiday. Good Friday would either bring a new chapter for the island, or send it back into its centuries-old cycle of tribalism and violence — a status quo from which it sometimes seemed Northern Ireland could never break free.

The long war had taken its toll on Northern Ireland. Its costs — and triumphs — were borne by ordinary people. The fathers who buried their sons. The children who lost their mothers. The brothers and sisters and soldiers and civilians, on all sides, who — finally — gave the notoriously turbulent region a chance, whether through votes, or politics, or the simple setting down of a gun.

There were countless everyday people who worked for such an ending. Among them was a small, trusted group of advisers that Adams had gathered together across the span of the peace talks. Many were local Sinn Fein volunteers from West Belfast; some were former Republican prisoners. They undertook a daunting, tedious task during that week in April 1998, leading up to Mitchell's deadline.

In the administration room on the eve of Good Friday, the group gathered to review the peace agreement's proposed language. Every word, every comma, every syllable had to be carefully vetted. No detail was too small, no mention too mundane. For Northern Ireland's peace to work, every component had to be tested, considered, and approved.

Among them was a strong-faced woman, a Belfast native with sharp eyes and a soft voice, poring over a large computer screen. She had been out of prison for more than a decade by then, raising her own family in West Belfast. There was no such thing, though, as a former IRA volunteer — was there?

Who has the right to answer such questions? Can a country, a region, a people, ever truly move past such a blood-soaked history? Or will the land always be bound to a tribal contract, its violent interest collecting for successive generations that are forced, willingly or not, to bear the cost? Even in peace, how does such a tortured, divided land start anew?

"There is someone I know who wants to give it up and lead a normal life," Geraldine Crawford once said, a few years before she arrived to the Stormont Complex in 1998. "The trouble is that here, what is a normal life?"

As morning dawned on Good Friday, Belfast and Northern Ireland took its first, tentative steps toward finding out.

The deadline that Mitchell had set for the peace talks worked. On April 10, 1998, all of the parties signed on to the Good Friday Agreement, a watershed peace accord that overhauled Northern Ireland's social and political structures, ensuring more fair representation of nationalist communities, an eventual withdrawal of British troops from Northern Ireland, and an end to paramilitary violence on all sides. It was a hard-won compromise — negotiations went far into the small hours — that ensured, among other things, that major paramilitary groups would put down their weapons. Such realities had seemed impossible not so long before.

A month after the Good Friday Agreement was reached, majorities of voters in both Northern Ireland and the Republic voted to ratify the accord. Under it, Northern Ireland would remain a separate, British territory, but with significant, permanent changes. A new Northern Irish government, housed at Stormont, would rule the state, this time with structures to ensure equal representation of both nationalists and Unionists. Residents of the territory could opt for British or Irish nationality, or both. And, for the island's future, there was an important carve-out: Northern Ireland could eventually unite with the Republic, if a majority of voters in the island's north and south concurrently voted for it to be so.

The agreement was a triumph, but the fight for peace was far from over. Over the next decade, there followed a long, painful, occasionally violent, usually distrustful process: Northern Ireland would undulate between periods of intense hope and intense wariness, periodically pulled back toward war by dissident breakaway groups who remained staunchly opposed to the Good Friday Agreement. In the tradition of the Republican movement — and just as Vince Conlon had predicted decades before — there were hard-line factions who opposed any political compromise short of a full British withdrawal from the island of Ireland. As the complicated compromise of the Good Friday Agreement was instituted, those factions refused to go quietly. In the years following the agreement, they carried on with periodic but brutal attacks, each one threatening to scuttle the agreement altogether.

A year after the Good Friday Agreement was struck, a new gun-trafficking case popped up in American courts. A group of Irish nationals — three men and one woman — were arrested for attempting to send pistols, shotguns, and ammunition into Northern Ireland via US mail, labeling the packages as toys, videos, and electronics. Among the defendants was a thirty-year-old from Northern Ireland who was working as a handyman in Philadelphia.

The Provisional IRA, in the midst of the nascent peace process, denied that the mission was sanctioned. Despite initial fears that the case could upend the Good Friday Agreement, the four defendants were eventually convicted and mostly forgotten. The ringleader, a Florida-based Belfast man who claimed to be a member of the Provos, said he had been buying guns, in case the peace process were to collapse, in an effort to brace Catholics for the eventual, inevitable return to violence.

That fear would never materialize. But the man's ominous warning to officers underscored the uncertainty that racked Northern Ireland in the midst of the Good Friday Agreement. They're still haunting today: "You didn't get all of us."

There was no shortage of controversy in the peace accords, but the most fraught involved the decommissioning of weapons, an endeavor that caused as many arguments between Unionist and nationalist factions as it did within the Republican movement itself. For nearly ten years after the signing of the Good Friday Agreement, there remained few clear explanations on the decommissioning of IRA weapons, and at times it nearly led to a complete breakdown and reversion to pre-1998 Northern Ireland. The process could not be seen as an act of surrender — such optics could isolate even pro–Good Friday Agreement Republicans. In one instance, the posterity of the document was threatened because Unionist politicians wanted a photographer present at the IRA's decommissioning, a proposal that was soundly rejected by Adams and his cortege.

Finally, in 2005, nudged by a series of rogue killings, Provisional IRA leadership announced "an end to the armed campaign." It was closely followed by a post facto announcement that members of both Protestant and Catholic clergy had overseen the secret, mass decommissioning of "huge amounts" of the IRA's explosives, ammunition, and guns. As with most things in Northern Ireland, the details—where, when, and how—were never revealed, but the act was seen, largely, as the end of the Provos' armed stance. Forty years after American prosecutors first interrupted the IRA's American arms network, the guns—if there were even any of them left—were rendered useless.

Vince Conlon did not live to see that ending. On an April morning in 1995, months after what would become the first in a string of pivotal IRA ceasefires, he was admitted to New York Hospital, his body riddled with cancer. He had been at the printing office past midnight the night before, working on Clan-na-Gael's latest newsletter.

Even stuck in a hospital bed, Conlon remained remarkably focused. Friends came and went, bringing news from Northern Ireland. "The talk always reverted to 'the struggle in the North,'" said a friend later, who had visited Conlon at his New York bedside. "He spoke of the past but stressed the future."

In what would become his final, transatlantic act, Vince Conlon traveled across the ocean to spend the last days of his life back in Rakeeragh, with his children and Marina. He died in Monaghan not long after his return, a few miles south of the border he had fought his entire life to erase.

Vincent Conlon was buried on a quiet hillside near his home, not far from the grave of Fergal O'Hanlon, the IRA volunteer who died on the raid that catapulted Conlon, Dave O'Connell, and the other Brookeborough survivors into IRA lore so many years before. In his crowded funeral was the story of Northern Ireland and the IRA, its intimate connections spooling out among the mourners. There were relatives of O'Hanlon, friends from the 1950s border campaign, Sinn Fein representatives from Belfast and Derry, and colleagues from America, although at least one notable personality was absent: Adams, who, in the midst of the early politicking that would eventually lead to the Good Friday Agreement, sent his regrets for missing the ceremony.

Northern Ireland—and the restless border that defined Conlon's life—would soon find enduring peace through the sort of compromise Conlon himself had the foresight to see decades before, when he first advocated for political conversations in the 1970s. It was a fitting tribute to one of the cause's most dedicated sons. His was a life that stretched across one of the Irish conflict's longest arcs, from the IRA's darkest days to its most violent, then, its most promising.

The reach of his influence, across borders and oceans, was reflected in the crowd gathered in the cemetery that day.

Among the people who came to pay their respects was Pat Doherty, Sinn Fein's vice president, there in Adams's stead. Such rituals, Doherty said, brought bittersweet memories, like another somber day in 1987.

"When I last stood in this graveyard we were gathered to lay to rest the remains of Volunteer Jim Lynagh," Doherty said. "The circumstances were different, then."

These names and graves, this tapestry of violent collisions. In such a small place, in such a long war, there are no strangers. Indeed, how much had changed, since 1987. How much change was still to come.

Today, from that hillside in Rakeeragh, the land is quieter. When you look north, you can see the green hills of Armagh spilling out before you until they dissolve into gray sky. Somewhere between, one country ends and another begins. But as you drive from Vince Conlon's gravesite into Northern Ireland, on winding country roads, there are no more soldiers or checkpoints, no more barricades or pointed guns. In fact, if you weren't paying attention, you wouldn't know you'd crossed a border at all.

EPILOGUE

ANDERSONSTOWN, NORTHERN IRELAND, 2023

I STEPPED OFF the bus in Andersonstown onto a busy street filled with schoolchildren and commuters. It was a beautiful day on the edge of the Christmas season, uncharacteristically sunny, the sky an electric, robin's-egg blue. Laughter was floating from a nearby elementary school and groups of friends were gathered at street corners, chatting and minding their children. I turned off the main road and wandered deeper into West Belfast's housing estates.

It had taken nearly three years of reporting to get to this moment, the end of a journalistic voyage that was filled with twists and turns, setbacks, watershed discoveries and crushing defeats. There had been chilling threats in rural pubs and emotional revelations shared around kitchen tables with strangers. The experience gave me a riot of color and context for an incredible story, but my driving purpose — what had set me on this journey in the first place — was to tell the story of a single American gun in Northern Ireland. On that day in Belfast, the mission still felt maddeningly incomplete.

It was a reporting target that I had naively believed would be easy to land, especially given the fact that I was armed with hundreds of serial numbers. Three years, thousands of documents, and hundreds of interviews later, I had only managed to connect the dots for one particular Philadelphia rifle. The reporting led me to that street corner on a winter day, down the hill from Lenadoon, not far from where the violent incident that led me there had happened in the first place.

I was always a bit on edge while reporting in Belfast, well aware that my intention — of telling a very specific story about a very traumatic time — was not necessarily a welcome one. But that day in Andersonstown, I felt especially uneasy and out of place, less like a reporter than a trespasser. The person for whom I had searched, for years, had politely but unequivocally turned me down. And yet I disregarded her declination and came back, hoping for one more chance. It was an act about which I felt professionally validated but personally nauseated.

The trail that led me to Geraldine Crawford's home was not the product of a sudden revelation. I knew by then that she was shot while holding one of the four hundred Philadelphia rifles that had been sent to the Provos in the early 1970s. But finding that simple fact had required painstaking reporting, first in fifty-year-old American court documents, then in old Belfast newspaper clippings, then in a box of documents squirreled away in a Philadelphia attic, then in partial public records in Northern Ireland. A name led to another name, which had led to a date, which led to a notion, which led to several newspaper offices, a few pubs, and a museum. But still, I hadn't been able to reach her directly. Having heard nothing, I was left to wonder whether the silence was due to missed connections or, rather, to Geraldine Crawford's quiet wish to be left alone.

Unable to let it go, I finally tracked down an address through the obituary of Crawford's husband, published locally in 2023. It's where I was headed on that strange, sunny day.

For months, I had told myself that if I could just speak to Geraldine Crawford face-to-face, I could convince her of the value of sharing her story. I had all of the pieces on the other side of the ArmaLite — using old documents from the American court case, I had been able to identify who had bought the gun she carried in 1973, and where it had come from. Surely, I thought, such details would interest the person whose life they had irrevocably changed. Surely Crawford would want her end of the gun explained, too. It was why I finally sent a long letter to her address, explaining this project and what I hoped to ask her, in person.

At the top of the hill, I saw the street where I ought to turn. I stopped at the corner, taking a moment for myself before I stepped into the housing development.

When this reporting journey started, the story of the Philadelphia guns was faded words on pages. But in the years since, those words have taken on a life of their own. That typewritten text from the Philadelphia courthouse basement led me across an ocean, to a real place with real consequence, and real, living people. How easy it was, when reporting from a distance, to forget such stakes. How much more simple it was to see a story in ink, rather than blood.

I thought all of this on that quiet street corner, the outline of Black Mountain crisp above me, as if punched through the sky. To the south, the horizon was clear of its usual mist, and the meandering streets of West Belfast sprawled before me. Beyond them, the outer limits of the city spread out until it dissolved into country. To the east, I could see the spindly outlines of Samson and Goliath, the Harland and Wolff cranes, standing like sleepy sentries at the city's docks.

I thumbed at my phone and reread an email that had arrived a few weeks before.

Hi Ali, just received your letter about doing interview, it read. **Please be advised that I'm not interested in participating.**

Regards, it was signed. **Geraldine.**

What right do we have to the stories people don't want to tell? I stood for a moment near the sign that said FÁILTE GO LÉANA AN DÚIN. Then I turned from the estate and went on up the hill, toward a bus that would take me away from West Belfast and toward home.

The curiosities that drove this reporting mission were organic and deeply human. In the strange haze of the 2020 coronavirus lockdown, I filled the empty hours trying to unpack a mystery that had bounced across generations of my mother's family, one that no one ever seemed keen to talk about: my great-grandfather — who hailed from Ireland's northern Ulster Province — had emigrated to America in 1922 under suspicious, rushed circumstances, supposedly on the run after serving in the Irish Republican Army. It's a story that many second- and third-generation Irish Americans have in their own histories, but many of those tales take root in New York and Boston. My great-grandfather, though, landed in Philadelphia, nursing sympathies for Irish nationalism — including the Provisional IRA's armed campaign — until his death in the 1980s.

Philadelphia means a lot to me, as a city. It's where my beloved grandmother grew up, where my mother was born, and where my brother and I both started our own adult lives. The perpetual underdog, as fiercely loyal as it is prickly, Philadelphia seemed forever sidelined in the grander conversations about Irish America, eclipsed by the size of New York and the ego of Boston. But in reporting my great-grandfather's story, I unearthed a sensational tale about the city I loved, and a history I never knew.

That my great-grandfather landed in Philadelphia was no accident; he gravitated toward like kind, settling into an insular Irish-American community that supported the same cause he had always believed in. Philadelphia, it turned out, was perhaps the most aggressively Irish of them all, the headquarters for some of the most militant Irish-American Republican groups and the center of one of the most sweeping — and little-known — gun-trafficking cells that had fueled the beginning of Northern Ireland's Troubles.

The great-granddaughter in me was intrigued; the reporter in me was obsessed. The curiosities eventually led me to a 1975 court case in which five men from my great-grandfather's old neighborhood were charged with smuggling hundreds of guns — mostly ArmaLite rifles — into the streets of West Belfast and Derry, an effort to which my great-grandfather had, according to family legend, donated money. In Vince Conlon, Danny Cahalane, and Neil Byrne, I saw the potential to tell a story about the Troubles that hadn't yet been fully tackled, one that many of us in Irish America would perhaps prefer stayed comfortably distant, close enough to co-opt but too far to confront.

The court documents from the Philadelphia Five case were buried in two decaying banker's boxes in a warehouse on the outskirts of Northeast Philadelphia, not far from where my mom grew up. Armed with these files, I spent months in Philadelphia asking anyone connected to the case if they remembered anything specific about the rifles that were sent to Northern Ireland. Did anyone ever mention specific names? I asked. Had anyone ever seen a document about the guns in Northern Ireland?

I got next to nothing. One person said they had helped defense lawyers page through the Northern Irish files back in 1975, and thought some of the guns were found in sheds and cars. Another thought many of them landed in Donegal, smuggled via a sympathetic pub. Another said he didn't remember anything at all.

The absence of evidence defied reason. How could such a sensational story lack such critical details? The Philadelphia men, after all, were accused of serious felonies: trafficking guns to the Irish Republican Army.

Looking for a break, I reached out to the Police Services of Northern Ireland, the successor to the RUC, created out of the Good Friday Agreement. My request for help was tricky, I acknowledged, because secrecy rules still governed many public disclosures related to the Troubles. Still, though, I explained, I already had half the story from American court documents. Surely it would make sense that Northern Irish authorities could help me connect the dots I already had.

It was a naive effort. After working with an officer to locate some of the documents ostensibly tied to the Philadelphia guns, a PSNI supervisor unceremoniously swooped in and dashed my hopes. There would be no disclosure of the Philadelphia files, regardless of how blasé the American justice system might be about the details of the case.

Just because they gave it to you in America, the man said, sounding both annoyed and offended, *doesn't mean we'll give it to you here.*

Even in the Western world's contemporary tilt toward government accountability and transparency, there is a significant gap when it comes to Northern Ireland. It's a void that is both maddening and understandable, given the recent, complicated history of the Troubles. According to statistics from the region's Information Commissioner's Office, in Belfast, there were only ninety-one requests filed in 2023 under the territory's Freedom of Information (FOI) statute. The numbers alone baffled me. American law-enforcement agencies are notoriously inundated with FOIA requests (under the corresponding US law, in effect since 1967), buried under years' worth of backlogs, so much so that an entire cottage industry has sprung up in the States to help journalists and members of the public navigate the clunky, byzantine process. There is an expectation among US citizens generally that the public ought to be given information — that we have the right — and there's a collective willingness to ask for it. But even in a significantly smaller country like Northern Ireland, a mere ninety-one FOI requests seemed like a shockingly low number. And in Northern Ireland, there is no comparable infrastructure in place to help members of the public navigate the process.

This diffidence is indicative of a broader trend around the Troubles, and specifically within Irish Republicanism, where the movement has created a stunningly successful messaging machine that manages to say both plenty and nothing at all. In Northern Ireland, discretion and secrecy are not just mechanisms for officials to avoid accountability; they amount to a cultural and social responsibility that much of Belfast and Northern Ireland still collectively

carries, with deadly seriousness. It's a strange sort of balancing act, one that —
admittedly — is almost impossible for an outsider who never lived through the
horror of the Troubles to understand.

But it is one I was warned about, early. Not long after I arrived in Ireland, I
followed the trail of the policeman's rifle up to Burnfoot, a village in Donegal. I
was led there by a single piece of paper from the FBI, released under the American FOIA, which suggested a Philadelphia gun might've turned up within the
town's perimeter, half a century ago. It was a desperate journey, undertaken
with no clear plan, no real backup, and no explanation for why a stranger was
asking around about a fifty-year-old case. But I hoped I might at least find a
willing ear at the local pub, where a stray Philadelphia connection or my own
family's history might lend some credibility to otherwise bizarre questions.

It was a clumsy, unpolished landing — one I would not have the luxury of
making twice. The bartender, having successfully plied me for my intentions,
had me wait around until some of the local men wandered in. What came next
was a brilliantly sharp maneuver, one I foolishly failed to foresee.

"Hiya boys. She's a journalist," the woman said, jerking her chin at
me, throwing me to the wolves. "Do you all know anything about guns in
Burnfoot?"

I knew then. The next time I arrived to Burnfoot — if there *was* a next
time — the whole town would know who I was, and what I was asking.

The man at the counter studied me, then turned, sharply, to the man at his
elbow.

"Say nothing," he muttered, the casual, final postscript that locks this
island's stories away, like ghosts in an endless purgatory.

Is it even possible, so many years on, for a single gun to tell the story of a war?
Maybe not. But maybe it *can* bring to life the scale and consequences of the conflict, and challenge us to carry its legacy differently.

Irish America remains proud of having armed the IRA, but how little we
know about the lives that these weapons touched, for better and worse. As one
disillusioned descendant of the Philly Five put it, there could be peace for years
in Northern Ireland, but given the opportunity, plenty of Irish Americans
would still shoot the Queen. It's easy, another remarked, to pull a trigger from
three thousand miles away.

EPILOGUE

And yet, the story of Northern Ireland and Irish America is inextricably linked. We know of the large ways, but we know less of the smaller ones, of the day-to-day, the people and faces whose fates were codependent. The further we get from those awful, violent years, the more of those stories we lose. I'm not sure how one chooses what's worth forgetting, but I do know this: peace is a difficult thing to find, without clear accountings of the past. The ambiguity of half-truths, perhaps, can be a more dangerous ending.

It took three years, three different countries, thousands of documents, and more than a hundred interviews to finally track just one of the Philadelphia ArmaLites to a real incident in Northern Ireland. Even then, certain details are probably lost forever — memories fade, people pass on, and government files on both sides of the Atlantic are aging out of their retention time frames. There were hundreds of those guns, each with a story that's either already lost to time, or will be, soon. Multiplied across the scope of the Troubles, it's an overwhelming amount of information that we may just never know.

The gun that Geraldine Crawford was holding that dark night in Belfast, on her first IRA mission, was a gun bought by Vincent Conlon, Neil Byrne, and Daniel Cahalane on March 21, 1972, snuck over on a ship in a box that was labeled as household supplies, and smuggled into West Belfast via a network of pickups that secretly moved the gun across the border. Who knows what other lives it impacted, in the months before the gun was recovered on that September night. I've wondered if Geraldine had any idea of the long journey that ArmaLite took to get to her, and I've wondered if Vince Conlon ever knew where it had landed. It's ironic and strange that the person who was hurt while brandishing that weapon was actually one of his own comrades.

Did they ever cross paths? Did they know of each other within Sinn Fein circles, never understanding how closely their fortunes were tied?

I've wondered, and then I've wondered if it matters. Somewhere, in the scattered continuum of Northern Ireland, perhaps two people crossed paths one day along the border, passing by each other like two atoms on different planes. Perhaps a restless IRA man and a quiet former prisoner from Armagh sat at the same table in the 1990s, or brushed shoulders on the street, or gathered at the same hillside graveyard to bury the North's dead. Or perhaps the two of them lived their respective stories never knowing that they shared such intimate triggers, that across the most traumatic years of their lives, a shadow character had followed them from the other side.

EPILOGUE

Not far from Vincent Conlon's grave is the plot of Jim Lynagh, a notably hard-line IRA man who succeeded Conlon as a Sinn Fein candidate in Monaghan in 1979. The pair of them were friends and remained so until Lynagh's violent death in 1987, when he was shot and killed during an IRA attack on a police station. Who knows how much the two men ever discussed about those early years of the 1970s? Who knows if they ever traded contacts, or compared tales of those confused days of 1973, when Lynagh was on the front and Conlon had just returned from America?

The dead may know these things, but we never will. Perhaps Jim Lynagh and Vince Conlon once spoke of their most passing, sensational connection. Perhaps Conlon knew of the bizarre clash of fates. Perhaps Lynagh mentioned the kind girl with the bandaged, bloody knees from the security wing of Belfast's Musgrave Park Hospital in the autumn of 1973. Perhaps Conlon and Crawford stood together on the same fresh dirt, on the same day, watching a friend be laid to rest.

Or perhaps none of this ever happened. Perhaps Northern Ireland could've gone on with its strange, unreckoned peace, without ever knowing these truths. Perhaps none of it really matters, and perhaps, like so many of this island's secrets, these minutiae of war are better left buried.

As discreet as the men from Philadelphia were in their lethal endeavors, the debacle remained an open secret among their friends and family, some of whom didn't realize the extent of their fathers' involvements until well into adulthood. It's a complicated thing, to find out your parents do more in life than simply parent. It's a particularly difficult one to find out their other pastimes involved gunrunning and international arms smuggling, and that they risked the livelihood and stability of their families. Some of the men's children understood the stakes, and many are deeply proud of their fathers' legacies. A few have even picked up their generational mission, albeit in far less illegal ways; many have stayed involved in Philadelphia's Irish community, and some even tried their hands at leading various iterations of NORAID before it fizzled out. Others, soured by the endless disagreements and traditional splits among Irish Americans, stay away. Many remain conflicted about their fathers' choices, subsequently proud of their principles and — now as parents themselves — disturbed at the lack of regard for their own well-being as children.

Vincent Conlon's son Sean, the boy who remembers the bloody slab at the morgue, never followed his father's path into armed conflict. But he did pick up what is perhaps a more lasting legacy: since 2004, Sean has held his father's old seat on the Monaghan County Council. As a Sinn Fein representative, he has helped champion cross-border conversations and post-conflict resolution strategies. He's a shocking mirror of his dad, lanky and tall with the same dark brow and the same restless gleam in his eye. In a recent conversation, we chatted about the challenges of a united Ireland and the growing realization that a referendum for a thirty-two-county island is likely nearer than it's ever been. That subject has grown increasingly likely, particularly as a united Ireland becomes more and more palatable to a post-Brexit generation of Northern Irish voters, free from the Troubles' immediate baggage.

It would be a sensational ending to a centuries-long saga. Sean Conlon, though, refused the kind of nativist language that might be associated with such outcomes. He recalled a line his father had once said, one that had gotten Vince sharply criticized but that Sean still holds close: he looked forward, Vince Conlon once said, to the day the Orange Order could parade peacefully in his adopted home of Monaghan. Such seemingly impossible events

Deep in the pine forests of the border, Sean Conlon unlocks the safe house where his father, Vince, hid out after the 1957 Brookeborough raid.

would prove for certain that the place had fostered a tolerant society, and was truly at peace.

Sean, too, has inherited such realism. When his father's dream of a united country finally comes to fruition, he says, it will not just be a victory for Irish Republicans. It can't be. When a united Ireland happens, it must be a solution for Unionists, too. It will be — it *must* be — a country, and an island, for everyone.

Vince Conlon, of course, died just before he could see where that first, hugely consequential 1994 visit from Gerry Adams would lead. Marina Conlon lived the rest of her days surrounded by family and loved ones in Monaghan, where she died in 2020.

Neil Byrne eventually returned to Ireland, too, though he did live to see the end of the conflict he had, for so long, helped fuel. He would spend the rest of his life back in Donegal's Glencolmcille, in a house by the sea, where he lived with his memories and his dog, Growler. In his later years, he was known to share stories at the local pub of his time in an American prison, and recollections of his and Vince Conlon's gunrunning antics. The two families stayed in touch until Neil Byrne's death in the early 2000s.

The other veterans of the NORAID network met a variety of ends, some more violent than others. John McCullough, the head of Philadelphia's roofers' union and a key ally for NORAID and its network of IRA fugitives, was killed in 1980, by a hit man who walked into his kitchen, posing as a flower deliveryman; it was a slaying the police believed to be mob-related, connected to disputes over casinos in Atlantic City. Hugh Breen went more quietly, passing away in 1985 at eighty-six. Even as Irish America frayed around him, he remained a dedicated supporter of the IRA and the Irish cause until he died. His last words to a NORAID colleague were "Keep up the fight."

Daniel Duffy passed away in the spring of 1999, the year after the Good Friday Agreement. The full details of his reported cooperation with federal authorities remain lost to history, but rumors of the arrangement have periodically haunted his children, who do not believe them; indeed, Duffy's own pronouncements and behavior suggest *he* may not have even known that the FBI ever considered him an informant — after all, it was well known that Duffy would talk about Ireland to anyone who would listen. After Duffy died, his remaining guns were disposed of privately — no one, it seemed, knew if they were legally purchased, and it was easier not to ask.

Danny Cahalane died in March 1980, at age fifty-five, of a heart attack. One day, not long after he was buried, a group of his friends gathered to take his old green work van into a mechanic's shop for a brief but critical cleanup. It was over quickly, and the van was returned to his family looking the same as it had, albeit a little lighter. Danny, after all, had never stopped doing the same things that had sent him to prison. Until the day he died, he got good use out of that false bottom he had welded onto his green van. It just needed to be cleared out one last time.

Marty Lyons worked as a plumber for thirty years in New York, though his profile in the Irish community remained shadowy, and he is rarely mentioned in relation to NORAID. After retiring, he moved to upstate New York, where he had his own farm, and eventually relocated to Myrtle Beach, South Carolina, to be closer to family and, according to his obituary, "his lifelong friends from 'the Old Country.'" He died at age eighty-three.

Bob Merkle had a long, illustrious career as US attorney for the Middle District of Florida, in Tampa. He went on to prosecute drug kingpins and political rivals, and do it with the delicacy of a raging bull. Among other things, he was once charged in a road rage incident in which he punched another driver. He died well known and, if not well liked, then at least well respected, in 2003. Brandon Alvey, for his part, went on to work several more IRA-related gunrunning cases before being unceremoniously fired from the Justice Department, supposedly due to an indiscretion committed while out drinking with some visiting authorities from Belfast. He is said to have died by suicide not long after.

At the time of this writing, Geraldine Crawford is alive and living in Belfast, where she still works closely with a community organization for women ex-prisoners of the Republican movement. Respecting her wishes not to be interviewed for this book, I opted instead to piece together her story using a collection of other sources, including photographs, news reports, and — critically — three lengthy, firsthand interviews she gave in later years to other researchers and community groups about her life in Belfast and her service in the IRA. They are cited in this book's Notes section in the back. She does not appear to have spoken publicly about her life in recent decades.

I don't know what might've happened that clear winter day if I had turned and walked into Lenadoon, marched up to an unwelcoming foyer, and knocked. The reporter in me says it might've been the crack that broke the dam. But the realist, the human, the great-granddaughter in me knows, and knew, probably, from the beginning: the other end of the Philadelphia gun was never going to talk. Expecting otherwise was perhaps its own exercise of Irish-American naivety. This is both the maddening and completely predictable ending of this path. The truth is, I'm not sure that any of us are owed her story, anyway.

And what of the guns themselves? Of the 378 Philadelphia firearms the men were charged with sending, 180 were recovered in Northern Ireland by 1976. One of them was Geraldine Crawford's. In a 1987 accounting of the Provisional IRA, writers Patrick Bishop and Eamonn Mallie quote security forces in Northern Ireland, who claimed 420 weapons thus far had been seized and traced back to the Philadelphia men. More almost certainly remained — the conflicting figures suggest that Vince Conlon, Danny Cahalane, and Neil Byrne sent far more guns than the 378 rifles the US government charged them with sending. It's impossible to know how many stayed in circulation, and how many went unaccounted for. Some of them were almost certainly recovered but not identified as being part of the Philadelphia Five trove. Whatever was left on the street, like most of the IRA's hardware, was likely neutralized in the mass decommissioning process that followed the Good Friday Agreement, left somewhere secret, useless and forgotten.

But in the years since the IRA's mass disarmament, rumors have persisted about the guns that weren't turned over, the rifles that were never given up but which instead sit, waiting, in oil drums and dirt, hidden in backyards and forest parks, just out of reach but ready, if the moment should ever come when they are needed again. Such whispers have been periodically validated, like when police officers uncovered a buried drum full of guns and bullets in 2023, suspected to have been hidden away by the New IRA, one of a handful of dissident groups that split from the Provos during the peace process. Even as Northern Ireland has stabilized, such dangerous discoveries are reminders that the wound of the Troubles has still not fully healed.

It is left to the living to bear this weight. Much has stayed with me from this reporting, but there is a line that still haunts me, said by an ex-combatant outside Derry. In it was a profound sense of resignation, that as Ireland imagines its future, it may abandon an entire generation to its unreconciled past.

"I suppose we are remnants," the person said, "of anxious and terrible times."

ACKNOWLEDGMENTS

MY GRATITUDE IS endless to Professor Ruan O'Donnell in Limerick and Professor Danielle Zach in New York, who have become not just colleagues, but friends in this work.

This book would not have been possible without the editing of Alexander Littlefield and Morgan Wu at Little, Brown, whose careful attention to this complicated story turned it into something worth reading. It would've never even gotten to their desks had it not been for Justin Brouckaert, who saw the potential in the Philadelphia Five before I did. I remain forever indebted to Mike Wilson, the greatest writer I know, for being a first reader.

To the staff at the Philadelphia federal courthouse, especially Steve, who looked after that box of documents for months: thank you. It would've taken so little for this story to have been lost forever; because of you, it wasn't.

There are librarians all over the world who facilitated this project — in Philly, New York, Derry, Belfast, Galway, Dublin, and lots of other places. Your work is so important, and it has been the greatest pleasure of this process to work with so many of you.

Thank you, to Trina Vargo, the US Ireland Alliance, and the George Mitchell Scholarship Program, which supported my initial relocation to Ireland, partly in pursuit of this project. Thank you especially to Abby Barton, the greatest Mitchell Scholar, who was my sidekick and supporter on many reporting missions to the border and beyond. There are not enough words in the English language to fully express my gratitude and support for the University of Galway's Masters in Writing program, and especially Elaine Feeney, whose friendship and instruction have made me a more thoughtful journalist and a more disciplined writer.

I have been humbled at the kindness of strangers across the world, many of whom have become friends over this long, lonely work of a book. To the

ACKNOWLEDGMENTS

Cahalane, Duffy, and Conlon families, and so many others in Irish Philadelphia: thank you for welcoming me into your clubs, bars, homes, and lives. I am honored to hear and tell your stories. To Patsy Kelly, Matt Regan, Joe McGettigan, and the MacSwiney Club, which is not only the most interesting Irish pub in Philly, but the best bar around — thank you.

Most importantly, to the countless people in Northern Ireland and along the border who showed me such kindness and grace, I am so grateful for your trust. Thank you to the staff at the *Andersonstown News,* who welcomed me into their offices, and the Derry Public Library, which was my second home for several weeks.

There are so many friends and loved ones who tolerated nearly three years of periodic disappearances, radio silence, and scattered rantings about serial numbers in the 1970s. Among them: Sopan, Wesley, Katie Bo, Jon, Nicole, Amy Julia, Akbar, Lauren, Rachel, Katie, and Kara. Thank you for still inviting me to things. And to Mike Wade, my friend, who first helped me go through the Philly transcripts when this was all just a hunch — thank you.

Finally, to my parents, two of the most loyal and generous people I've ever known; to Josh, whose friendship, support, and air mattress made this happen; and to Dylan — I moved to Ireland to write this story, and found ours. Thank you all for so graciously bearing the burden, of loving a writer. I am so lucky. You are my world.

AUTHOR'S NOTE

To RECONSTRUCT THE story of the Philadelphia Five, I relied on more than one hundred original interviews across Philadelphia, New York, Ireland, and Northern Ireland, dozens of trips to West Belfast, Derry, and Donegal, and thousands of pages of historic documents from Ireland, Great Britain, and America, including court transcripts, internal government correspondence, and the personal papers of several characters. Much of this story, though, remains lost to time and fading memories. More than fifty years have passed, and many records have been lost, purposefully destroyed, or forgotten. Critically, the evidence file of the Philadelphia Five case — which belonged to the Bureau of Alcohol, Tobacco, and Firearms, the case's investigating agency — was not preserved by the ATF when the agency moved from the Treasury Department to the Justice Department in 2003. The agency, now known as the Bureau of Alcohol, Tobacco, Firearms, and Explosives, says it retains no documents pertaining to either this particular case or this critical period of IRA-related prosecutions more broadly.

In converting this research into a narrative, I have described exact scenes and circumstances to the best of my ability, and sought to corroborate witness accounts, interviews, and memory through multiple sources where possible. In many cases, anecdotes were relayed without specific dates or places, and were simply described as having happened around the same time as the events described in this book. Some details of scenes and conversations have been pieced together from multiple accounts.

Many of my sources requested anonymity for fear of potential legal consequences surrounding the events of this period, or ostracization within their communities if it was revealed that they spoke to a journalist. In almost every interview, subjects expressed concern related to the doomed Belfast Project at Boston College from the early 2000s, in which dozens of Troubles-era combatants gave recorded interviews with the assurance that such transcripts would only be released posthumously; instead, the recordings were obtained by legal authorities in the United Kingdom and used to build legal cases against former IRA combatants. Such incidents have made it even more difficult to record interviews within these communities. The burden of secrecy surrounding this subject remains vividly alive, particularly in West Belfast and Derry, where memory is long and tensions short.

Language is a delicate thing when it comes to Northern Ireland, where the very use of certain terms or titles implies certain loyalties. For the purposes of narrative clarity, except where otherwise noted, I have used "Provos," "Provisionals," and "IRA" mostly interchangeably; after the IRA split in 1970, I clearly denote when the contingent of volunteers about whom I'm speaking is the Official IRA.

I often refer to British-affiliated authorities in Northern Ireland as Northern Irish or Unionist officials and I describe authorities who are primarily based in Westminster or London as British. I also use "British security forces" to describe the collective efforts of the British Army and the Royal Ulster Constabulary in Northern Ireland. I use the word "volunteer" to describe those who joined the IRA or other Republican paramilitary groups, and "cause" to describe the IRA's goal of uniting Ireland's thirty-two counties, but use of these words is not intended to imply support, for or against, that which they describe. I often refer to the island's southern twenty-six counties as "the Republic" or "the Republic of Ireland"; and use "Northern Ireland" and "the North of Ireland" interchangeably, to describe the separated six counties in the island's North.

In some cases, particularly where requested by friends or family of the characters, I have used traditional Irish spellings and names on first reference, along with the corresponding Anglicized, English name. To that end, in most instances, I have referred to Clan-na-Gael by its full, formal title; periodically, I also refer to it as "the Clan" or "the Brotherhood." Use of the gendered term — which comes from Clan-na-Gael's own documentation — is not meant to overlook its small but extremely active contingent of women members.

Early on in this project, I sought to reach a former representative of NORAID to discuss this reporting. The man did not respond to my messages, and given the length of time since the events described in this book — and that the organization no longer exists in any unified or discernible form — those efforts were abandoned.

Finally, in an important distinction for American readers, I often refer to adherents of the IRA's beliefs as "Republicans," a political term that bears no resemblance or connection to American Republicanism. Instead, Republicanism in Ireland is traditionally aligned with leftist politics.

NOTES

THIS BOOK WAS greatly aided by more than one hundred interviews conducted by the author across the course of four years, from Philadelphia to New York to Ireland and Northern Ireland. In an effort to respect the privacy of those who spoke, most of those conversations are not specifically cited in these endnotes.

PROLOGUE

The operation in Andersonstown is described by Geraldine Crawford to Eileen MacDonald, in *Shoot the Women First* (Reading, UK: Cox & Wyman Ltd., 1991), 160–164; additional details are found in a series of articles in the *Belfast Telegraph* from October 1973, April 1974, and September 1974. The security conditions in Andersonstown are described in *A Tough Nut to Crack: Andersonstown,* by Steve Corbett (West Midlands, UK: Helion, 2015); *The Troubles: Ireland's Ordeal 1969–95 and the Search for Peace,* by Tim Pat Coogan (London: Hutchinson, 1995), 187; and a series of articles in the *Andersonstown News* from 1972 through 1974, including its republished series "As Others See Us."

The economic, social, and security conditions in 1970s Northern Ireland are described in *Making Sense of the Troubles: A History of the Northern Ireland Conflict,* rev. ed., by David McKittrick and David McVea (London: Penguin/Viking, 2012), 8–14 and 19–25; *Say Nothing: A True Story of Murder and Memory,* by Patrick Radden Keefe (London: HarperCollins, 2018; New York: Doubleday, 2019), 12–15; and Coogan, *The Troubles,* 14. Economic conditions are also addressed in John Bradley's paper "The History of Economic Development in Ireland, North and South" (British Academy, 1999). The American perspective on Catholic oppression in Northern Ireland is described in an internal CIA briefing paper from 1949, released as part of the Freedom of Information Act ("Ireland," Central Intelligence Agency, SR-48, April 1, 1949).

Details on the IRA's border campaign are found in *Armed Struggle: A History of the IRA,* by Richard English (New York: Oxford University Press, 2003), 71–76; Coogan, *The Troubles,* 64–66; and Ed Moloney's *A Secret History of the IRA* (New York: W. W. Norton, 2003), 49–52.

Northern Ireland in the early 1970s is described in McKittrick and McVea, *Making Sense of the Troubles*; Coogan, *The Troubles;* Moloney, *Secret History of the IRA;* Keefe, *Say Nothing;* English, *Armed Struggle;* Ed Moloney, *Voices from the Grave: Two Men's War in Ireland* (London: Faber & Faber, 2010); *We Don't Know Ourselves: A Personal History of Ireland Since 1958,* by Fintan O'Toole (UK: Head of Zeus, 2021); *Daughter of Derry: The Story of Brigid*

Sheils Makowski, by Maggie Bernard (Bloomington, IN: Author's Choice Press, 1989); *Provos: The IRA and Sinn Fein,* by Peter Taylor (London: Bloomsbury, 1997); *War and an Irish Town,* third ed., by Eamonn McCann (Chicago: Haymarket Books, 1974); and *The Provisional IRA,* by Patrick Bishop and Eamonn Mallie (London: Heinemann, 1987). Descriptions can also be found in the daily coverage of the *Derry Journal,* the *Belfast Telegraph,* and the *Andersonstown News.*

CHAPTER 1

The letter that arrived at Vincent Conlon's Philadelphia home was part of his personal papers, which were provided to the author in September 2022. The cited correspondence is part of a collection of undated, unsigned letters whose contents line up with the 1969 IRA split. Occasionally, the letters are signed "SMcS," which is likely Seán MacStíofáin, a compatriot of Conlon's who went on to be a leader in the Provos.

Included with these papers is a series of letters between Conlon, Cathal Goulding, and IRA leadership in Dublin across the 1960s.

Vincent Conlon's life is described in an eighteen-page commemorative pamphlet published by Clan-na-Gael upon Conlon's death in 1995 and available as part of Indiana University's Irish Republican Movement Collection.

Conlon was also described in interviews conducted by the author with his son Sean, which took place over a period of years. The 1957 Donegal gun-smuggling incident is described in Clan-na-Gael's commemorative pamphlet and in two articles in the *Philadelphia Bulletin* — Carol Ritch, "I Love Ireland Like My Mother," December 23, 1975, and "Former Upper Darby Man Arrested as IRA Member," April 14, 1957 — and a partial clipping from an unknown source ("Arms Find in Donegal Border Town," April 15, 1957) provided by Professor Ruan O'Donnell, University of Limerick.

The IRA's 1950s border campaign is described in Coogan's *The Troubles,* 65; English's *Armed Struggle,* 72–73; and Moloney's *Secret History of the IRA,* 50–51. The American perspective on the IRA's stature leading up to the border offensive is found in "Ireland," an internal 1949 CIA briefing paper.

CHAPTER 2

Clan-na-Gael's history is described in Jack Holland, *The American Connection* (Niwot, CO: Roberts Rinehart, 1987); Wilson's *Irish America and the Ulster Conflict 1968–1995,* 8–16; Bernard, *Daughter of Derry,* 42–45; *The McGarrity Papers: Revelations of the Irish Revolutionary Movement in Ireland and America 1900–1940,* by Sean Cronin (County Kerry, Ireland: Anvil Press, 1972), 14–17; and Coogan, *The Troubles,* 12. The group's history is also detailed in Villanova University's Joseph McGarrity Collection and in the personal papers of Vincent Conlon. The FBI describes its understanding of Clan-na-Gael in internal briefing papers from the 1950s and 1960s, released as part of the Freedom of Information Act.

Clan-na-Gael's botched Fenian campaign is described by Robert Collins in *NORAID and the Northern Ireland Troubles 1970–1994* (Dublin: Four Courts Press, 2022), 17; and its broader role in the Irish War for Independence is explored by Francis M. Carroll in *America and the Making of an Independent Ireland: A History* (New York: New York University Press, 2021).

The history of the Irish in the city of Philadelphia is described in Dennis Clark, *The Irish in Philadelphia: Ten Generations of Urban Experience* (Philadelphia: Temple University Press, 1973);

NOTES

Dennis Clark, *Irish Blood: Northern Ireland and the American Conscience* (Port Washington, NY: Kennikat Press, 1977); and Michael L. Mullan, *The Philadelphia Irish: Nation, Culture, and the Rise of a Gaelic Public Sphere* (New Brunswick, NJ: Rutgers University Press, 2021). The concentration of Northern Irish émigrés is detailed in *The Philadelphia Irish*, 92–93; and in *The Irish in Philadelphia*, 33–34. In a 1974 article in *Philadelphia Magazine,* Mike Mallowe notes cultural differences: "The Boston Irish became politically precocious and the New York Micks permeated every level of society, but in Philadelphia they remained largely on the construction trades, on the police force, and among the ranks of saloon-keepers" ("The Rising of the Moon").

Descriptions of the contemporary 1970s Irish diaspora in Philadelphia can be found in Mullan's *The Philadelphia Irish;* Clark's *The Irish in Philadelphia* and *Irish Blood;* Holland's *American Connection;* and Bernard's *Daughter of Derry.* The concentration of Northern Irish immigrants in Philadelphia is described in Mullan, *The Philadelphia Irish,* 93; and Clark, *The Irish in Philadelphia,* 34. The phrase "the thirty-third county" is claimed by a handful of other heavily Irish enclaves, including Boston.

Conlon's impact on the clan was noted in several FBI cables from the early 1960s. The role of the MacSwiney Club is described in the club's own literature, including a commemorative anniversary pamphlet. Brigid Makowski describes her initial nomination into Clan-na-Gael as having happened at the MacSwiney Club in Bernard, *Daughter of Derry,* 43; and an advertisement in the *Philadelphia Daily News* in 1972 and preserved by the FBI lists Clan-na-Gael's headquarters as "The MacSweeney [*sic*] Club."

Vince Conlon was banned permanently from the United Nations alongside his friend Brendan Kerr when the pair traveled to New York to see Irish prime minister Seán Lemass. During LeMass's speech, Conlon shouted from the balcony: "Ireland is not free. You do not represent all the Irish people" ("UN Ejects 2 City Men for Heckling," *Philadelphia Bulletin,* October 18, 1963).

Hugh Breen and John McCullough were described to the author in several interviews. Breen's IRA service history is described in a biography published in a 1974 NORAID pamphlet for a dinner in Astoria. Breen is separately described in an article in *Philadelphia Magazine* in March 1973 (Mike Mallowe, "My Life and Times with the IRA").

John McCullough's tenure as leader of the Philadelphia and South Jersey Roofers Union is described in "Union Terror in the Building Trades" (Mark Frazier, *Reason,* October 1972). The arrangement to place Irish fugitives within unions in Philadelphia and other cities was described by several sources during interviews by the author in the Philadelphia area and Ireland.

CHAPTER 3

The split between the Provisional and Official IRA in 1969–70 is described in McKittrick and McVea, *Making Sense of the Troubles,* 69; Moloney's *Secret History of the IRA,* 68–73; Moloney's *Voices from the Grave,* 17–20, 44–46; English's *Armed Struggle,* 103–8; Coogan's *The Troubles,* 90–105, 112–13; Taylor's *Provos,* 59–68; and Bishop and Mallie, *Provisional IRA,* 119–49. Gerry Adams's presence at the Provisional walk-out is historically disputed. Cathal Goulding's faction long claimed Adams was present; Adams has maintained he wasn't.

Belfast's economic fluctuations, including its shipbuilding and linen industries, are described in McCann, *War and an Irish Town,* loc. 3760; Bradley's "The History of Economic Development in Ireland," 42; and Coogan, *The Troubles,* 14. The city's population numbers are detailed in the *New York Times* article "Population of Belfast Drops 25% in Decade," January 2, 1983.

The Apprentice Boys march and the Battle of the Bogside on August 12–14, 1969, are described in Coogan, *The Troubles,* 87–90; McKittrick and McVea, *Making Sense of the Troubles,* 61–65; McCann, *War and an Irish Town,* loc. 2236; and a series of articles in the *Derry Journal,* August 1969. The quote "There is hope in the future" was published in an article in the *Derry Journal,* August 15, 1969. The *Derry Journal,* like many other papers in the north of Ireland, has its own bias; it is known to be a nationalist paper and is anti-unionist in its writing.

The deployment of British troops to Northern Ireland is described in Coogan, *The Troubles,* 91–97; and Moloney, *Voices from the Grave,* 16. The violence in Belfast the night of August 14 is described in Coogan, *The Troubles,* 99–100; and Moloney, *Voices from the Grave,* 15–20. The IRA's lack of guns is described in Bishop and Mallie, *Provisional IRA,* 168–69; Moloney, *Voices from the Grave,* 17, 90; and Coogan, *The Troubles,* 90.

CHAPTER 4

Joseph McGarrity's Thompson machine-gun shipments are described in Cronin, *McGarrity Papers,* 98–100.

Further history of gunrunning from America to the IRA is described in Wilson, *Irish America and the Ulster Conflict,* 3–16; Holland, *American Connection,* 11–21; and Clark's *Irish Blood,* 3–14. Irish-American efforts to arm the IRA during its Easter Rising in 1916 are described in the feature "Easter Rising 1969: How an Irish Rebellion Sought International Help" (BBC, March 24, 2016).

The fight between the Officials and the Provos over guns is addressed in Moloney, *Voices from the Grave,* 49; and Bishop and Mallie, *Provisional IRA,* 168–71.

The use of the word "Stickies" or "Sticks" to describe the Official IRA can be found in Coogan, *The Troubles,* 113; and Moloney, *Voices from the Grave,* 11–14.

Daithi O'Connell's New York trip is described in Holland, *American Connection,* 81; and more broadly in Collins, *NORAID and the Northern Ireland Troubles,* 23.

Brigid Makowski puts the visit of the Provos to Philadelphia "about three weeks" after she was released from the hospital following the birth of her son in October 1969, and says the delegation included Sean Keenan and Joe Cahill (Bernard, *Daughter of Derry,* 73). Separately, in *Irish America and the Ulster Conflict,* 87, Wilson says this trip happened in December 1969: "The I.R.A. sent Sean Keenan to America to coordinate the purchase of arms. He contacted a group of Irish-Americans in Philadelphia." This trip is further described in Bishop and Mallie, *Provisional IRA,* 294–95.

Cathal Goulding's subsequent visit to discredit their efforts is described in Bernard, *Daughter of Derry,* 74: "The visit prompted Goulding to travel to the U.S. to discredit them.... Golding [sic] said that there had been a secret attempt by certain members of Jack Lynch's cabinet to take over and undermine Sinn Fein and the IRA, and that Keenan and Cahill were being used by these people."

When one thinks of the Armalite the contemporary association is with the Armalite AR-15, the civilian version of the M16 military rifle that was introduced to the market in the 1960s. Lesser known is the Armalite AR-18 series, which included the AR-18 and the AR-180, the semi-automatic version. The origins of the AR-180 are detailed in the National Rifle Association magazine *American Rifleman:* Dave Campbell, "A Look Back at the Armalite AR-18/180" (August 9, 2018); and Guy J. Sagi, "Armalite AR-18: The Forgotten AR" (September 1, 2021). Although it appears the IRA showed little preference between the Armalite models, the AR-180 was the American gun that the group more regularly received, and the main gun that the Philadelphia men shipped over. (Most accounts that describe the IRA's guns at the time simply refer to the weapons as "Armalites"; those that do describe them further tend to call them AR-15s; court testimony and firearms records as part of the Philadelphia trial show this was not always the case.) The AR-180's specifications are additionally detailed in the testimony of ATF agent Frank A. Moyer at the Philadelphia trial (*United States of America v. Neil Byrne et al.* (75-773 E.D. Pa. 1976)).

Michael Flannery is profiled in Holland, *American Connection;* Collins, *NORAID and the Northern Ireland Troubles,* 21–28; and Nate Lavey's *Foreign Agent* podcast ("The New World and the Old Country," 2022, Novara Media), from which Flannery's direct quote beginning "The sword" is taken.

The Official and Provisional IRA's respective welfare structures for volunteers' dependents are described in an internal 1987 briefing paper from the Northern Ireland Office, "The IRA: Finance and Weapons," accessed via Ulster University's digital Conflict Archive on the Internet, or CAIN.

Bernadette Devlin's disastrous visit to the United States is detailed in Collins, *NORAID and the Northern Ireland Troubles,* 30–31; Wilson, *Irish America and the Ulster Conflict,* 31–40; and Holland, *American Connection,* 205–6.

The beginnings of NORAID are detailed in Holland, *American Connection,* 27–62; Collins, *NORAID and the Northern Ireland Troubles,* 22–44; and Wilson, *Irish America and the Ulster Conflict,* 42–43. NORAID's early expansions are also described in court transcripts on the fourteenth day of the Philadelphia Five trial (*United States of America v. Neil Byrne et al.*). The term "the inner circle" is used by Martin Lyons, in a recorded 2014 interview about NORAID with New York University's Tamiment Library, available as part of its Ireland House Oral History Collection.

The structure of NORAID was described to the author in dozens of interviews with former members of its Philadelphia chapters. It is also described by Danielle A. Zach in "'It Was Networking, All Networking': The Irish Republican Movement's Survival in Cold War America" (*Journal of Ethnic and Migration Studies,* January 24, 2019), 8–9.

Details of the Irish-American schisms following the IRA's split are described in Wilson, *Irish America and the Ulster Conflict,* 46–48. The acrimony within Philadelphia's Clan-na-Gael is described in Bernard, *Daughter of Derry,* 43–44, 74–75.

In interviews, Daniel Cahalane's children said they still don't know the roots of their father's radicalism, though they believe his views changed after he arrived in America, and that he was likely recruited to lead Delaware County's NORAID chapter by Hugh Breen, whose premises he frequented.

CHAPTER 5

The opening anecdote of the chapter was described in varying detail in two interviews conducted by the author.

Daniel Cahalane was described by his children in interviews conducted by the author over several years. His immigration path is detailed in an internal FBI document from 1974, obtained via the Freedom of Information Act. The quote that closes this chapter is from Cahalane's acceptance speech for NORAID's Man of the Year award in 1976 (Larry McMullen, "Weighing the Scales of Justice," *Philadelphia Daily News,* August 25, 1978).

Bill Corry was described by his son in several interviews with the author over a period of years.

CHAPTER 6

Martin Lyons's trip to the New York docks, dressed as a priest, was described by John Casey in his testimony during the Philadelphia Five trial (*United States of America v. Neil Byrne et al.*). Separately, William Kavanaugh, an undercover ATF agent, testified that Lyons told him the illicit guns and ammunition were crated as plumbing supplies.

NORAID's reliance on ships as a primary means of gun smuggling was described by Dan Duffy to John Nigro, who testified to the exchange at the Philadelphia trial (*United States of America v. Neil Byrne et al.*).

Martin Lyons is an enigmatic figure in the greater story of NORAID. He is mentioned only in passing in Collins, *NORAID and the Northern Ireland Troubles*, 20. In the podcast *Foreign Agent*, Nate Lavey profiles Lyons ("The New World and the Old Country," Novara Media, 2022). Basic details about Lyons's life appear in an obituary published online by the Farenga Brothers Funeral Home in 2020, and an undated NORAID pamphlet describes Lyons as having been on NORAID's board of directors from 1970 to 1973. A comprehensive profile of Lyons can be gleaned over the course of the Philadelphia Five trial (*United States of America v. Neil Byrne et al.*), in which multiple undercover ATF agents testified about the time they spent infiltrating NORAID. They engaged often with Lyons and observed him across a number of months as he directed the group's inner circle.

Lyons's role in NORAID is described by John Casey in testimonies at both the Philadelphia trial (*United States v. Neil Byrne et al.*) and before a grand jury panel in 1976, the transcript of which was found in a box in a Philadelphia attic and provided to the author in spring of 2022.

The Falls Road Curfew is a touchstone for most histories of the Troubles. Descriptions of the incident can be found in McKittrick and McVea, *Making Sense of the Troubles*, 71; Coogan, *The Troubles*, 127–29; Moloney, *Secret History of the IRA*, 90–91; Bishop and Mallie, *Provisional IRA*, 161; Moloney, *Voices from the Grave*, 55–59; and McCann, *War and an Irish Town*. The direct quote from Brendan Hughes is taken from an interview published by Ed Moloney in *Voices from the Grave*, 57.

The quote about John McCullough's roofers' union comes from Zach, "It Was Networking, All Networking," 15.

There is some debate about how the ArmaLite first arrived to the Provos. The more mainstream version, described by Brendan Hughes in Moloney, *Voices from the Grave*, 76–79, says that the Provos didn't know about ArmaLites until the winter of 1970, and that Hughes didn't travel to America to get them until the spring of 1971. However, the Philadelphia trip by Sean Keenan and Joe Cahill described in Wilson, *Irish America and the Ulster Conflict*, 87, and further sourced in chapters 3 and 5, predated that by a year, and according to both Richard English in *Armed Struggle*, 116, and A. R. Oppenheimer in *IRA: The Bombs and the Bullets: A History of Deadly Ingenuity* (Kildare, Ireland: Irish Academic Press, 2009), 137, that trip resulted in a large shipment of ArmaLites received by the Provos in the autumn of 1970, direct from Philadelphia. This information is supported in Bishop and Mallie, *Provisional IRA*, 169. According to the authors, the shipment of those 1970 ArmaLites was arranged by nameless operatives eventually prosecuted in Philadelphia and took six months to organize. The primary source for this is listed in the book's endnotes as "private information." A possible explanation for the discrepancy in timeline between Hughes's version and Bishop and

Mallie's is that Keenan and Cahill's endeavor predated the formal IRA split, and the pair represented an older generation of Provos with whom the Belfast brigade did not immediately align (Moloney, *Secret History of the IRA*, 73). Further bolstering this theory is that Keenan was a Derry man, and communication between the two cities' dissident IRA contingents was haphazard at best, especially during the chaotic months surrounding the split.

Catholic dislocation following the Falls Road Curfew can be found in McKittrick and McVea, *Making Sense of the Troubles*, 71; Coogan, *The Troubles*, 91; and Niall Gilmartin's "Dislocation, Unsettledness, and the Long-Term Consequences of Forced Displacement in Northern Ireland's 'Troubles'" (*Space & Polity* 27, no. 1, 17–34). According to Gilmartin, around sixty thousand people were forced to leave their homes in Belfast from 1969 to 1973. In Donegal, an article ("Donegal Organizes Refugee Relief Measures," *Derry Journal*, August 22, 1969) describes a refugee intake center being established to process the number of Catholics fleeing south.

The demographics of Lenadoon are described in a 1974 community case study published on Ulster University's CAIN website (John Darby, "Intimidation in Housing," compiled by Fionnuala McKenna).

CHAPTER 7

The 1971 meeting between Marjorie Palace, Vince Conlon, and Harry Rutherford was described by Marjorie Palace in her testimony before a federal grand jury in January 1975.

Quotes from BBC broadcasts were taken from the BBC's own archives on Northern Ireland.

Details about Vincent and Marina Conlon's lives in Philadelphia were described to the author by their son Sean in interviews over a number of years.

The NORAID donation poem is found in Clark's *Irish Blood*, 48.

George Harrison's role as an IRA gunrunner is described in English's *Armed Struggle*, 115–17; and Holland, *American Connection*, 63–114. Glimpses into the IRA's pre-1970 gunrunning network in America can also be found in Vince Conlon's personal papers. One letter from Cathal Goulding, dated January 1, 1963, reads: "Re the machinery left by Harrison in a New York cellar, see Manus and go ahead and get it to a safe place." The "Harrison" to whom Goulding refers is almost certainly George Harrison, and the "machinery" is almost certainly guns.

CHAPTER 8

The FBI's first visit to NORAID headquarters and its ensuing analyses are described in Holland, *American Connection*, 33–40.

Details about the Foreign Agents Registration Act can be found in a January 2024 report published by Congressional Research Service, "Foreign Agents Registration Act (FARA): An Overview." Additional information can be found in a briefing paper from the CIA, prepared for Congress in 1976, "Statutes Affecting Domestic Activities of Foreign Agents." Details of NORAID's first registrations under FARA are contained in a set of FBI documents obtained via the Freedom of Information Act. The fight between NORAID and the Justice Department over FARA is detailed in Holland, *American Connection*, 45–48; and Collins, *NORAID and the Northern Ireland Troubles*, 52–54.

The first contacts between British and American officials over Irish America and NORAID are described in Holland, *American Connection*, 38–39; and Wilson, *Irish America and the Ulster Conflict*, 53–56. Further details are found in internal FBI correspondence from the same period, obtained via the Freedom of Information Act, and internal security documents from British officials in London and Northern Ireland available at the British National Archives. One, a newsletter clipping from 1976, states: "Security chiefs in Northern Ireland had been in contact with the agents since 1970."

Among other initiatives, the British documents also describe the British Information Services, a public-facing organization that sought to influence messaging in the United States about NORAID.

The quote beginning "The greatest joke" can be found in Kit Konolige, "The Greening of Ulster," *New Paper,* February 7, 1976.

CHAPTER 9

John Casey describes his experience in the Bronx during his testimony in the Philadelphia trial, and his 1976 grand jury testimony. The incident at the J&J bait shop would go on to be the primary charging incident in the case against NORAID member Frank Grady, in New York (*United States v. Frank Grady,* 544 F.2d 598).

Frank Grady's exchange with Martin Lyons is described in the testimony of John Casey at the Philadelphia trial (*United States v. Neil Byrne et al.*).

CHAPTER 10

Descriptions of the killings listed as having occurred in 1971 can be found in McKittrick and McVea, *Making Sense of the Troubles,* 74. The killing of the three off-duty British Army soldiers is also described in Coogan, *The Troubles,* 139.

Details on internment can be found in Coogan, *The Troubles,* 149–52; McKittrick and McVea, *Making Sense of the Troubles,* 77–87; Moloney, *Secret History of the IRA,* 98–103; and Moloney, *Voices from the Grave,* 95. In *A Tough Nut to Crack,* Steve Corbett, a former gunner for the British Army stationed in Andersonstown, described how soldiers were instructed to buy "Granny books" — small photo albums that fit in the pockets of their jackets, in which they kept pictures of IRA suspects (46). Statistics on the disproportionate application of internment can be found in Collins, *NORAID and the Northern Ireland Troubles,* 38; McKittrick and McVea, *Making Sense of the Troubles,* 81–82; and Coogan, *The Troubles,* 151. Descriptions of West Belfast under internment can be found in the *Andersonstown News* coverage from 1972 through 1975.

Maudling's quote about internment can be found in McKittrick and McVea, *Making Sense of the Troubles,* 77.

The shift among southern Republicans following the introduction of internment is detailed by Gearóid Ó Faoleán in *A Broad Church: The Provisional IRA in the Republic of Ireland, 1969–1980* (Kildare, Ireland: Merrion Press, 2019), 70.

Internment's effect on NORAID is described in Collins, *NORAID and the Northern Ireland Troubles,* 36–44; Wilson, *Irish America and the Ulster Conflict,* 53–57; and Holland, *American Connection,* 35–36. According to Holland (35), from August 1971 to January 1972, NORAID collected $128,099; in the period following that, which included Bloody Sunday, it collected $313,000.

The quote from an IRA officer can be found in the *Andersonstown News* ("Recruitment Soaring — IRA Claim," August 1, 1973).

The details of Dessie Healey's killing can be found in a newspaper article from December 2022 from *Belfast Media,* "Dessie Healey Inquest Opens 51 Years after Killing."

NOTES

The days leading up to the Civil Rights Association march in Derry on January 30, 1972, are followed in a series of articles in the *Derry Journal* published on January 25, 1972, and January 28, 1972.

CHAPTER 11

Dan Duffy was described by his family over months of interviews by the author in Philadelphia and Ireland. His experience of Bloody Sunday was described in an interview with the author in Philadelphia.

The horrific events of Bloody Sunday are a touchstone moment of the Troubles. They are included in nearly every retelling of the conflict, including: McCann, *War and an Irish Town;* Coogan, *The Troubles;* McKittrick and McVea, *Making Sense of the Troubles;* Moloney, *Secret History of the IRA;* Taylor, *Provos;* English, *Armed Struggle;* and Bernard, *Daughter of Derry.* The tragedy is also described in coverage in the *Derry Journal* across January and February 1972. For decades, the British government carefully defended the paratroop regiment, beginning with the government's Widgery Report in 1972, which not only defended the soldiers' actions but also praised their credibility: "Witnesses could not fail to be impressed by the demeanor of the soldiers of 1 Para." In 2010, British prime minister David Cameron fully reversed that judgment, issuing a formal state apology and calling the killings "unjustified and unjustifiable." His apology followed a separate government inquiry that found the British soldiers had lied about their role in the killings and that all of the victims that day had been innocent.

Derry's sectarian tensions in the 1970s are discussed in McCann, *War and an Irish Town;* by Brigid Makowski in Bernard, *Daughter of Derry;* and in the local nationalist newspaper, the *Derry Journal,* which published twice a week during the start of the Troubles.

Daniel Duffy's quote "I love Ireland like my mother…" is from Ritch, "I Love Ireland Like My Mother" (*Philadelphia Bulletin,* December 23, 1975).

The interactions between Dan Duffy and Jeffrey Reh were testified to by Reh at the Philadelphia Five trial (*United States of America v. Neil Byrne et al.*).

The surge of interest in NORAID and Irish America following Bloody Sunday is detailed in Collins, *NORAID and the Northern Ireland Troubles,* 44–50; and Wilson, *Irish America and the Ulster Conflict,* 61–76.

Dan Duffy's politics — and his aversion to Vince Conlon — were described to the author in an interview in Philadelphia.

CHAPTER 12

A list detailing the serial number, purchase date, and the date the weapon was received by the Department of Industrial and Forensic Science in Northern Ireland for many of the Philadelphia guns was discovered in a box of old case documents in a Philadelphia attic. The list, part of defense lawyer Jack Levine's papers, contains Levine's handwritten notes on the Northern Irish gun seizure documents that would be largely ruled inadmissible from the case. According to Levine's documents, the first of the Philadelphia guns — serial numbers 26693, 26658, and 26656 — were received by the Department of Industrial and Forensic Sciences in Belfast in November 1971.

Brigid Makowski's experience of Bloody Sunday is described in Bernard, *Daughter of Derry,* 92–98.

The movement of the Philadelphia guns into Northern Ireland was described to the author by someone familiar with the procedure, and further in Bishop and Mallie, *Provisional*

IRA, 295–96. The connections between gun smugglers and sympathetic US customs agents is described in an article in *Newsweek* preserved by the CIA and released via the Freedom of Information Act (Nicholas Horrock, "A Feud Among US Agents," August 13, 1984).

The scene at the Montgomery Loan Company is described by Marie Hallowell, the secretary at the company, in her testimony at the Philadelphia trial (*United States of America v. Neil Byrne et al.*).

The relationship between the IRA and Sinn Fein is perhaps one of the most convoluted, complicated ones in contemporary politics. In *The Troubles,* Tim Pat Coogan writes that it "is intricate in the extreme" (391). The relationship is explored at length in Taylor, *Provos;* and Moloney, *Secret History of the IRA.*

CHAPTER 13

The ArmaLite that was recovered in Burnfoot, County Donegal, was traced through a collection of documentary sources and author interviews, in Ireland and America. The first was a document released by the FBI via the Freedom of Information Act as part of its packet on Daniel Cahalane; in it is a letter dated February 26, 1972, between American and British legal attachés. Its subject line is "Arms found in Drumbroggan, Burnfoot, Co. Donegal." "Drumbroggan" does not exist as a townland, but Burnfoot does. The letter goes on to detail an ArmaLite, serial no. S-11522, purchased by Cahalane on March 10, 1972. After being shown the FBI's file, two individuals familiar with County Donegal recalled the specific incident, and separately confirmed the name of the officer, a former Garda who was reclusive and solitary. The author has decided not to name the officer, given the lack of documentary evidence confirming his identity.

Details about the Northern Ireland border can be found in the program "The Hardest Border" (Nuala McCann and Christina McSorley, BBC, May 31, 2017).

Neil Byrne was described to the author over the course of multiple interviews in Philadelphia and Ireland.

An internal FBI document (97-5299) from February 1973 details the history of the agency's FARA investigation. In it, an agent writes: "On January 10, 1972, MATTHEW HIGGINS and MICHAEL FLANNERY turned over a large carton of books and records of the INAC in the presence of their attorneys."

The history of the Bureau of Alcohol, Tobacco, Firearms and Explosives can be found on the agency's website. Its feud with the FBI is detailed in the following articles: Eric Lichtblau, "F.B.I. Attacks Firearm Agency in Draft Report," *New York Times,* November 12, 2002; Stephen Labaton, "The Nation; How the A.T.F. Became a Demon," *New York Times,* May 14, 1995; and Dan Eggen, "Move to Justice Department Brings ATF New Focus," *Washington Post,* January 22, 2003.

The 1971 incident in which Frank Grady takes a copy of the New York *Daily News* and points to an article about the IRA, saying "That is one of our guns," is recounted by John Casey in his 1976 grand jury testimony.

Accounts of British Army raids, IRA shoot-outs, and skirmishes in Andersonstown are described in daily coverage by the *Andersonstown News* in November and December of 1972. They are further described in Corbett, *A Tough Nut to Crack.*

Northern Ireland's population in 1972 is estimated by the UK's Office for National Statistics to have been 1,539,000. It is widely reported to be the deadliest year of the Troubles; according to Ulster University's CAIN Archive, 472 people died in 1972 as a result of the violence; 321 of those were civilians.

A table of gun seizures and home raids was published in the *Andersonstown News* on February 21, 1973.

Bloody Friday and the adoption of the car bomb as an IRA strategy is described in McKittrick and McVea, *Making Sense of the Troubles,* 100–101.

The various political options considered by Stormont politicians in the months following Bloody Sunday are described in McKittrick and McVea, *Making Sense of the Troubles*, 90.

CHAPTER 14

The mystery of the six Cobh suitcases is detailed in the podcast *Foreign Agent* ("The American Front," Novara Media, 2022); Holland, *American Connection;* and Andrew Blake, "The American Connection Running Guns to the IRA," *Washington Post,* September 4, 1979.

The ATF's visit to the Montgomery Loan Company is described by ATF agent Robert L. Doyle on the third day of the Philadelphia trial. Doyle testifies that he visited the shop on June 16, 1972 (*United States of America v. Neil Byrne et al.*).

CHAPTER 15

The Fort Worth Five case is discussed at length in *Foreign Agent* ("The American Front," Novara Media, 2022) and in James Markham, "Gun-Running Case in U.S. Embitters I.R.A. Supporters," *New York Times,* July 17, 1972. Seymour Hersh first revealed the case's link to NORAID in a small, untitled news item in the *New York Times* on March 14, 1973: "The Justice Department disclosed today that the reason it had subpoenaed and then jailed five New Yorkers of Irish descent in Texas was that it had information about the purchase of Mexican weapons for shipment to Northern Ireland."

Irish-American support for the embattled Fort Worth Five, as the men became known, is described in Clark, *Irish Blood,* 65–67.

Brandon Alvey and Bob Merkle were described in interviews conducted by the author, newspaper articles, and internal documents of both the American and British governments, which included years' worth of correspondence between the two prosecutors and legal officials in the United Kingdom. Alvey was also described in Jeremy Campbell, "The Quiet Man Who Bust the IRA Gun Runners," *Liverpool Daily Post,* January 24, 1975; and in an interview conducted by the author with a person familiar with Alvey's career.

Robert Merkle is described in several obituaries and articles that paid tribute to him after his death, including: William R. Levesque, "Bulldog Attorney Merkle Dies," *Tampa Bay Times,* May 7, 2003; and Mary Jo Melone, "Prosecutor Was a Bull, Tampa Was a China Shop," *Tampa Bay Times,* May 8, 2003.

The quote from British investigators lamenting the lack of proven connection between NORAID and gun purchases can be found in a May 1976 letter included in the British National Archives files on American gunrunning to the IRA.

The shuttering of NORAID chapters under federal scrutiny can be found in Holland, *American Connection,* 39.

Richard M. Weronik, an ATF agent, testified at the Philadelphia trial that he had reviewed the financial records of the Cahalanes, the Duffys, and the Conlons. His conclusion: Cahalane "would have had to have saved all of his money for the whole three years and it still wouldn't add up to $14,040" (*United States of America v. Neil Byrne et al.*).

CHAPTER 16

Eugene Marley was described in an interview conducted by the author in Philadelphia. The
botched arrangement at the Kirkwood Motel was testified to by multiple ATF agents during
the Philadelphia trial (*United States of America v. Neil Byrne et al.*).

CHAPTER 17

The scene at the apartment in the Bronx, in which Bill Kelly, an apparent gun dealer, courts Martin Lyons, is described by ATF agent William Kavanaugh in his testimony at the Philadelphia
trial (*United States of America v. Neil Byrne et al.*).

"The boys in Philly really came through for us" was a statement from Martin Lyons to John Casey
and Frank Grady in 1971, recalled by John Casey in his testimony at the Philadelphia trial
(see above). Asked if Casey understood what Lyons was implying, Casey said: "I knew what
he meant. He was talking about guns."

CHAPTER 18

Jeff Reh described his dealings with Dan Duffy and John Nigro on the eleventh day of the Philadelphia trial (*United States of America v. Neil Byrne et al.*).

It's difficult to say when Dan Duffy first crossed the threshold from being a NORAID member to
buying guns for the IRA. His lawyer claimed he never bought a gun, and his name does not
appear on any of the firearms records used to prosecute the Philadelphia Five. According to
Duffy's own defenses at the time, he claims to have not even met Dan Cahalane until the fall
of 1972. But his own conversations with Jeff Reh — bolstered by interviews the author conducted with his children and documents that suggest Duffy was well acquainted with Vince
Conlon and Neil Byrne as early as the 1960s — imply that Duffy was involved in procuring
guns far more often and earlier than his legal defenses claimed.

The connection between US military bases and smuggled guns for the IRA is described in Holland, *American Connection,* 83; and Wilson, *Irish America and the Ulster Conflict,* 88. Details
of the US military's report on stolen guns can be found in "Pentagon Says I.R.A. Stole Arms
at U.S. Bases," *New York Times,* September 2, 1972.

John Nigro's interactions with Dan Duffy are described by Nigro in his testimony at the Philadelphia trial. The quotes from their initial phone call are described by Nigro in his testimony,
but are also drawn from what Nigro — a paid government informant — said was a homemade
transcription of the call, taken from a secret coil recording he set up before calling Duffy back.
The recording would be the grounds for a yearslong appeal shepherded by Dan Cahalane's
and Neil Byrne's lawyers.

The strange case of George Fassnacht was described in John Nigro's testimony, and further in
an article in the *Philadelphia Inquirer,* June 22, 1971, which was headlined "Diversified
Arms Cache Has Police Baffled," and stated, "Police can't figure out what George Fassnacht
was doing with all those guns and explosives in his basement, and say only he can supply
the answer." A separate article in the *New York Times* said Fassnacht worked as a ballistics
expert for the Philadelphia Police Department before resigning to join the CIA from 1967 to
1969. The case is further explored in the article "A Look into the Twilight World of George
Fassnacht," published in the *Philadelphia Bulletin* in June 1971 and contained in a file about
Fassnacht that was released by the CIA under the Freedom of Information Act. There is nothing besides Duffy's passing inquiry that connects him to the Philadelphia men.

According to a February 1993 article from United Press International, Fassnacht was never charged with a crime, but the city of Philadelphia refused to return his arsenal to him unless he promised not to sue for damages; the cache was eventually returned, but was damaged and missing several pieces. A federal jury awarded him $260,000 in 1993.

CHAPTER 19

ATF agent Charles Wunder described his surveillance of Danny Cahalane as he made his way to Bill Corry's home in testimony at the Philadelphia trial (*United States of America v. Neil Byrne et al.*).

There are no primary sources confirming that the meetings in December 1972 through February 1973 among Danny Cahalane, Neil Byrne, and the New York NORAID men specifically involved the securing of Marjorie Palace as a gun dealer; there are no recordings of their conversations, and Palace's presence in Philadelphia's gun-smuggling lexicon was not new. However, circumstantial evidence would suggest that the pattern of contact lined up with their various engagements with Palace, and that her role in late 1972 was a more significant one than she had yet played.

The scene of Danny Cahalane and Neil Byrne in the George Washington Inn lounge is described by Dennis Dutch and Thomas Clark, two ATF agents, in their respective testimonies at the Philadelphia trial.

The scene at Breen's bar was described in testimony by ATF agent Harvey Straus on the thirteenth day of the Philadelphia trial.

The scene of Dan Cahalane and Neil Byrne at Cowan's, in the Bronx, and their subsequent trip to Marty Lyons's apartment are described by ATF agent Thomas Clark in his testimony at the Philadelphia trial.

The scenes at Breen's bar and the Commodore Barry Irish center, in which ATF agent James Loughery watched the Philadelphia men have a secret meeting near the stage, are described by several ATF agents on two separate days of testimony.

Father Sean McManus, a well-known voice in Irish America in the 1970s, is described in a profile published in the *Andersonstown News* in October 1974 and by Wilson, *Irish America and the Ulster Conflict*, 100–102. His presence at the Commodore Barry club the evening of James Loughery's surveillance was noted by Loughery, but the event was further advertised in *The Irish People* on December 9, 1972, a date that lines up with the events detailed in the Philadelphia trial.

CHAPTER 20

John Rugg describes his experience in his own testimony at the Philadelphia Five trial (*United States of America v. Neil Byrne et al.*). While Rugg does not say that he called the ATF — he nearly does, but is cut off by lawyers — his contact with officials is confirmed by Bob Merkle and recorded by the court reporter in the transcript of a sidebar conversation.

The scene outside Danny Cahalane's house was described by ATF agent J. M. Kelly on the thirteenth day of the Philadelphia trial.

ATF agent Thomas Lydon describes seeing the boxes of guns in the back of Danny Cahalane's work truck in testimony at the Philadelphia Five trial.

CHAPTER 21

I first reached out to the Forensic Services of Northern Ireland, or FSNI, in March of 2022; I was working on a project about American guns in Northern Ireland in the 1970s, I said, and the American court case I was investigating relied on documents created by the Department of Industrial and Forensic Sciences, FSNI's precursor. I included relevant sections of the Philadelphia court case as reference. What I hoped to find, I explained to FSNI, were specific incidents of violence connected to the Philadelphia guns. What followed was a maddening process. One officer at FSNI said they had identified a box of documents in an off-site warehouse that was related to the Philadelphia case; they had ordered it to be delivered to them, and expected to be able to provide some information to help. Not long after, the FSNI refused to answer any more questions, and instead passed my request on to the Police Services of Northern Ireland, or PSNI, the police organization that succeeded the Royal Ulster Constabulary. In no uncertain terms, PSNI denied my request, both the unofficial one and the one I had submitted through the Freedom of Information Act. Among the official reasons, they cited Section 17(5) and Section 30(3) of the Freedom of Information law of 2000, which give exceeding "appropriate cost limit" and ongoing investigations as reasons for the denial. In a phone conversation, the PSNI officer handling my request explained that it didn't matter what information the American courts had given me; in Northern Ireland, they did not believe such information should be public. An official with the Public Records Office of Northern Ireland, which is the custodian of Troubles-related court cases, later explained that authorities are forbidden from releasing the serial numbers of weapons, regardless of how long ago the incidents may have taken place. Such facts, the person explained, could help researchers, journalists, and members of the public "triangulate" information to identify specific people and crimes. Even if court records were released as part of the declassification procedures, the official said, the serial numbers of weapons are redacted from the court file. This was the case, they said, because such information "could affect other outstanding cases." However, this stands in stark contrast to the British government's own documents. In files maintained at the British National Archives, in Kew Gardens, outside London, there are several files that touch on American gunrunning to the IRA, and the Philadelphia case specifically. In the back of one of those files are four sheets of paper that detail ten specific weapon recoveries, and tie those recovered guns directly to specific killings and shootings in Northern Ireland. Several of the entries list specific weapons and their serial numbers, and two point out potential purchasers and locations in America. The incidents detailed in this chapter — including the killing of Constable Robert Megaw, Constable Raymond Wylie, Constable Ronald Mcauley, and Private Phillip Drake — are included in the list of incidents in the files at the British National Archives. In a separate British government document, a lawyer refers to one of the Philadelphia guns having been used to kill an unnamed police officer.

The internal wrangling of the Justice Department over NORAID is described in Holland, *American Connection*, 39–40; and in Wilson, *Irish America and the Ulster Conflict*, 84–99. It was described by Robert Merkle to British embassy officials in March 1977, according to an internal British briefing paper on the conversation.

The formal launch of the FBI's FARA case against NORAID is described in Holland, *American Connection*, 40–41; and in internal FBI documents from 1971 and 1972, released as part of a request under the Freedom of Information Act.

CHAPTER 22

The union event at John McCullough's Olney hall is described in Mallowe, "My Life and Times with the IRA."

NOTES

Patrick Radden Keefe dissects the phenomenon of informers within Irish Republicanism in *Say Nothing*. Brendan Hughes's recounting of his own childhood experience is included in Moloney, *Voices from the Grave*, 38.

CHAPTER 23

The arrival of the grand jury subpoenas in Philadelphia is described in the article "Subpoena Quashing Denied Philadelphia Men," *The Irish People*, June 23, 1973.

The response of Irish Philadelphia to the grand jury summonses is described in Clark, *The Irish in Philadelphia,* 49; and Holland, *American Connection,* 43.

The transcript of Danny Cahalane's grand jury testimony was located in a box of papers in a Philadelphia attic, including notes from his lawyer, Jack Levine, on the case. Cahalane's immunity offer is described in Ritch, "I Love Ireland Like My Mother."

Vince Conlon's last gun purchase in Philadelphia was with Neil Byrne and Daniele Cahalane on March 21, 1972, at the Montgomery Loan Company, described in Counts XIII, XIV, and XV of the federal indictment *United States of America v. Neil Byrne et al.*

CHAPTER 24

Descriptions of Geraldine Crawford in the 1970s can be found in an article published in the *Belfast Telegraph* in September 1974; in the book *In the Footsteps of Anne: Stories of Republican Women Ex-Prisoners* (Belfast: Shanway Press, 2011), compiled by Evelyn Brady, Eva Patterson, Kate McKinney, Rosie Hamill, and Pauline Jackson; and in Danny Morrison, "The Times of Laura Crawford," *An Phoblacht,* January 5, 2016.

The atmosphere of Lenadoon and Andersonstown is described in a series of articles in the *Andersonstown News* between April 1973 and June 1974, and the *Belfast Telegraph* between October 1973 and April 1974. Further descriptions can be found in Corbett, *A Tough Nut to Crack;* and in McKittrick and McVea, *Making Sense of the Troubles,* 127.

The Provisional IRA's recruiting boom in 1973 is described in an interview with IRA operatives published in the *Andersonstown News,* August 1, 1973.

The shooting incident at the Woodbourne barracks on September 22, 1973, is described by Geraldine Crawford in an interview in MacDonald, *Shoot the Women First,* 160–64; and in a series of articles published in the *Belfast Telegraph* between October 1973 and September 1974.

Loyalist incursions into Lenadoon were described by an IRA officer in an interview in the *Andersonstown News,* August 22, 1973.

A table of complaints filed against the Royal Ulster Constabulary ran in the *Andersonstown News,* March 28, 1973.

CHAPTER 25

The Crawford family's history in Belfast before 1970 is described in Morrison, "Life and Times of Laura Crawford." The article appeared in the newspaper *An Phoblacht,* which is closely associated with the Provisional movement; Morrison served as the national director of publicity for Sinn Fein in the 1980s.

Geraldine Crawford also spoke about her childhood as part of the Dúchas Oral History Project in Belfast, organized by the Falls Community Council. Though her full interview is not publicly available, excerpts were published in *Living through the Conflict* (Belfast: Dúchas Oral History Archive, 2014), 16.

The role of women in the Republican movement is described in Brady et al., *In the Footsteps of Anne,* 17; MacDonald, *Shoot the Women First,* 134–35; and the documentary *A Kind of Sisterhood* (directed by Michele Devlin and Claire Hackett, 2015). Patrick Radden Keefe explores the novelty of personalities like the Price sisters in *Say Nothing,* 48–53.

It's difficult to find any hard statistics for how many men and women were charged with gun possession or membership in the IRA in the early 1970s. However, the pages of the *Belfast Telegraph* and the *Andersonstown News* are filled with updates on court cases of women who were accused of weapons possession or membership in the IRA.

Geraldine Crawford addressed her feelings about the specific British soldiers with whom she interacted in MacDonald, *Shoot the Women First,* 161–63: "He threw a bandage over to me and I put it on myself. He was not violent or abusive in any way, very professional." And, later: "She did not hate the soldiers, but she did feel sorry for them."

CHAPTER 26

It took two years, dozens of interviews, hundreds of newspaper articles, and thousands of pages of American and Northern Irish government documents to identify Geraldine Crawford as one of the IRA volunteers convicted for carrying a Philadelphia rifle. The incident in Andersonstown on the evening of September 22, 1973, was first identified through the transcript of a sidebar conversation as part of the Philadelphia trial (*United States of America v. Neil Byrne et al.*). Bob Merkle, the prosecutor, is attempting to introduce documents that prove certain individuals found with Philadelphia guns were convicted of membership in the IRA. In explaining those documents, Merkle reads off four defendants' names: Anthony McKiernan, Patrick Duffy, Paul Christopher Girvan, and Aine McCotter. Although the names were not admissible in open court, they were unredacted in the case transcript. Those names were then run through the e-catalog for Public Records of Northern Ireland, or PRONI, which maintains Troubles-era criminal cases. Such cases are closed and must be requested via the Freedom of Information Act. However, in the PRONI case locator, one can find basic details confirming the existence of a file. Those details include the charge, name, and date of a conviction. Attempts to locate Duffy and Girvan failed. McKiernan's case was located in this database. He was convicted of possession of a firearm and ammunition, and with belonging to an illegal organization in 1974. But McKiernan's story took a fatal turn: he was murdered in 1988 amid rumors that he was an informer; later, his case would be tied to Freddie Scappatici, a high-ranking IRA man who was allegedly a British agent code-named Stakeknife. Reached by the author, McKiernan's family did not want to speak. Finally, a search for McCotter revealed she died in 2015 in Dublin. She is described in her brief obituary as "Republican and socialist," and two contacts confirmed that she would eventually split from the Provos over the peace process. Through an intermediary, her family declined to speak. But in the PRONI case locator, McCotter's case was listed as dual-defendant. She and Geraldine Crawford were convicted of possession of a firearm and ammunition with intent, carrying a firearm in a public place, and possession of a firearm and ammunition. McCotter was convicted of belonging to Cumann na mBan, the illegal IRA women's organization, which was likely why she was included in the Philadelphia transcript and Crawford was not; as described by British officials to Merkle and Alvey, the charge of membership to the IRA or Cumann na mBan was often dropped when possible in favor of more serious charges like weapons possession, which is the charge that Crawford, as the woman holding the rifle, faced. The date of the incident was cross-referenced with a handwritten sheet of serial numbers from

Jack Levine, which showed that ArmaLite serial no. S11981 was recovered by security forces in Northern Ireland on September 25, 1973. The discrepancy in the date of official processing is likely due to the clunky, byzantine paperwork described by Northern Irish officials at the time in testimony at the Philadelphia trial (*United States of America v. Neil Byrne et al.*).

Understaffing in Northern Ireland's labs and legal offices is described by Victor Leslie Beavis, an employee of the Department of Industrial and Forensic Science in Belfast, in his testimony at the Philadelphia trial (*United States of America v. Neil Byrne et al.*).

Geraldine Crawford's experience in Royal Victoria Hospital is described in MacDonald, *Shoot the Women First*, 161–62. The security situation at Royal Victoria can be found in Ruth Coon, "Working in a Warzone: The Challenges Faced by Medical Staff Working during the Troubles," *Epidemic Belfast*, Ulster University.

Geraldine Crawford's friendship with Jim Lynagh, a notoriously hard-line IRA man, is described in an interview with Crawford, published in Brady et al., *In the Footsteps of Anne*, 302–3.

Geraldine Crawford's trial is described in coverage by the *Belfast Telegraph* between October 1973 and September 1974. The articles include: "Girls on Arms Charges," October 18, 1973; "Belfast Girl Is Remanded," November 1973; "Stone-Thrower Sentenced," December 6, 1973; "Conditional Discharge," January 10, 1974; "Girl in Custody," January 17, 1974; "Girls Sent for Trial on Rifle Charges," April 19, 1974; and "Jail for Belfast Gun Girls," September 6, 1974. The trial is also described in MacDonald, *Shoot the Women First*, 160–61.

An internal 1987 briefing paper from the Northern Ireland Office on IRA fundraising says: "Unlike Provisionals, members of the Official IRA do not refuse to plead when brought before the court." The paper was accessed via CAIN at Ulster University.

Descriptions of Armagh Gaol in the 1970s come from Devlin and Hackett's documentary, *A Kind of Sisterhood;* Raymond Murray, *Hard Time: Armagh Gaol, 1971–1986* (Dublin: Mercier Press, 1998); and Brady et al., *In the Footsteps of Anne*. Descriptions are also drawn from several visits to the Eileen Hickey Irish Republican History Museum in West Belfast.

CHAPTER 27

Descriptions of Armagh Gaol's Dr. Cole and his nurse, nicknamed "Ratchet," can be found in Brady et al., *In the Footsteps of Anne*, 269–70. The incident with the home brew is described by Geraldine Crawford in the same book, 302–3.

Brigid Crawford's discovery of Laura Crawford's blond wig is described in Morrison, "Life and Times of Laura Crawford."

CHAPTER 28

The dinner honoring Danny Cahalane's return from prison is described in articles published in *The Irish People* (Nancy McGibney, "Dan Cahalane Thanks Defense Fund," March 16, 1974) and the *Philadelphia Daily News* (Chuck Stone, "Irish and Indians Remember," March 5, 1974).

Danny Cahalane describes his experience in prison in letters to his daughter between 1974 and 1978, provided to the author in 2022.

The Philadelphia Defense Fund is described in an article in *The Irish People*, August 4, 1973.

Irish America's response to the IRA's 1975 ceasefire is described in Wilson, *Irish America and the Ulster Conflict*, 108–9; and McKittrick and McVea, *Making Sense of the Troubles*, 128–29.

The establishment of the Irish National Caucus is described in Wilson, *Irish America and the Ulster Conflict*, 102; and Clark, *Irish Blood*, 68.

NOTES

CHAPTER 29

John Casey details his decision to cooperate with federal investigators in grand jury testimony given in New York in March 1976: "[Federal agents] told me if I didn't tell the truth at this trial they would really prosecute me, really give me a hard time."

The shooting of the three-year-old boy in Belfast is described in a document from the Northern Ireland office held at the British National Archives, part of a list of incidents tied to American guns that were provided to American investigators as part of the Philadelphia Five case. It correlates to an article published in the *Irish Times* on November 6, 1975 (Conor O'Clery, "Republicans Seek Mediator to End Bitter Conflict"). The news article just says the boy was rushed to the hospital; the RUC documents — which are undated, but include information up to 1976 — say he died. His true fate could not be confirmed.

CHAPTER 30

Internal documents at the British National Archives detail months of consternation among British officials over the politics of thanking American officers. They stop short of directly criticizing Merkle or Alvey, but they do periodically voice concern that Merkle is not entirely aware of the delicate politics surrounding NORAID.

The end of internment is described in a *New York Times* article in December 1976 and in a summary paper published by Ulster University's CAIN center, which also details statistics on the religion of the interned. The reaction within Irish America at the end of internment — including paranoia, that the end of the policy would lead to increased prosecutions in the states — is described in Clark, *Irish Blood,* 71.

The visit to America by two members of the Royal Ulster Constabulary is described in an internal British security memo dated January 1976. The visit is further detailed in an RUC memo from the same month. Both were accessed at the British National Archives.

CHAPTER 31

Rumors about Dan Duffy's relationship with the FBI have persisted in Philadelphia Irish circles for years, so much that some say IRA officials were eventually enlisted to help tamp down on such chatter. Still, certain facts are clearly stated in US government files. Duffy did have a relationship with the FBI. This is stated in a handwritten note entitled "Additional Overt Acts," filed in federal court on May 28, 1976. In a list of facts related to the trial, fact ten states: "During 1971 Daniel Duffy conversed with agents of the F.B.I." Duffy's children recall a visit by the FBI around that time. As part of the visit, his daughter said, Duffy instructed his children to hide his firearms in a laundry washing machine. Duffy's interactions with the FBI are further detailed during the course of the Philadelphia trial, though such references occurred in sidebar conversations that might not have been within earshot of the entire courtroom, or the defendants themselves. In one instance, Jack Levine is discussing discovery materials with the judge, defense lawyers, and prosecutors: "We received from the government… a series of FBI 302 reports concerning contacts they had with Daniel Duffy who is one of the defendants in this Court," he says. Later that day, Levine mentions those FBI reports again: "There are some F.B.I. interview reports with Mr. Duffy when he was an informant for the F.B.I., and appended to one of those reports was an F.B.I. teletype which referred to a meeting that my client had with an I.R.A. official at an airport in New York in 1963." The client to whom Levine is most likely referring is Neil Byrne. Internal surveillance reports from the FBI detail a meeting matching most of that description as having occurred in November 1963, at which Vince Conlon brought Cathal Goulding via train to Philadelphia — almost certainly from New York — and met Neil Byrne, along with several other Clan-na-Gael members there. A separate FBI memo dated 1964 lists eight people whom the FBI considered informants within Philadelphia's Irish circles. Among them is PH T-1, who appears to be described in a separate FBI memo dated February 9, 1965, as "a mechanic by trade" and who immigrated to the United States in 1963. Among other comments, PH T-1 shows a clear distaste for Vince Conlon and Neil Byrne: "PH T-1 advised that the majority of Irish in the Philadelphia area did not hold them in high regard and were not supporting their aims and purposes." It may be impossible to ever know if PH T-1 was indeed Dan Duffy, and indeed, some of the details about PH T-1 do not exactly align with Duffy, though discrepancy in these emigration dates could be due to Duffy's eventual naturalization as an American citizen. Further complicating this uncertainty is that it's difficult to know whether Duffy considered himself an informant. He appeared to have disagreed sharply with Vince Conlon's direction for the Clan-na-Gael, and his efforts may have been less sinister and more — in his view — in service of Irish America, which he believed had been harmed by Conlon's work. It's important to note that at the time of his reported relationship with the FBI, Irish America was not in the Justice Department's crosshairs, and Northern Ireland was not particularly volatile. Duffy's position was further confirmed in an interview by the author with an individual familiar with the trial, who confirmed what FBI agents detailed in their reports: Duffy considered Conlon and his more radical colleagues to be communists. How far this cooperation with the FBI went, though, remains unclear. Regardless, Duffy's relationship with the FBI was over by 1972, around the same time that he became more deeply involved with NORAID. Even in the FBI's retelling, he never gave them information on guns or gun smuggling. In an interview with the author, Dan Duffy's daughter described hearing about her father's indictment on the radio a few days before Christmas.

The indictment of the Philadelphia men is described in the following articles: "5 Area Men Indicted in IRA Arms Case," *Philadelphia Inquirer,* December 23, 1975; "5 Indicted on IRA Charge," *Philadelphia Bulletin,* December 22, 1975; and "5 Indicted in Philadelphia in Ulster Gunrunning," *New York Times,* December 23, 1975.

The *Philadelphia Daily News,* in its account of the indictment of the Philadelphia men on December 23, 1975, also reported: "A leading Protestant yesterday denounced as 'fiends' the two killers who shot and killed a Roman Catholic mother of eight as she was putting up Christmas decorations at her home in Belfast. Two masked gunmen fired through the glass front door late Sunday as Mrs. Christie Hughes, 43, was decorating the hallway."

In "The Greening of Ulster," Kit Konolige says: "They looked ordinary, even boring, at their arraignment in a federal district court on December 31." The same article contains the direct quotes by and about Dan Duffy, and about his receipt of a bullet in the mail. That incident was confirmed by Duffy's daughter in an interview by the author; she also provided parts of the note in question, which included the quote beginning "You are brave enough." She recalled there being an additional part of the note that said, "The next one is for you," but that portion could not be located.

CHAPTER 32

The NORAID event at Incarnation Parochial School is described in Joseph McCaffrey and John Morrison, "Irish Dance for a Cause: Does Phila. Money Buy Guns for the I.R.A.?," *Sunday Bulletin,* January 11, 1976.

John McGee's letter to the editor, and others, can be found in the *Philadelphia Inquirer,* January 6, 1976, and April 7, 1976.

Details of Raymond Broderick's life are described in obituaries: "Judge Raymond Broderick, Architect of Pennhurst Decision," *Main Line Times & Suburban,* August 9, 2000; "Raymond J. Broderick, 86, Federal Judge," *New York Times,* August 17, 2000; and "Judge Broderick Dies at 86 Years Old," *Legal Intelligencer,* August 14, 2000.

Brandon Alvey's concern over Judge Broderick's assignment to the Philadelphia trial is described in an internal memo from the British embassy to Northern Irish officials, dated January 13, 1976. Discussion of Vince Conlon's whereabouts and the possibility of extradition is detailed in a separate letter from January 21, 1976, held at the British National Archives.

Brandon Alvey's quote about NORAID can be found in "British Say Irish American Donations Are Blood Spattered," *Baltimore Sun,* January 24, 1976.

Descriptions of Vince and Marina Conlon's lives back on the border were shared by their son Sean in interviews with the author.

The quote suggesting a possible attack while Queen Elizabeth was expected to visit Philadelphia in the summer of 1976 can be found in Konolige, "Greening of Ulster."

CHAPTER 33

The mechanics of returning the Philadelphia guns from Belfast for the trial of the Philadelphia men is described in a series of dispatches between Northern Irish and American authorities in the spring of 1976. These processes are also described in the testimony of Victor Beavis and Richard Anderson at the Philadelphia trial (*United States of America v. Neil Byrne et al.*).

CHAPTER 34

The documents detailing the Philadelphia gun seizures in Northern Ireland were not provided to Bob Merkle and Brandon Alvey until February 1976, according to letters contained in the British National Archives. Among them is a letter from Nigel Kerr, the RUC's legal adviser, to Bob Merkle in April 1976, saying he had little success in identifying cases in which the Philadelphia guns led to convictions for violent incidents.

The description of those Northern Irish documents can be found in a memo filed on June 15, 1976, with the Philadelphia Federal Court.

CHAPTER 35

Raymond Broderick's ruling on the admissibility of the Northern Irish documents is a convoluted legal maneuver that spools out across days of the Philadelphia trial. A key session of oral arguments related to the decision — which occurred on the fourth day, in the afternoon — is missing from the case's transcripts. However, subsequent comments from Broderick make clear the court's ruling: the Northern Irish officials could testify to the date that the Philadelphia guns were received at the forensics lab, but not anything prior, including circumstances under which the guns were recovered. "These documents will not be admitted to show who recovered them under what circumstances, but they may be admitted to show the limited information that the rifle was in the possession of the police....I would not permit the document in to show, for instance, that the weapon was, according to Corporal So-and-So, seized down in the Bogside," Broderick says.

The retelling of the Philadelphia case is taken from transcripts detailing the day-to-day of the trial. Details can also be found in the following articles: "1 Man Acquitted, 2 Held in Gun Case,"

Delaware County Daily Times, June 22, 1976; "Lawyers Seek Delay in Arms Case," *Philadelphia Bulletin,* May 11, 1976; "Irish Arms Trial Opens," *Philadelphia Inquirer,* May 25, 1976; "Law Fought as Obscure in IRA Arms Trial," *Philadelphia Inquirer,* May 26, 1976; "Justice Dept. Is Criticized in IRA Case," *Philadelphia Inquirer,* May 27, 1976; "Irishman Charged with Arms Exports to North," *Irish Times,* May 26, 1976; "200 Smuggled Weapons 'Found in the North,'" *Irish Times,* May 28, 1976; "Arms Exported to NI Identified in US Court," *Irish Times,* June 2, 1976; "The Philadelphia Five," *The Irish People,* June 5, 1976; "The Philadelphia Five" and "Philadelphia Perspective," *The Irish People,* June 12, 1976.

Daniel Duffy's quote can be found in Jim Smith, "Pair Found Guilty of Arms Smuggling," *Philadelphia Daily News,* June 22, 1976.

CHAPTER 36

The Philadelphia appeal is the only court document associated with the case that is available online, and can be reviewed on the law website *Justia,* which publishes current and historic court briefs, under *United States of America v. Neil Byrne et al.*

Mick Haggerty's transport of Danny Cahalane to the Philadelphia airport was described to the author in an interview in Philadelphia. Haggerty and his business partner and Mike Doyle would later be convicted of helping to smuggle Irish fugitives across the US–Canada border. They were caught in the middle of the night in 1987, sneaking two men in a boat across the Saint Lawrence River. The case was detailed in the aforementioned interview, and in court documents (*United States v. Doyle et al.,* Criminal no. 88-00191-01) provided to the author.

Neil Byrne's quote following the trial can be found in Jim Smith, "2 IRA Backers Get Year in Jail for Arms Smuggling Plot," *Philadelphia Daily News,* October 28, 1976.

The quote about NORAID membership shrinking is from a memo dated November 12, 1977, held by the British National Archives.

Michael O'Rourke's case is described in an article in the *New York Times* in November 1979; "IRA Bomber Back in Dublin," *Washington Post,* June 20, 1984; a UPI article published on February 18, 1983; and several interviews conducted by the author in Philadelphia.

Danny Cahalane's funeral is described in Jack McKinney, "Not All Irish Eyes Smile Today," *Philadelphia Daily News,* March 17, 1980.

CHAPTER 37

The British government's request to export submachine guns from America is detailed in internal British government correspondence held at Kew Gardens.

CHAPTER 38

The scene in which Geraldine Crawford is stopped by a British soldier in an army jeep is described by her in an interview in MacDonald, *Shoot the Women First,* 163–64.

The establishment of the Falls Taxi Association is described in a 1987 briefing paper from the Northern Ireland Office, accessed via the CAIN website at Ulster University.

The end of political status for IRA prisoners is described in McKittrick and McVea, *Making Sense of the Troubles,* 142–45; Coogan, *The Troubles,* 263–66; and *The Hunger Strike of 1981,* a briefing paper published by CAIN, at Ulster University.

Father Raymond Murray describes his assignment to Armagh Gaol in *Hard Time,* 7.

Laura Crawford's death is described in "Two Die as Car Explodes," *Belfast Telegraph,* December 2, 1975; and an excerpt in *An Phoblacht,* December 6, 1975. The incident is further detailed in

"The Times of Laura Crawford," which includes this reference to Geraldine Crawford: "Geraldine, who thought that the extent of Laura's involvement was as a member of Sinn Fein, recalls the prison chaplain Fr. Raymond Murray, coming into Armagh Prison the following morning and breaking the news to her."

Laura Crawford's funeral is described in "The Times of Laura Crawford" and Geraldine Crawford's interview in Brady et al., *In the Footsteps of Anne*, 302–3.

Details of strip-searching at Armagh, including Geraldine Crawford's experience, were described in a copy of a letter, written by Father Raymond Murray and discovered in the attic of the MacSwiney Club (Raymond Murray to Armagh Parochial House, 14 December 1982).

Descriptions of the incident at Joe McDonnell's funeral are found in the following articles: "Five Face Funeral Arms Charges," *Belfast Telegraph,* July 4, 1981; "No Bail for Gun Charge Girl," *Belfast Telegraph,* August 11, 1981; "Combat Jackets Shown in Court," *Belfast Telegraph,* November 26, 1982; "Adams' Brother Denies Rifle Charges," *Belfast Telegraph,* November 25, 1982; "The Final Salute," *An Phoblacht,* July 18, 1981; and "Thatcher's Madness" and "Instability Threat Pushes Establishment," *An Phoblacht,* July 18, 1981. The incident is further described by Geraldine Crawford in MacDonald, *Shoot the Women First,* 162–63.

CHAPTER 39

Vince Conlon's return to America is detailed in his personal papers. Conlon's work is also traced in a series of FBI surveillance reports from 1988 through 1993, when the bureau was scrambling to understand how Irish America was responding to the peace process. Among the papers is a dispatch from the FBI's New York office to FBI headquarters: "NY wishes to express its concern in being required to discontinue investigation of captioned subject and his activities within CLAN NA GAEL (CNG)." The cited letter, between Marty Lyons and Conlon, was discovered in Conlon's personal papers.

Details of Michael Flannery's and George Harrison's prosecutions can be found in Holland, *American Connection,* 102–8; "A Marshal with a Very Martial Air," New York *Daily News,* March 17, 1983; and "Turning the Tables on the CIA," *National Law Journal,* October 18, 1982. Both articles were released by the CIA as part of the Freedom of Information Act.

Gerry Adams securing a visa in 1994 is seen as a critical moment in the peace process. It is discussed at length in the podcast *Foreign Agent* ("Our Day Will Come," Novara Media, 2022); Taylor, *Provos,* 344–46; Moloney, *Secret History of the IRA,* 420–22; and Trina Vargo, *Shenanigans: The US–Ireland Relationship in Uncertain Times* (New York: Cavan Bridge Press, 2019). Various newspaper articles underscore how critical the visit was to what would eventually become the Good Friday Agreement: "Gerry Adams: New York in 1994 Visit 'Pivotal to Peace,'" says one headline from the BBC in February 2019. Details on the British reaction to the decision are recounted in *The Journal* (Dublin), "British Officials Were 'Apoplectic' After Gerry Adams Was Granted a US Visa in 1994," December 28, 2021.

Vince Conlon's role in Adams's visit becomes clear through his personal papers, which include several letters back and forth to the Sinn Fein offices in Belfast regarding the trip, and an original draft of Adams's 1994 speech.

CHAPTER 40

The fraught months leading up to the Good Friday Agreement are described in McKittrick and McVea, *Making Sense of the Troubles,* 250–68; Taylor, *Provos,* 363–79; Moloney, *Secret History of the IRA,* 437, 485–86; and Vargo, *Shenanigans*.

The rise of dissident voices within the IRA is described in Keefe, *Say Nothing;* McKittrick and McVea, *Making Sense of the Troubles;* Moloney, *Secret History of the IRA;* and Taylor, *Provos,* 355–62.

Geraldine Crawford's role in the 1998 Good Friday Agreement negotiations was noted by Gerry Adams during his speech at the twenty-fifth-anniversary commemoration of the agreement, held at Queens University in Belfast. Her role is further detailed in the article "Rebels in the Castle," *An Phoblacht,* April 9, 1998.

Adams is a complicated figure in the course of the Troubles, a man who was both invaluable as a political arbiter for peace and subsequently linked to some of the IRA's most brutal killings. Whatever one's opinion of Adams — right, wrong, indifferent, or perhaps a little bit of everything — it is impossible to overlook his role in past and present Republicanism as a whole. This is why I approached Adams as he wandered Queens University in Belfast one evening during the twenty-fifth-anniversary commemorations of the Good Friday Agreement. It's simply hard to tell any story about the Troubles or the IRA without him. I've wondered in hindsight what Adams thought in that moment, twenty-five years since he had managed to somehow thread the delicate political needle that had eluded Irish leaders before him. He stood among the Clintons and Tony Blair, Rishi Sunak and George Mitchell. He seemed light and unbothered walking around the campus, the day's events having wrapped. I introduced myself as a writer for the *New York Times,* working on a book about American support to the IRA in the 1970s. Adams smiled. I should send Sinn Fein an email, he said, an endeavor that I predicted — correctly — would go nowhere beyond the superficial (Sinn Fein, the contact told me, could speak broadly about Irish America but wouldn't talk about guns). I thanked Adams for the suggestion and let him wander on into the dusk, toward whatever strange, complicated legacy he's built for himself.

Details about the contemporary gunrunning case, which included a Philadelphia-based defendant, are described in the following: Michael Ellison, "IRA Arms Trial Ends in Confusion," *Guardian,* June 14, 2000; Darwin Templeton and Chris Thornton, "Provos 'Tried to Smuggle in More Weapons,'" *Belfast Telegraph,* June 14, 2000; and "Post Office Cameras Caught IRA Gunrunners," *Irish Times,* June 14, 2000.

Descriptions of Vince Conlon's funeral can be found in "Vincent Conlon Laid to Rest," *An Phoblacht,* June 15, 1995.

EPILOGUE

Statistics and context of Northern Ireland's Freedom of Information policies were provided by the Public Records Office of Northern Ireland and the Information Commissioner's Office in Belfast. Statistics can be found in the office's annual report ("TEO FOI/EIR Annual Report," The Executive Office, 2023).

Descriptions of the seized Philadelphia guns can be found in Bishop and Mallie, *Provisional IRA,* 294.

The discovery of an oil drum containing weapons associated with the New IRA is described in Martin McCullough, "Guns and Ammo Found in Suspected New IRA Arms Cache Discovered in Co Tyrone," *Belfast Live,* March 22, 2023.

ILLUSTRATION CREDITS

Page 8, Vincent and Marina Conlon, wedding photo: Provided by Conlon family

Page 19, Vincent Conlon, 1969: Provided by Conlon family

Page 20, Clan-na-Gael at the St. Patrick's Day Parade, 1970: Provided by Conlon family

Page 36, ArmaLite AR-180: Photo courtesy of Morphy Auctions, www.morphyauctions.com

Page 47, Danny Cahalane, 1949: Mary Jane Coughlin

Page 59, NORAID pamphlet: Photo courtesy of author

Page 89, Daniel Duffy in Philadelphia: Provided by Duffy family

Page 109, IRA fighters, 1972: Brian Hamill / Premium Archive via Getty Images

Page 181, Geraldine Crawford: Courtesy of Shanway Press

Page 230, Danny Cahalane and his daughter, Mary Jane: Mary Jane Coughlin

Page 243, Car bomb: Victor Patterson

Page 246, Laura Crawford's funeral: anphoblacht.com

Page 273, Sean Conlon at his father's safe house: Author's personal collection

INDEX

INDEX

ABOUT THE AUTHOR

ALI WATKINS IS a journalist for the *New York Times,* based out of the London bureau. Previously, she covered crime and law enforcement on the Metro desk and national security in Washington, also at the *New York Times.* She has also worked for BuzzFeed and at McClatchy Newspapers, where she was a finalist for the 2015 Pulitzer Prize in national reporting for coverage of the Senate's report on the CIA's post-9/11 torture program. Watkins is a graduate of the University of Galway's Masters in Writing program and Temple University in Philadelphia, where she began her journalism career as an intern at the *Philadelphia Daily News.* She grew up in Fleetwood, Pennsylvania.